LOTUS 1-2-3 MODES

MODE	DISPLAYS WHEN. . .
EDIT	An entry is being edited or a formula has been incorrectly entered.
ERROR	An error message is on screen. Esc or ⏎ will clear the error indicator; F1 (Help) will provide assistance.
FILES	A menu of file names is in the control panel.
FIND	/Data, Query, Find is being used to query a database.
FRMT	A format line is being edited.
HELP	A Help screen is being displayed.
LABEL	A label is being entered.
MENU	A menu is on the screen.
NAMES	Graph names, add-in names, or range names are on the screen.
POINT	You are prompted to specify a range or are highlighting a range to create a formula.
READY	You are entering data or choosing a command.
STAT	A status screen is displayed.
VALUE	A number or formula (a value) is being entered.
WAIT	1-2-3 is executing a process or command.

1-2-3 MACRO KEYSTROKE INSTRUCTIONS

There are certain 1-2-3 keystroke operaitons that are activated in macros by typing a command name and enclosing it within { } (braces). This table lists the most commonly used keystroke instructions.

KEY	MACRO INSTRUCTION	KEY	MACRO INSTRUCTION
↓	{DOWN} or {D}	Ins	{INSERT} or {INS}
↑	{UP} or {U}	F1 (Help)	{HELP}
→	{RIGHT} or {R}	F2 (Edit)	{EDIT}
←	{LEFT} or {L}	F3 (Name)	{NAME}
Backspace	{BACKSPACE} or {BS}	F5 (Goto)	{GOTO}
Del	{DELETE} or {DEL}	F6 (Window)	{WINDOW}
End	{END}	F7 (Query)	{QUERY}
/	/ or {MENU} or <	F9 (Calc)	{CALC}
Esc	{ESCAPE} or {ESC}	F10 (Graph)	{GRAPH}

Teach Yourself
Lotus 1-2-3 Release 2.2

Teach Yourself
■ *Lotus 1-2-3® Release 2.2*

■ **Jeff Woodward**

San Francisco

■

Paris

■

Düsseldorf

■

London

Teach Yourself book concept: David Kolodney
Acquisitions Editor: Dianne King
Editor: Cheryl Holzaepfel
Technical Editor: Michael Gross
Word Processors: Scott Campbell, Deborah Maizels, and Chris Mockel
Book Designer: Ingrid Owen
Technical Art: Jeffrey James Giese
Screen Graphics: Delia Brown
Page Layout: LUCID PRODUCTIONS
Desktop Publishing Operations: Dan Brodnitz
Proofreader: Lisa Jaffe
Indexer:Ted Laux
Cover Designer: Kelly Archer

dBASE is a trademark of Ashton-Tate Corp.
IBM PC/XT, IBM PC/AT, PS/2, and PC-DOS are trademarks of IBM Corp.
Multiplan and MS-DOS are trademarks of Microsoft Corp.
LaserJet Series II is a trademark of Hewlett-Packard Co.
Lotus 1-2-3, Symphony, and VisiCalc are trademarks of Lotus Development Corp.
WordPerfect is a trademark of WordPerfect Corp.
SYBEX is a registered trademark of SYBEX, Inc.

TRADEMARKS: SYBEX has attempted throughout this book to distinguish proprietary trademarks from descriptive terms by following the capitalization style used by the manufacturer.

SYBEX is not affiliated with any manufacturer.

Every effort has been made to supply complete and accurate information. However, SYBEX assumes no responsibility for its use, nor for any infringement of the intellectual property rights of third parties which would result from such use.

Library of Congress Card Number: 89-51855
ISBN: 0-89588-641-3

Manufactured in the United States of America
10 9 8 7 6

■ *Acknowledgments*

Teach Yourself Lotus 1-2-3 Release 2.2 is a new concept in computer book tutorials, and a tremendous effort by many people has gone into its creation. There are many people to whom I wish to extend my most grateful thanks:

To all those people who work so hard behind the scenes to complete their individual parts of a large and complex project. I do not know these people by name, but I am very appreciative of their hard work.

To Cheryl Holzaepfel, my developmental editor. Her encouragement, support, and guidance, along with her ever cheerful and positive demeanor, aided me greatly in the completion of this book.

To Michael Gross, my technical editor. His diligent and detailed technical review contributed greatly to the accuracy of the many exercises covered in this book.

To Dianne King, Acquisitions Editor, for thinking of me for this book, and for being cheerfully responsive to every request for assistance I made during the process of putting this book together.

To Dr. Rudy Langer, Editor-in-Chief, for entrusting me to write this book, my third, for SYBEX.

To the fine people at Lotus, for developing such a sensational program. May they continue to have much success with future releases of Lotus 1-2-3.

Jeff Woodward
30 November 1989
Los Angeles, California

∎Contents at a Glance

■ *Table of Contents*

■ *4 Formatting Your Worksheet*   *105*

■ 5 *Working with 1-2-3's Advanced Features*   *131*

■ *8 Using 1-2-3 as a Database Manager*

■ 9 Speeding Up Your Work with Macros   *357*

∎*Introduction*

Welcome to *Teach Yourself Lotus 1-2-3 Release 2.2*, a guide to the powerful tools available in Lotus 1-2-3 Release 2.2. If you are new to computerized number crunching, are familiar with other versions of 1-2-3, or would like to make the transition from another spreadsheet program to 1-2-3, then this book is an excellent place to begin.

The unique visual approach of this book enables it to reflect as closely as possible the actual experience of using 1-2-3 at the computer. *Teach Yourself Lotus 1-2-3 Release 2.2* is an efficient and effective tool for those who want to learn how to create spreadsheets as they work at the computer, but don't really want to read pages and pages of text to accomplish their goal. The exercises are not lengthy, providing the most benefit in the least amount of time.

Why, you ask, is this book any better than the documentation that came with my 1-2-3 program? The 1-2-3 documentation, excellent as it is, is primarily a reference manual listing the many functions of the program. *Teach Yourself Lotus 1-2-3 Release 2.2* is designed to be a learning aid to guide you through the basic features of 1-2-3. You are directly involved from the first moment, activating keystroke commands and creating sample worksheets step by step. Each step is followed by an illustration of what appears on your monitor, to help you stay on the right track. You will be surprised at how easy it is to get up and running with 1-2-3 Release 2.2.

While there are several versions of 1-2-3, and different models of computers they work with, this book concerns itself with Release 2.2 for the IBM PC/XT, AT, and PS/2 family of computers and those that are compatible with them.

■ *What's New in Release 2.2*

Lotus has made many powerful enhancements in this latest release of 1-2-3, while maintaining compatibility with earlier releases of 1-2-3. This compatibility enables the transfer of files from Releases 1A, 2.0, 2.01, and Symphony into Release 2.2. Files created in Release 2.2 can also be used in 1-2-3 Releases 2.0, 2.01, 3.0, and Symphony versions 1.1 and later. To use Release 2.2 files in 1-2-3 release 1A or Symphony 1.0 or 1.01, you must convert the files with the 2.2 Translate utility. Let's take a look at some of the improvements in Release 2.2.

File linking is one of the major enhancements. It enables you to pull data into the current worksheet from worksheets stored on the disk. You also can automatically update worksheet data in worksheets that are linked to a source worksheet when the source worksheet is edited. File links can be established with worksheets created in Releases 3.0, 1A, 2.0, and 2.01.

Release 2.2 now incorporates minimal recalculation, which means only the formulas or cells that are affected by a change in the worksheet are calculated. This results in faster calculation speeds and increased performance.

Undo is an exciting new feature. It allows you to correct changes made to the worksheet by returning the worksheet to the way it looked before the error was made.

With Release 2.2 you can set and reset the column widths for a range of columns.

Release 2.2 introduces settings sheets that display on one screen all the settings for global defaults, printing, parse, sort, regression, query, worksheet status, and graphs. This makes it easy to keep tabs on the options you have chosen for these particular operations.

There also are many graphic enhancements in Release 2.2. Improvements have been made in the crosshatching patterns used to shade bars and pie slices. Long legends now wrap to two or more lines. Grid lines can be drawn behind bar and stacked bar graphs. X-axis labels that are long enough to overlap are staggered along the axis. Also, the Allways Spreadsheet Publisher is now included with 1-2-3 as an add-in program to make presentation-quality graphs available to every user.

■ *How to Use This Book*

Unlike most computer books, the format for this book relies on graphics, not text, to present the material. Each chapter is broken up into practical exercises that present graphic and written instructions, followed by an illustration of what you should actually see on your computer screen.

Each numbered step has two parts. Text and key graphics explain what to do or which keys to press. Directly following the step is an illustration of what you should see on your screen. The sequence looks like this:

■ *4*   Type **+D8+D9+D10+D11** and press ⌐ 💿

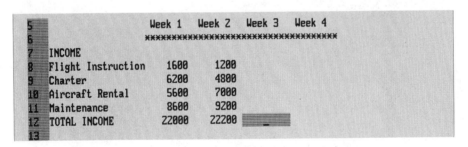

Descriptions of the keyboard and the keys you'll use most often are found in this Introduction.

Some screen illustrations include notes that provide additional information about the screen you are viewing, as in this example:

■*3*   ⬇ to move the pointer to cell D11.

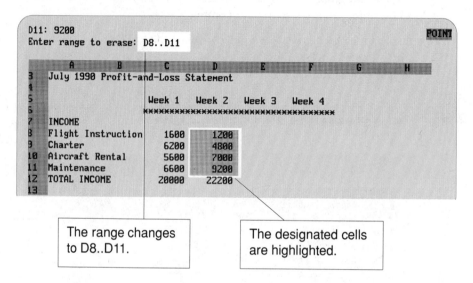

The range changes to D8..D11.

The designated cells are highlighted.

So, the step-by-step flow of these next two instructions:

■*4*   ⏎

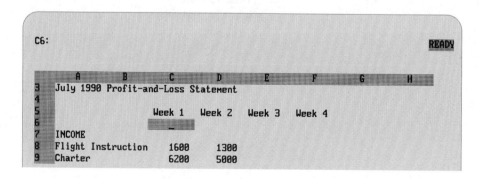

■ *5* [ALT] [F4] to restore the asterisks to
the worksheet.

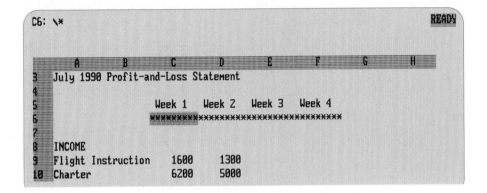

would be: Step 4 of this exercise is to press the [↵] (Enter) key. Your screen
should now look like the one shown below the step. Step 5 is to press [ALT] [F4],
which will produce the screen shown below that step.

You will also see notes such as this one throughout the book:

Note You may also start the 1-2-3 program directly from a DOS prompt without
going through the Access System menu. Simply type 123 at the A or C prompt and
press m. The 1-2-3 program will start and the worksheet screen will be displayed.

Notes give you supplementary information about the feature you're learning.
They might refer you to a related section in the book, give you a helpful hint or
warning, or offer a useful or interesting observation.

There is another graphic element in this book that you should become familiar with before you start the exercises. When you see two keys connected, like this:

ALT F4

it means you should press and hold down the first key (the ALT key in this case), press the second key (the F4 key here), and then release them both.

A Quick Tour
■ through the Chapters

Before you start with Chapter 1, there are a few preliminary tasks that you'll need to take care of. You should make backup copies of your 1-2-3 program disks and properly install 1-2-3 on your computer. Appendices A and B contain instructions for completing these tasks. Once you've done so, you're ready to start with Chapter 1. The best way to use *Teach Yourself Lotus 1-2-3 Release 2.2* is to follow the exercises from beginning to end. However, if you wish to skip ahead for information about a particular feature, feel free to do so. You may also substitute one of your own documents in place of the ones used in the exercises.

Chapter 1 guides you through starting your computer and the 1-2-3 program. You'll also learn about the 1-2-3 worksheet, where you enter your data, how to move around the worksheet, and how to exit from the program.

Chapter 2 introduces you to the procedures for entering data into a worksheet. You'll enter text, numbers, and formulas into worksheet cells, use functions to streamline formulas, and save your worksheet.

Chapter 3 shows you how to edit your worksheets. You'll make corrections, use 1-2-3's Help feature, work with rows and columns, and copy data from one area of a worksheet to another.

Chapters 4, 5, and 6 guide you through some of the advanced features offered by 1-2-3. You'll learn how to format cell entries, fix titles so they don't scroll off the screen, add comments to the worksheet, perform advanced printing procedures, share files with other programs, and link worksheets.

Chapter 7 shows you how to create worksheet graphs. In this chapter you'll create a bar graph, a stack-bar graph, a line graph, and a pie chart.

In Chapter 8 you'll create and work with a 1-2-3 database.

Chapter 9 covers the use of 1-2-3 macros, which are helpful for speeding up certain operations you perform on a regular basis.

Appendix A guides you through the procedures for installing the 1-2-3 Release 2.2 program. If you are upgrading from a previous release of 1-2-3, consult your 1-2-3 *Upgrader's Handbook* documentation.

Appendix B shows you how to make backup copies of your 1-2-3 program disks. You can use the same procedures to make copies of other program and document disks.

Inside the covers of this book you will find material that provides you with instant reference to information such as pointer-movement keys, function keys, cell format options, mode and status indicators, and macro key instructions.

■ *Computer Basics*

Before you begin working with 1-2-3, there are a few things you should know about your computer. In this section you'll learn about hardware and software, floppy disks, and a little about how your computer uses DOS, its operating system.

About Software

The term *software* refers to the many programs that are run on your computer. Examples of software are Lotus 1-2-3, WordPerfect, dBASE, and DOS. The variety and amount of software on the market is practically endless—everything from word processing and business applications to banner makers and games is available. If you have a hard disk (see "About Hardware" in this Introduction), you will probably copy your programs from the floppy disks to the hard disk. If you have a computer with only floppy drives, you must use the program floppy disks each time you run the program.

About Hardware

The main components that you will need to operate 1-2-3 are a monitor and a display card, a printer, disk drives, and the computer itself. This equipment is referred to as computer *hardware*.

Monitors

A monitor is the screen where you view your document. Monitors come in a multitude of models that vary in shape, size, and quality of *resolution* (the clarity of the display image). You may have a monochrome, composite, or color monitor. 1-2-3 will run on all of them.

The most common monochrome monitors display images in green or amber on a black background. Composite monitors are also monochrome, but they can display different shades of green or amber. This gives you shading variations that can be used in the same way that color differences can be used on color monitors. For instance, the setting for yellow displays a lighter shade of amber or green than the setting for red.

Display Cards

The display card is an important part of your computer system. It links the computer with the monitor, allowing the images that you create at the keyboard, or program information, to be processed and displayed on the monitor screen. Each type of monitor requires its own display card, so be sure your system is set up properly. This is especially important if you purchase your monitor and computer separately and connect them yourself.

The display card also determines the resolution that can be displayed on the screen. The degree of resolution is an important consideration if you plan on working with 1-2-3's and Allways's graphics features.

Disk Drives

Disk drives operate the hard or floppy disks that contain your software applications and store the documents you create. There are essentially two types of disk drives—floppy disk drives (5¼- or 3½-inch diameter) and hard drives.

If your system has two floppy drives, they are situated either side by side (with a vertical drive slot) or stacked (with a horizontal drive slot). The topmost horizontal drive or left-hand vertical drive is called drive A. The other drive is drive B.

The hard drive is normally called drive C and is mounted internally in the computer; however, external hard drives are also available. Internal hard drives aren't removable from your computer. If your system has both a hard and a floppy drive, you have an A and a C drive. Hard drives work basically the same as floppy drives, except the disks used in them are thicker and harder and hold a great deal more information. Hard disks also process information faster than floppy drives.

Printers   1-2-3 will work with hundreds of different printers. To give you a general overview, there are basically three types of printers: dot-matrix, daisy-wheel, and laser printers. Dot-matrix printers print text or graphics by grouping hundreds of small ink dots into the correct shape or design. The print from these printers is not usually of a high quality, although several brands achieve letter-quality print. Consequently, documents printed on dot-matrix printers are often limited to rough drafts, lists, memos, and graphics.

Daisy-wheel and laser printers are both letter-quality printers. A daisy-wheel printer, like most electric typewriters, uses a plastic print element called a daisy-wheel to print characters. These printers are usually slow and noisy, and are limited to printing text. Laser printers are more expensive, but they can print both letter-quality text and graphics, and do it quietly and quickly.

Caring for Floppy Disks

Care must be taken when using floppy disks, especially those disks that contain 1-2-3 and your operating system. It is important that you make backup copies of all your software. (See Appendix B, "Making Backup Disks of 1-2-3".) Use the backup copies and store the originals in a safe place in case the backups get damaged. Take care never to bend your disks, expose them to magnetic fields, or subject them to extreme heat or cold, cigarette smoke, or any chemicals that give off vapors. Store your disks in plastic or cardboard boxes.

When placing a floppy disk into a horizontal drive, open the drive latch and slide the disk into the slot with the label facing up and the write-protect notch facing left. On side-by-side vertical drives, the label should face to the left with the write-protect notch facing down. The write-protect notch on a 5¼ inch disk is the rectangular cutout on one edge of the disk. The write-protect notch on a 3½ inch floppy disk is the small square window with the tab that can be moved back and forth.

Be careful not to touch the portion of the disk exposed by the long oval slot; you can lose valuable information stored on the disk. Be sure to close the drive latch after placing the floppy disk in the drive.

DOS — The Disk Operating System

DOS can be mystifying if you're new to computers. I'll try to shed a little light on this subject and put you at ease.

DOS is a master program that controls the flow of information between the components of your computer system, such as between the computer and the storage disks, or between the computer and the printer. DOS is a software program that must be loaded into your computer each time you start the computer in order to run 1-2-3 or any other program. Hard-disk users will have to install DOS on their hard disks if the computer manufacturer hasn't already done so. Once installed, DOS is automatically loaded when you start the computer. Floppy-disk users must place a DOS disk in a floppy-disk drive before they start the computer.

Understanding Computer Memory

Computers have two types of memory—temporary and permanent—and there are important differences between them. As a beginner, you may think that the information you type into the computer is there forever, to be called upon whenever you need it: you type a document, turn off the machine, and return later for editing. It's not quite as simple as that. Let me explain.

The area of the computer where your data is initially stored is called *RAM* (random access memory) and is referred to as temporary storage. If you turn your machine off, or if there is a power failure of some sort, you would immediately lose data stored in RAM because the data is only temporarily stored there until you record it permanently. Until the data is recorded, or *written* on a disk, it can be lost.

Why have temporary memory? Why not have it recorded permanently as you enter the data into the computer? Recording information on a floppy or hard disk is a physical process and is much slower than manipulating the data electronically, which is what RAM is used for. The constant recording of data on a floppy or hard disk as you work would be very time consuming and would defeat one of the main benefits of having a computer—speedy data processing.

The final objective, of course, is to store, or *save*, your hard-wrought data permanently for future use. Permanent memory is the recording of the data onto a floppy or hard disk. You can compare it to making a recording of a favorite song from the radio. Once you listen to the song it's gone, but if you record it on a tape, you can replay it and listen to it as often as you want. So, if you are wise, you will save your data on a disk often while you work so you will not lose valuable information.

Keeping Track of Your Data

The location of your data is an important concept when working with computers. Knowing how to manipulate data is important, but you must also know *where* the information is in order to save, retrieve, and edit it.

If you have a dual floppy-disk system, the location possibilities are fairly clear: your documents are located on either the A or B drive. If you have a hard-disk drive, it's a bit more complex. All your information is usually on drive C because it can hold much more data than a floppy disk. However, drive C has a vast amount of storage space, so the space is usually divided into separate groups to make it easier to find your data. To find data on your hard disk, you must know which group it is stored in.

Try to visualize the monitor as your work area and the A, B, or C drives as file drawers in an electronic file cabinet. (A *file* is data that is saved as a unit, and has a specific name, just like a labeled manila folder.) Your files are located in these "file drawers." Some of the files are organized into separate groups called *directories* and *subdirectories*. When you want to bring a file to your work area (monitor), you have to tell the computer to look in the correct file drawer (the A, B, or C drive) and directory. This route the computer follows to find the file is a *path*. For example, if you gave your computer this path to find a file when working in 1-2-3

    C:\123\REPORT.WK1

the computer would go to drive C (C:), then to the 1-2-3 directory (123), and retrieve the worksheet REPORT.WK1. If you wanted to store the file in that location, you would type in this same path when you save the file.

A hard drive can hold literally hundreds of files. Knowing which directory your file is located in, and how to get there, is vital to your efficient use of the computer. As you work through the exercises in this book, you will learn how to tell the computer where you want files saved, and how to find files once you've saved them in a directory. Talking about this subject and understanding it are two different things. Don't be concerned; as you gain experience using your computer, you will soon become comfortable with these ideas. A light bulb will click on in your mind and you will understand them perfectly.

■ *The 1-2-3 Keyboard*

The keyboard you have for your computer works much like a typewriter, with several important differences. The illustration below shows three common styles of keyboards. There are some keys that work the same as typewriter keys, but when used in combination with other keys, they perform special tasks. In addition to these special keys, there are function keys that are not found on typewriters. Just as a pilot must be familiar with the instrument panel and controls of any new airplane he or she flies, so must you become familiar with the keyboard, for that is where you control 1-2-3.

Special Keys

Look at your keyboard and locate the following keys:

TAB   This is the Tab key. It is used in conjunction with Arrow keys and the Shift key to move the pointer or cursor.

↵   This is the Enter (or Return) key, one of the most frequently used keys on the keyboard. It is used when entering data into worksheets and to execute certain 1-2-3 commands.

BKSP ←   This is the Backspace key. You use it to delete unwanted characters, *not* to move backwards through text.

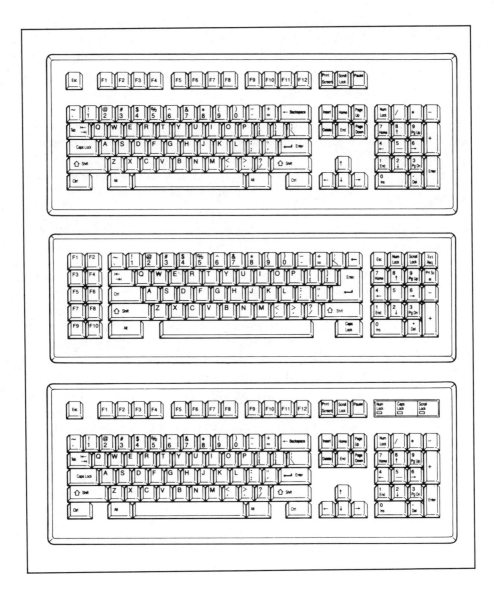

INS   The Insert (Ins) key is used to switch between Insert and Typeover modes. In the Insert mode, existing characters will move to the right to make room for the new ones that you type. In the Typeover mode, the new characters you type replace the existing ones.

SHIFT   This is the Shift key. It is used to create uppercase letters. When it is used in conjunction with the Tab key, it moves the pointer.

ALT   The Alt key is used in conjunction with function keys to execute certain 1-2-3 features, programs, or commands.

ESC   This is the Escape (or Esc) key. It will step you backwards, one level at a time, through the 1-2-3 menus.

DEL   When you press the Delete key you erase the character that exists at that cursor position.

↑
↓
→
←   These Arrow keys allow you to move the pointer and cursor throughout your worksheet. (The pointer is a highlight that identifies a specific cell or range of cells, and the cursor is a small flashing underline character that indicates the location where each character you type will appear.) All keyboards have a set of these keys on the numeric keypad on the 2, 4, 6, and 8 keys. Some keyboards have a second set of dedicated Arrow keys.

HOME   The Home key moves the pointer back to the top-left corner of the worksheet from anywhere in the worksheet. It is also used in conjunction with Arrow keys to move the pointer.

CTRL   The Control key (usually called Ctrl), like the Alt and Shift keys, is used in conjuction with the function keys.

Function Keys

The function keys are labeled F1 through F10 or F12, depending on which style of keyboard you are using. They are located along the top of the keyboard or in two rows on the left side of the keyboard. No matter the location, they perform the same tasks.

These keys have been programmed to perform many of the same tasks that the 1-2-3 menu system performs. Instead of pressing several keys to execute a menu command, you can press a function key by itself, or a function key in conjunction with the Alt key. You will find that you'll remember the key combinations you use regularly. For those 1-2-3 features that you use less frequently and may need to look up, 1-2-3 provides a Help feature that will tell you the command and function key combination needed to activate the feature. The 1-2-3 package also includes a keyboard template that sits on the keyboard above the function keys on the enhanced keyboard, or fits over the function keys on the older-style keyboards.

The Numeric Keypad

The numeric keypad is located on the right side of your keyboard. It is usually easier to manipulate the number keys from the keypad than it is to reach up for the numbers along the top of the keyboard.

To activate the numeric keypad, you simply press the Num Lock key. An indicator (NUM) along the bottom of the worksheet screen lets you know when Num Lock is activated. On some keyboards, a light on the Num Lock key or in the upper-right corner of the keyboard will indicate that the numeric keypad is in use. When Num Lock is active, the cursor keys on the numeric keypad (on the 2, 4, 6, and 8 keys) will no longer move the pointer or cursor; the keys produce numbers instead. To deactivate the numeric keypad, you press the Num Lock key again. The NUM screen indicator will disappear.

■ *Before You Begin*

Many people become intimidated when they have to read instructions of any sort. Here's some quick advice about intimidation for those of you who are new to computers. Forget it! This book is designed to make getting started with 1-2-3 as easy and as painless as possible. So relax and begin at the beginning; by the time you complete the first two chapters, you will have created your first worksheet, printed it, and saved it for future editing. I think you will be surprised by how easy it is.

ONE

Getting Started with 1-2-3

This chapter is the place to begin if you are new to Lotus 1-2-3. By this time you should have read the Introduction and the appendices and have 1-2-3 installed and ready to operate. If not, please read these important chapters, for they contain valuable information about setting up your 1-2-3 program and how to effectively use this book.

Starting the Computer

Starting 1-2-3

Finding Your Way around the 1-2-3 Worksheet

■*Starting the Computer*

This section is for those of you who are new to computers. Starting your computer is simple— once you've done it a few times, it'll be as easy as turning on your television or video recorder.

Let's jump right in. If you have a hard-disk computer, the start up is very simple. If you have a dual floppy-disk computer, you will need a disk that contains the disk operating system (DOS). Also, you need to have your 1-2-3 program back-up disks handy (see Appendix B, "Making Backup Copies of Floppy Disks").

■*1*   If you have a floppy-disk computer, place your DOS system disk in drive A and close the latch. Turn on the monitor and computer. Hard-disk users, simply turn on your monitor and computer.

```
Current date is Thu  8-10-1990
Enter new date (mm-dd-yy): _
```

■*2*   Type in the current date and press ⏎. If the date is correct, just press ⏎.

```
Current date is Thu  8-10-1990
Enter new date (mm-dd-yy):
Current time is 12:00:00.00
Enter new time: _
```

■ *3*   Type in the current time and press ⏎. If the time is correct, just press ⏎. The DOS C prompt appears for hard-disk users. (If you're using a floppy-disk system you'll see an A prompt instead of a C prompt.)

```
Current date is Thu  8-10-1990
Enter new date (MM-dd-yy):
Current time is 12:00:00.00
Enter new time:

C>_
```

Some computers are configured to bypass the date and time prompts and immediately display the DOS prompt. Some DOS prompts will also include the directory name, for example, C:\123 or C:\dBASE, and so on.

When the DOS C or A prompt appears, the operating system is ready to use. From here you can start up, or *execute* Lotus 1-2-3.

Note   Incorrect entries will result in an error message. Don't worry, the screen will display the previous prompt at which you made the incorrect entry. Simply enter the correct information at the prompt.

∎*Starting 1-2-3*

1

To execute the 1-2-3 program, floppy-disk users should start with step 1 below. Hard-disk users can begin with step 2.

∎ *1*   Floppy-disk users, remove the DOS disk from drive A and replace it with the backup 1-2-3 System Disk. Then, skip step 2 and proceed with step 3.

∎ *2*   Hard-disk users, type **CD 123** at the C prompt and press ⏎.

```
C>CD 123

C>_
```

You must
install 1-2-3
before you
can start
it—see
Appendix A.

■ *3*   Type **LOTUS** and press 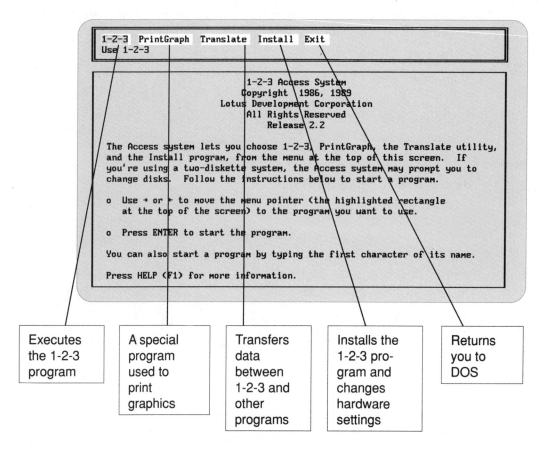. The Access
System screen appears.

```
1-2-3  PrintGraph  Translate  Install  Exit
Use 1-2-3

                    1-2-3 Access System
                  Copyright 1986, 1989
                Lotus Development Corporation
                   All Rights Reserved
                      Release 2.2

      The Access system lets you choose 1-2-3, PrintGraph, the Translate utility,
      and the Install program, from the menu at the top of this screen.  If
      you're using a two-diskette system, the Access system may prompt you to
      change disks.  Follow the instructions below to start a program.

      o  Use → or ← to move the menu pointer (the highlighted rectangle
         at the top of the screen) to the program you want to use.

      o  Press ENTER to start the program.

      You can also start a program by typing the first character of its name.

      Press HELP (F1) for more information.
```

| Executes the 1-2-3 program | A special program used to print graphics | Transfers data between 1-2-3 and other programs | Installs the 1-2-3 program and changes hardware settings | Returns you to DOS |

Note   You may also start the 1-2-3 program directly from a DOS prompt without going through the Access System menu. Simply type **123** at the A or C prompt and press 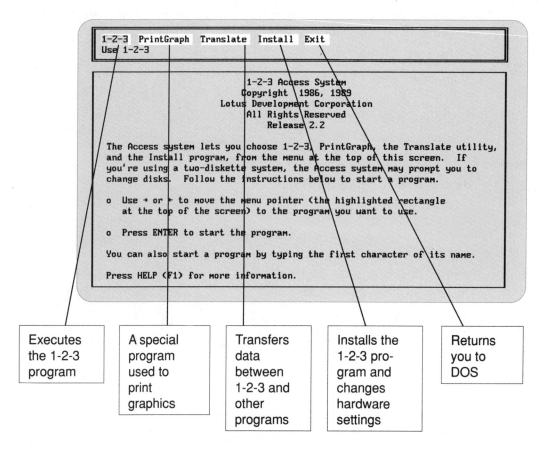. The 1-2-3 program will start and the worksheet screen will be displayed.

■*4* Use ⬅ and ➡ to move the highlight to the
option you wish to run. To start 1-2-3, place
the highlight on "1-2-3" and press ⏎ . The
1-2-3 worksheet appears.

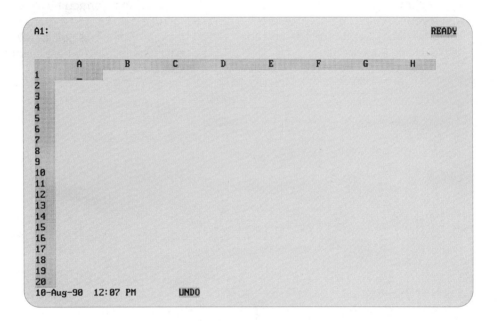

Finding Your Way
■*around the Worksheet*

The 1-2-3 worksheet has three distinct areas: the *worksheet area*, the *control
panel*, and the *status line*. Let's take a brief look at what each area is used for.

The Worksheet Area

The worksheet area is where you display and calculate your worksheet entries. It is constructed of rows and columns.

These numbers indicate the *rows* in which you can place data. Rows are numbered from 1 to 8,192. The screen displays only 20 rows at one time.

This is a *cell*. It is formed by the intersection of a column and a row and is named after both. This cell is called E5 since it is the location where column E and row 5 meet.

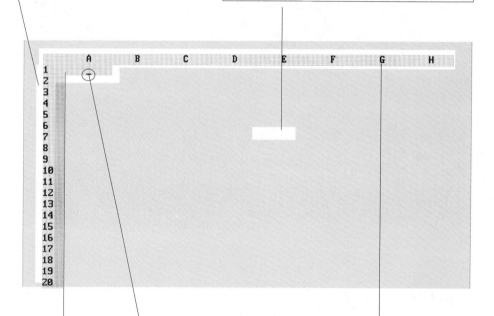

This is the *cell pointer*. It highlights the cell you are currently working with. You can move the pointer to any cell in the worksheet.

This is the *cursor*. It marks the location where characters are typed to, or deleted from, the screen.

These letters indicate the *columns* in which you can place data. There are a total of 256 columns. Columns are lettered from A-Z, then AA-AZ, then BA-BZ, CA-CZ, and so on to IV, the 256th column. You can now see only eight columns on the screen, but you can change the screen width.

The Control Panel

The control panel is where you initially enter and edit data to be displayed on the worksheet, enter the formulas you want 1-2-3 to execute, and where you select commands to execute 1-2-3's many powerful features.

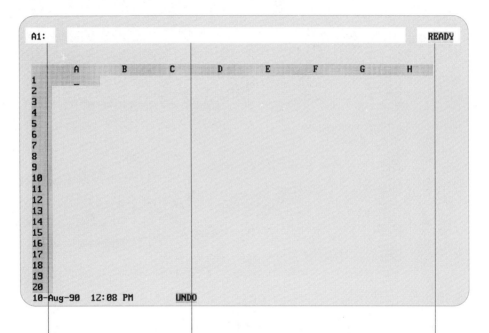

This is the *cell address*. It displays the location of the cell pointer. Any data that is entered in the selected cell will also be displayed here. This cell is blank because it does not contain any data.

This area displays the current entry data as you create it or edit it. It also displays a command line menu from which you can select program features.

This is the *mode indicator*. It tells you the mode, or current state of activity, that 1-2-3 is running in. Ready means 1-2-3 is ready for you to type data or select a command. See inside the cover of this book for a list of mode indicators.

The Status Line

The status line displays information about the current status of a work session.

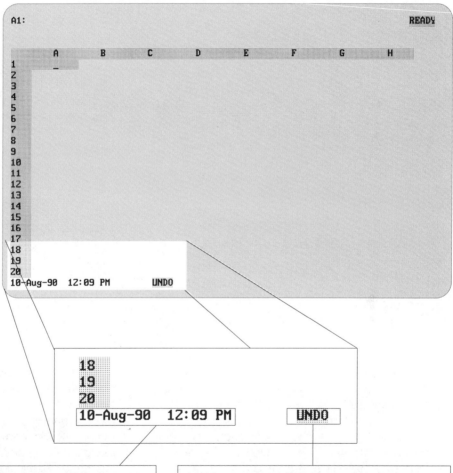

The date and time of the current work session are displayed here. Error messages also appear here when 1-2-3 detects an erroneous entry or cannot execute a command.

In this area you will find *status indicators* that show whether certain 1-2-3 operations are activated. For example, the UNDO indicator alerts you that the Undo feature is activated. See inside the covers of this book for a list of status indicators.

■*Moving the Cell Pointer*

In order to place data in the many cells that make up the worksheet, you must be able to move the cell pointer to the desired locations. There are a multitude of ways in which to move the cell pointer, but we will cover only the basic pointer movements in this entry-level book.

> **Note** Chapter 1 of your 1-2-3 documentation provides a complete listing of cell pointer movements. Look inside the covers of this book for a listing of the pointer-movement keys discussed in this book.

Let's experiment with the pointer-movement keys. You should still have a blank worksheet displayed on your screen with the cell pointer located in cell A1.

■ *1* Press ⊡ 10 times to move the pointer one cell at a time to cell K1. Notice that columns A-C disappear off the left side of the worksheet.

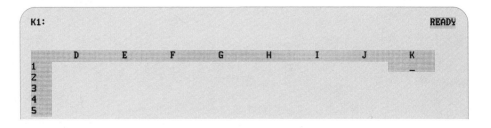

Note *The Num Lock Key* If you use the Arrow keys that are collocated with the numeric keypad, be sure the Num Lock key is off. When Num Lock is on, you will see *NUM* highlighted on the status line in the bottom right corner of your screen. If Num Lock is on, numbers will appear on your screen and the pointer will not move. If this happens, delete the numbers by pressing the ⬅ and press the Num Lock key to toggle it off.

■2   Press ⬇ 24 times to move the pointer one cell at a time to cell K25. Notice that rows 1-5 disappear off the top of the worksheet.

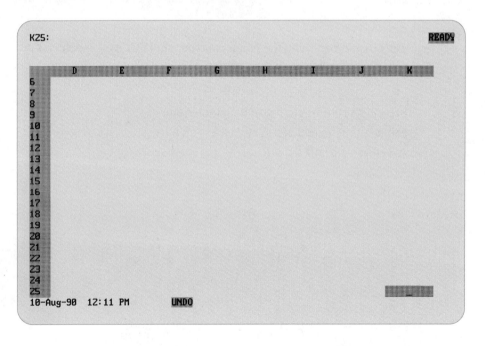

1

■*3* Press ⬅ five times to move the pointer to cell F25.

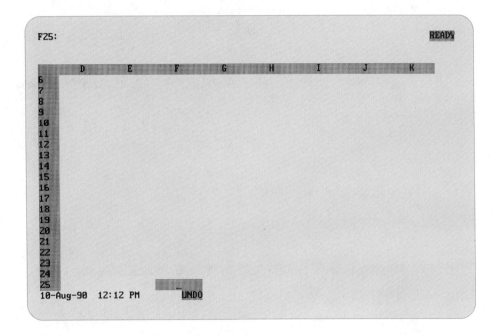

■*4* Press ⬆ 15 times to move the pointer to cell F10.

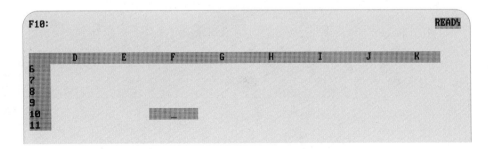

■ *5*   Press HOME to return the pointer to cell A1.
(You can do this from anywhere on the
worksheet.)

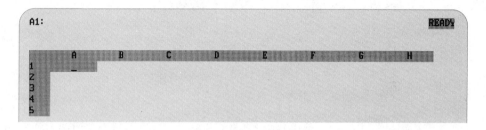

■ *6*   Press END → to move the pointer to cell IV1.

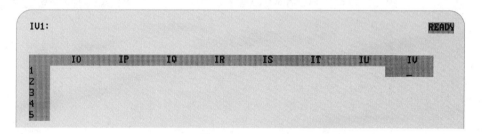

■ *7*   Press END ↓ to move the pointer to cell
IV 8192. Row 8192 is the last row of the
worksheet.

Note Pressing [END] and any Arrow key will move the pointer in the direction of the arrow to the nearest cell containing data, to the furthest cell containing data if this movement is made across consecutive data-containing cells, or to the furthest blank cell if no data is encountered.

■ *8* Press [HOME] to return to cell A1.

■ *9* Press [PG DN] to move the pointer one full screen—20 rows—to cell A21.

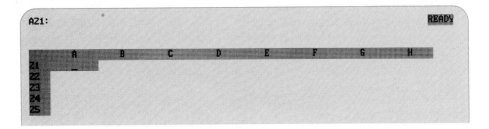

■ *10* Press [PG UP] to move the pointer one full screen or 20 rows to cell A1.

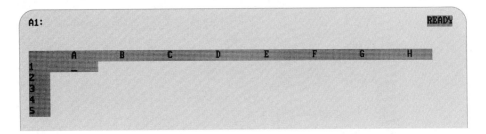

■ *11* Press F5. This is the Go To key, which allows you to type in a specific cell address and
move the pointer to that location.

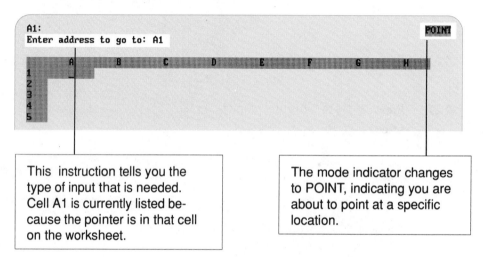

This instruction tells you the
type of input that is needed.
Cell A1 is currently listed because the pointer is in that cell
on the worksheet.

The mode indicator changes
to POINT, indicating you are
about to point at a specific
location.

■ *12* Type **G13** and press ⏎ to move the pointer
to cell G13.

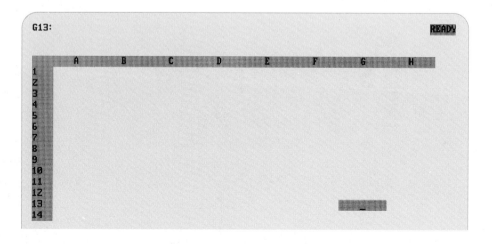

At this point, you may continue on with Chapter 2 where you will create your first 1-2-3 document. If you want to take a break, the following section will show you how to exit the 1-2-3 program.

■ *Quitting 1-2-3*

To exit 1-2-3, you must select the Quit option from the Main menu. The Main menu is displayed in the control panel when you press the slash key (□). Try it.

■ *1*   Press □ to display the Main menu.

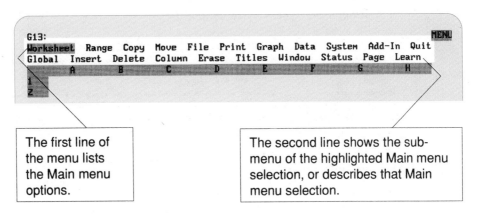

The first line of the menu lists the Main menu options.

The second line shows the sub-menu of the highlighted Main menu selection, or describes that Main menu selection.

■ *2*   Press ▭ 10 times or ▭ once to move the highlight to Quit.

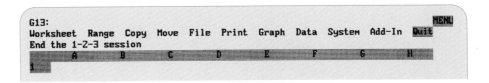

■*3*   Press ⏎. You are given the opportunity to remain in the program.

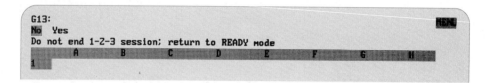

■*4*   Move the highlight to Yes and press ⏎. You return to the Access System menu. (If you started 1-2-3 directly from the DOS prompt, you will return to the DOS prompt without going through the Access System menu.)

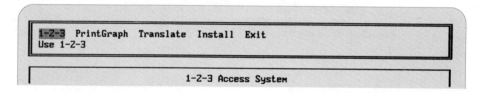

■*5*   Move the highlight to Exit and press ⏎.

■*Summary*

In this chapter you learned how to start your computer and the 1-2-3 program. Floppy-disk users should always use their backup disks when running 1-2-3 and should store the original disks in a safe place. You also learned about the 1-2-3 worksheet and how to move the cell pointer with the pointer-movement keys. Lastly, you saw how to exit the 1-2-3 program.

Chapter 2 will introduce you to the basics for entering data into the worksheet.

TWO

Creating and Printing a Worksheet

In this chapter you will enter data into a worksheet. There are many types of documents that can be constructed using 1-2-3, more than can be presented in this introductory book, so we'll confine our discussion to the development of a simple profit-and-loss statement.

- Labeling Your Worksheet
- Entering Numerical Values
- Using Formulas
- Using Functions to Streamline Formulas
- Understanding Order of Precedence
- Saving Your Worksheet
- Printing Your Worksheet

■ *Labeling Your Worksheet*

The columns and rows of numbers that make up a spreadsheet have no meaning unless you give them names that describe what the numbers represent. 1-2-3 calls these names *labels*. You can place any kind of label on a worksheet: years, months, days, dates, subject titles, budget items, and so on.

In the following exercise, you will create a worksheet with labels that title the spreadsheet, specify time periods, and identify several income and expense items.

If you took a break after Chapter 1, please start your computer and the 1-2-3 program. If you are continuing from Chapter 1, press HOME to return the pointer to cell A1.

Caps Lock is a
toggle key—press
it once to turn it
on, press it again
to turn it off.

■ *1* With the pointer in cell A1, type
BRIARCLIFF AVIATION. (Pressing Caps
Lock will allow you to type all capital let-
ters.) Use [BKSP ←] to correct any typos.

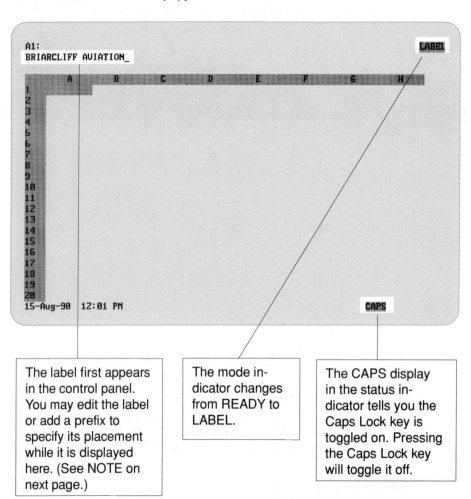

The label first appears
in the control panel.
You may edit the label
or add a prefix to
specify its placement
while it is displayed
here. (See NOTE on
next page.)

The mode in-
dicator changes
from READY to
LABEL.

The CAPS display
in the status in-
dicator tells you the
Caps Lock key is
toggled on. Pressing
the Caps Lock key
will toggle it off.

2

> **Note** *Label Prefixes* Label prefixes allow you to position a label within a cell. Type the prefix as you type the label into the control panel. You may edit the prefix anytime after it's placed on the worksheet.
>
> - Typing an apostrophe (') aligns the label with the left edge of the cell.
> - The caret (^) centers the label in the cell.
> - Quotation marks (") align the label with the right edge of the cell.
> - A backslash (\ ) repeats the label across the width of the cell.
> - Omitting a prefix will automattically align a lable with the left edge of the cell.

If the label name begins with a number or a numeric symbol — + – @ . (# or $ — always type a label prefix in front of the label number. If you don't, 1-2-3 will interpret the numeric entry as a value. If you forget the prefix, 1-2-3 will beep at you and not accept the entry unless it is a bona fide value entry.

■ *2* Press ⏎ to place the label on the worksheet in cell A1. The pointer remains in cell A1.

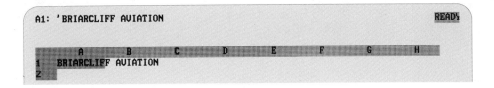

■ *3* Press ↓ to move the pointer to cell A2.
Type **Santa Clarita, CA.** and press ⏎.

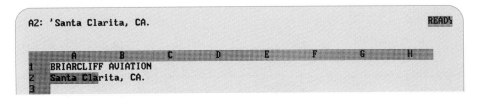

■4 Press ⬇ to move the pointer to cell A3.
Type **August 1990 Profit-and-Loss Statement** and press ⬅ .

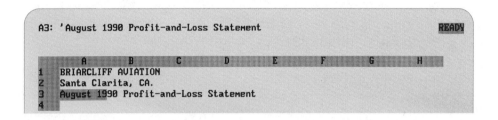

■5 Press F5 (the Go To key), type **C5**, and press
⬅ . The pointer moves to cell C5.

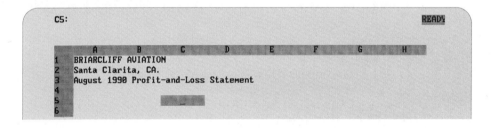

■6   Type **^Week 1** and press ⮕. The pointer
moves to cell D5 and the label is placed in
cell C5.

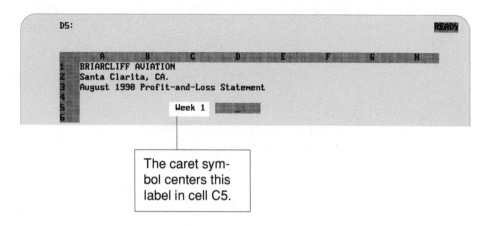

The caret sym-
bol centers this
label in cell C5.

■7   Type **^Week 2** and press ⮕. Then type
^Week 3 and press ⮕. Finally, type **^Week
4** and press ⮕. All the column labels are
now entered on the worksheet.

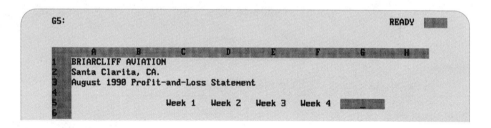

■ *8* F5 , type **C6**, and press ←.

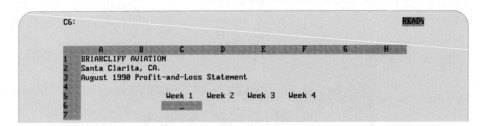

■ *9* \ * → (If you mistakenly press / , you
will see the Main menu in the control panel.
Press ESC to get rid of the menu and try again.)

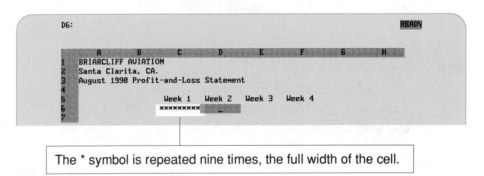

The * symbol is repeated nine times, the full width of the cell.

■ *10* Repeat step 9 three more times to place
asterisks across cells D6 through F6.

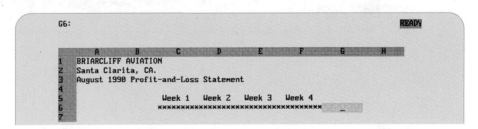

■ *11* Move the pointer to cell A7. Type **INCOME**
and press ⬇.

```
A8:                                                              READY

        A        B        C        D        E        F        G        H
1   BRIARCLIFF AVIATION
2   Santa Clarita, CA.
3   August 1990 Profit-and-Loss Statement
4
5                              Week 1   Week 2   Week 3   Week 4
6                              xxxxxxxxxxxxxxxxxxxxxxxxxxxxxxxxx
7   INCOME
8
9
```

■ *12* Type in the remaining labels as shown below.
Double-check to make sure you type the correct
label in the correct cell. Remember, after you
type the label, press ⬇ to place the label in the
cell and move the pointer to the next cell.

```
A22:                                                            READY

        A        B        C        D        E        F        G        H
3   August 1990 Profit-and-Loss Statement
4
5                              Week 1   Week 2   Week 3   Week 4
6                              xxxxxxxxxxxxxxxxxxxxxxxxxxxxxxxxx
7   INCOME
8   Flight Instruction
9   Charter
10  Aircraft Rental
11  Maintenance
12  TOTAL INCOME
13
14  EXPENSES
15  Wages
16  Fuel/Oil/Parts
17  Rent
18  Insurance
19  TOTAL EXPENSES
20
21  TOTAL PROFIT/LOSS
22
15-Aug-90  12:12 PM          UNDO
```

Note *Long Labels* A long label contains more characters than will fit in a single cell. If the cells to the right of the label are empty of data, the label will overlap into those cells. If data exists in the adjacent cells, the label will be cut off at the left edge of the first cell containing data.

▪*Entering Numerical Values*

You have labeled the worksheet and are ready to place the numerical data into the appropriate cells. We will place the raw income and expense data on the worksheet first. Then, in the next section, "Using Formulas," we'll apply the formulas necessary to analyze the raw data.

▪*1*   Move the pointer to cell C8 and type **1600**.
Do not press ⏎ or an Arrow key.

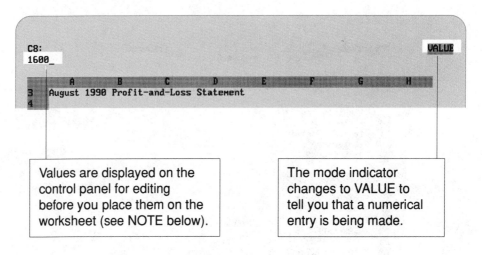

Values are displayed on the control panel for editing before you place them on the worksheet (see NOTE below).

The mode indicator changes to VALUE to tell you that a numerical entry is being made.

Note These basic guidelines must be followed when entering values onto the worksheet.

- Begin entries with numbers or numeric symbols: + −@ . (# or $. Dollar signs will not be displayed on the worksheet.
- Do not include commas or spaces in an entry.
- Do not type more than one decimal point in a single entry.

See Chapter 3, "Editing Your Worksheet," for instructions on how to display dollar signs and commas in numerical entries.

■*2*   ⊡ The value of 1600 is placed in C8 and
the pointer moves to D8.

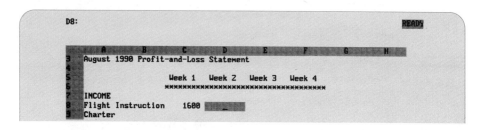

■*3*   Type **1200** and press ⊡ .

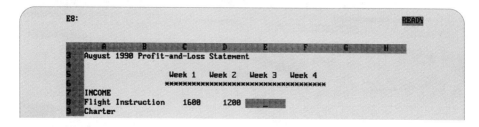

■*4* Using this same procedure, place the remaining values shown below in the appropriate cells. Don't try to change a value after it has been placed on the worksheet. I'll show you how to do this later. Use [BKSP ←] to correct any value still displayed on the control panel.

```
E18:                                                             READY

            A      B        C        D       E       F       G       H
 3  August 1990 Profit-and-Loss Statement
 4
 5                          Week 1   Week 2   Week 3   Week 4
 6                  xxxxxxxxxxxxxxxxxxxxxxxxxxxxxxxxxxx
 7  INCOME
 8  Flight Instruction     1600     1200
 9  Charter                6200     4800
10  Aircraft Rental        5600     7000
11  Maintenance            8600     9200
12  TOTAL INCOME
13
14  EXPENSES
15  Wages                  6800     6600
16  Fuel/Oil/Parts        10300     8400
17  Rent                   2000     2000
18  Insurance              1200     1200
19  TOTAL EXPENSES
20
21  TOTAL PROFIT/LOSS
22
15-Aug-90   12:16 PM            UNDO
```

Using Formulas
■ *to Manipulate Data*

Thus far you have used labels to construct the container that holds your income and expense figures. Now it is time to shake up the container and see how the figures come together. How you shake the container depends on the formulas you use to manipulate the numbers.

Formulas can be as simple or as complex as necessary to get the job done. Many mathematical computations, from simple addition to trigonometric functions, can be performed by 1-2-3. In this book, we will restrict our calculations to the more basic mathematical formulas you will deal with on a day-to-day basis.

Let's compute the total income, expense, and profit / loss figures for the worksheet you've just created.

2

■ *1*   Move the pointer to cell C12.

```
5                            Week 1   Week 2   Week 3   Week 4
6               ×××××××××××××××××××××××××××××××××××
7   INCOME
8   Flight Instruction  1600     1200
9   Charter             6200     4800
10  Aircraft Rental     5600     7000
11  Maintenance         8600     9200
12  TOTAL INCOME
13
```

■ *2*   Type **+C8+C9+C10+C11** (do not press ⏎).
You are telling 1-2-3 to add the values stored
in these four cells.

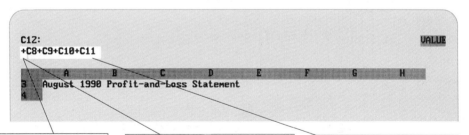

```
C12:                                                        VALUE
+C8+C9+C10+C11

        A         B         C         D         E      F      G      H
3   August 1990 Profit-and-Loss Statement
4
```

| This is an *operator*. Operators tell 1-2-3 what mathematical function to perform on a cell or group of cells. (See NOTE next page.) | The formula must begin with a number or numeric symbol. If not, 1-2-3 reads the formula as a label and will not perform the mathematical function. | Each of these cell entries represents the numerical value in its respective cell. For example, the value of cell C8 is 1600. |

> **Note** *Some Common Operators* There are several operators you need to be familiar with in order to construct 1-2-3 formulas.
>
> - The plus sign (+) denotes addition or a positive number.
> - A minus sign (–) indicates subtraction or a negative number.
> - An asterisk (*) shows multiplication.
> - A slash (/) denotes division.
> - A caret (^) indicates exponentiation.
> - A < sign is the less-than logical operator.
> - The > sign is the greater-than logical operator.

■*3* ⟶ to place the formula in cell C12. The total income appears in cell C12.

```
5                        Week 1   Week 2   Week 3   Week 4
6                        xxxxxxxxxxxxxxxxxxxxxxxxxxxxxxxxxxx
7    INCOME
8    Flight Instruction    1600     1200
9    Charter               6200     4800
10   Aircraft Rental       5600     7000
11   Maintenance           8600     9200
12   TOTAL INCOME         22000
13
```

■*4* Type **+D8+D9+D10+D11** and press ⟶.

```
5                        Week 1   Week 2   Week 3   Week 4
6                        xxxxxxxxxxxxxxxxxxxxxxxxxxxxxxxxxxx
7    INCOME
8    Flight Instruction    1600     1200
9    Charter               6200     4800
10   Aircraft Rental       5600     7000
11   Maintenance           8600     9200
12   TOTAL INCOME         22000    22200
13
```

■5 Move the pointer to cell C21. Type
+C12–C19 and press ⟶ .

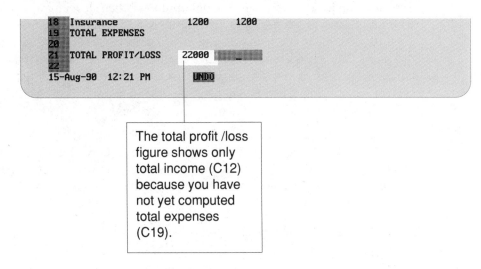

```
18  Insurance              1200      1200
19  TOTAL EXPENSES
20
21  TOTAL PROFIT/LOSS      22000
22
15-Aug-90  12:21 PM              UNDO
```

The total profit /loss
figure shows only
total income (C12)
because you have
not yet computed
total expenses
(C19).

■6 Type **+D12–D19** and press ⟶ . This computes the total profit / loss for Week 2.

```
18  Insurance              1200      1200
19  TOTAL EXPENSES
20
21  TOTAL PROFIT/LOSS      22000     22200
22
15-Aug-90  12:22 PM              UNDO
```

Keep this worksheet on your screen and proceed to the next exercise. If you want
to take a break at this point, go to the section "Saving Your Worksheet."

▪*Streamlining Formulas*

Typing formulas can be a cumbersome process when developing worksheets with many rows and columns of figures. Imagine having to type each cell address for 10 columns containing 20 rows of numbers. 1-2-3 provides functions that streamline the operation of your formulas. *Functions* are abbreviated formulas that perform a specific operation on a set of values. They consist of the @ symbol and a single word that identifies the function. Consult your 1-2-3 documentation for information about 1-2-3 functions.

This section introduces you to 1-2-3 operations using the @SUM function. @SUM tells 1-2-3 to add together a designated group, or *range*, of cell values. If you took a break after the last exercise and saved your worksheet, retrieve the worksheet file (see Chapter 3) and proceed with this exercise.

▪ *1*   Move the pointer to cell C19. Type **@SUM(**
but do not press ⏎.

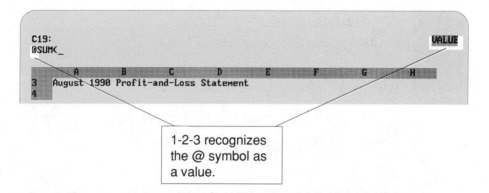

1-2-3 recognizes the @ symbol as a value.

Now, instead of typing in the individual cell values to be added together, you'll designate a range of cells by *pointing* at the first cell in the range, anchoring it into the formula, then pointing at the last cell in the range.

■*2*   Move the pointer to cell C15.

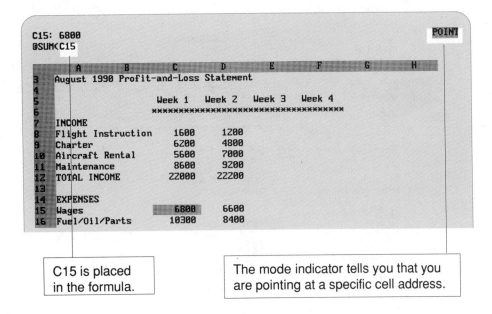

C15 is placed
in the formula.

The mode indicator tells you that you
are pointing at a specific cell address.

■*3*   ⌊.⌋ (period). This anchors cell 15 into
the formula.

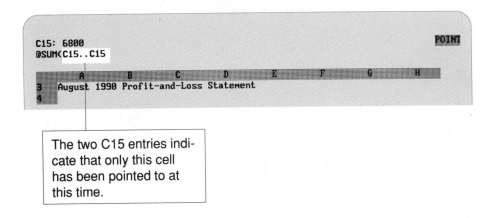

The two C15 entries indi-
cate that only this cell
has been pointed to at
this time.

■ *4*   Move the pointer to cell C18. Do not press ⏎.

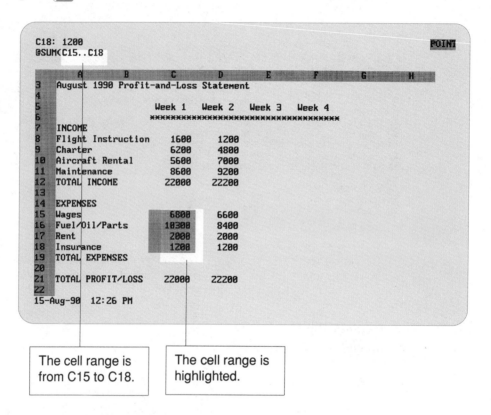

C18: 1200
@SUM(C15..C18

POINT

	A	B	C	D	E	F	G	H
3	August 1990 Profit-and-Loss Statement							
5			Week 1	Week 2	Week 3	Week 4		
6			************************************					
7	INCOME							
8	Flight Instruction		1600	1200				
9	Charter		6200	4800				
10	Aircraft Rental		5600	7000				
11	Maintenance		8600	9200				
12	TOTAL INCOME		22000	22200				
14	EXPENSES							
15	Wages		6800	6600				
16	Fuel/Oil/Parts		10300	8400				
17	Rent		2000	2000				
18	Insurance		1200	1200				
19	TOTAL EXPENSES							
21	TOTAL PROFIT/LOSS		22000	22200				

15-Aug-90 12:26 PM

The cell range is from C15 to C18.

The cell range is highlighted.

■ *5*   〔) 〕 to complete the formula.

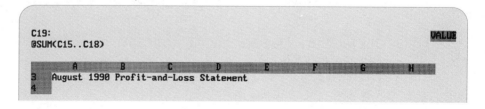

C19:
@SUM(C15..C18)

VALUE

	A	B	C	D	E	F	G	H
3	August 1990 Profit-and-Loss Statement							

2

■6   Move the pointer to cell D19.

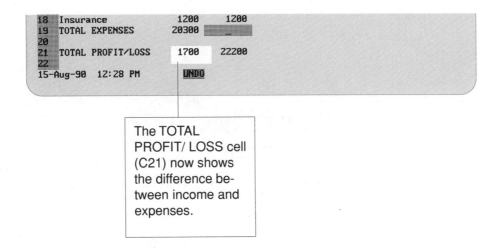

```
18  Insurance              1200      1200
19  TOTAL EXPENSES        20300
20
21  TOTAL PROFIT/LOSS      1700     22200
22
15-Aug-90  12:28 PM           UNDO
```

The TOTAL
PROFIT/ LOSS cell
(C21) now shows
the difference be-
tween income and
expenses.

■7   Follow the procedures in steps 1 through 5
and create this formula: @SUM(D15..D18).
After you type the closing parenthesis, move
the pointer to cell E19 in order to place the
computed profit-and-loss data in cell D21.

```
18  Insurance              1200      1200
19  TOTAL EXPENSES        20300     18200
20
21  TOTAL PROFIT/LOSS      1700      4000
22
15-Aug-90  12:29 PM           UNDO
```

■ *8*   Your worksheet should now look like this. If
you entered the wrong data in any cells, don't
worry. Chapter 3 will give you the editing procedures to correct these mistakes.

```
E19:                                                                    READY

            A        B        C        D        E        F        G        H
   3   August 1990 Profit-and-Loss Statement
   4
   5                          Week 1   Week 2   Week 3   Week 4
   6                 xxxxxxxxxxxxxxxxxxxxxxxxxxxxxxxxxxxxxx
   7   INCOME
   8   Flight Instruction    1600     1200
   9   Charter               6200     4800
  10   Aircraft Rental       5600     7000
  11   Maintenance           8600     9200
  12   TOTAL INCOME         22000    22200
  13
  14   EXPENSES
  15   Wages                 6800     6600
  16   Fuel/Oil/Parts       10300     8400
  17   Rent                  2000     2000
  18   Insurance             1200     1200
  19   TOTAL EXPENSES       20300    18200
  20
  21   TOTAL PROFIT/LOSS     1700     4000
  22
   15-Aug-90  12:30 PM          UNDO
```

When you begin to develop your own worksheets, you will build your own formulas. When you do, look through the functions in the documentation provided
by Lotus to see which functions can streamline your computations.

How 1-2-3 Computes Formulas
■ Using Order of Precedence

Order of precedence is the order in which 1-2-3 performs mathematical calculations. Instead of calculating a formula from left to right as it is written, 1-2-3 will apply algebraic rules of computation.

Note *Operator Order of Precedence* The following basic operators are listed in the order in which 1-2-3 performs them.

Precedence	Operator
1st	^ (exponentiation)
2d	+ or − (for positive or negative values)
3d	* or / (multiplication or division)
4th	+ or − (for addition or subtraction)
5th	<, or >, or = (less than, or greater than, or equal to tests)

Operators that have the same order of precedence are executed from left to right as written. Your 1-2-3 documentation contains a complete listing of operator order of precedence, including more advanced operators.

You may override the order of precedence by enclosing parts of a formula in parentheses. 1-2-3 always executes operations within parentheses first. For example, multiplication normally occurs before addition, but in the following formula, the addition takes place before the multiplication:

    C5*(A1+A2+A3)

The values in cells A1 through A3 are added first because they are enclosed in parentheses. The result of this addition is then multiplied by C5. Without the parentheses, C5 would first be multiplied by A1, then that result added to A2, which is then added to A3.

■*Saving Your Worksheet*

After you create your worksheet, you will want to save it for future editing. The beauty of 1-2-3 is that you can update a previously developed worksheet with fresh data and 1-2-3 will automatically recalculate new results. Remember, the work you see displayed on your screen only exists in "temporary memory" (RAM). A power failure of any sort will result in the information being totally lost. Therefore, you must record the worksheet into "permanent memory" on a hard or floppy disk. I recommend you save your worksheet every few minutes while you work in order to prevent losing a large amount of work.

Let's save the worksheet you have been working on in the previous exercises. If you saved this file previously, go to the end of Chapter 3 and do the exercise in the section "Saving an Existing File."

The illustrations you see in this exercise are for a hard-disk computer. However, they show the same information a floppy-disk user will see on the monitor, except the drive letter and directory display will be different.

If you have a dual floppy-disk computer, place a blank formatted disk in drive B and close the latch before you begin this exercise.

■ *1*   ⌿ to display the Main menu in the control panel.

```
E19:                                                              MENU
Worksheet  Range  Copy  Move  File  Print  Graph  Data  System  Add-In  Quit
Global  Insert  Delete  Column  Erase  Titles  Window  Status  Page  Learn
      A       B       C       D       E       F       G       H
3    August 1990 Profit-and-Loss Statement
4
```

The mode indicator changes to MENU.

■*2*   [→] four times to move the pointer to File.

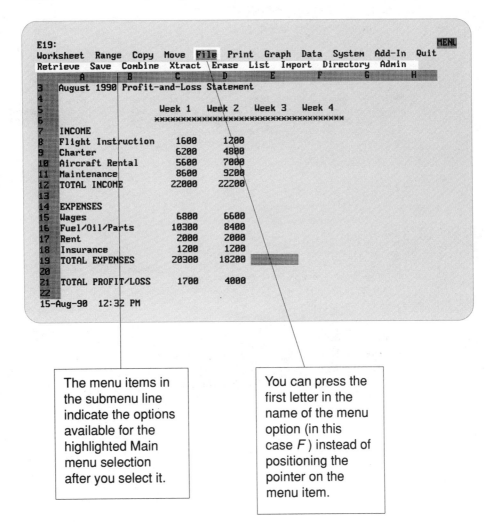

2

The menu items in the submenu line indicate the options available for the highlighted Main menu selection after you select it.

You can press the first letter in the name of the menu option (in this case *F*) instead of positioning the pointer on the menu item.

■ *3*   ⏎ to select the File option. You now have
access to the submenu options shown in
step 2 above.

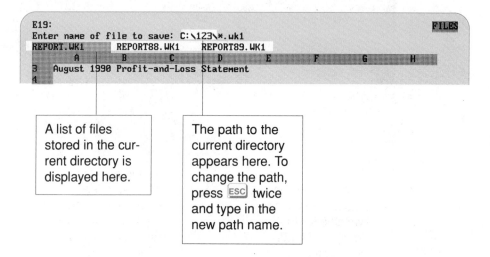

■ *4*   Ⓢ to select Save.

A list of files
stored in the cur-
rent directory is
displayed here.

The path to the
current directory
appears here. To
change the path,
press ESC twice
and type in the
new path name.

■5 If you have a hard disk, type **AUGPL1**. Do not press ⏎. If you have a floppy disk, press ESC and type **B:AUGPL1**. Do not press ⏎. In neither case do you type in a file extension (see NOTE below).

2

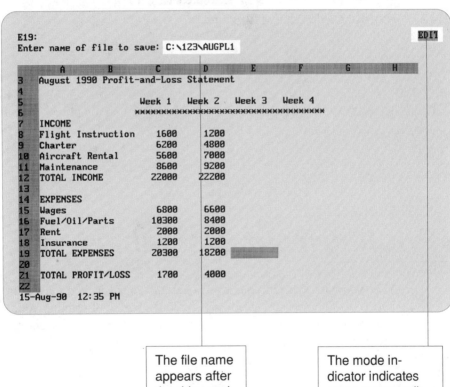

```
E19:                                                    EDIT
Enter name of file to save:  C:\123\AUGPL1

        A       B        C        D      E      F      G      H
3    August 1990 Profit-and-Loss Statement
4
5                         Week 1   Week 2  Week 3  Week 4
6                     ***************************************
7    INCOME
8    Flight Instruction    1600     1200
9    Charter               6200     4800
10   Aircraft Rental       5600     7000
11   Maintenance           8600     9200
12   TOTAL INCOME         22000    22200
13
14   EXPENSES
15   Wages                 6800     6600
16   Fuel/Oil/Parts       10300     8400
17   Rent                  2000     2000
18   Insurance             1200     1200
19   TOTAL EXPENSES       20300    18200
20
21   TOTAL PROFIT/LOSS     1700     4000
22
15-Aug-90  12:35 PM
```

The file name appears after the drive and directory path name.

The mode indicator indicates you can now edit the path and file name.

Follow these rules when naming files: use no more than eight characters; characters may be letters, numbers, or an underscore; use no blank spaces or punctuation marks; type either upper- or lowercase characters.

■*6*   ⏎ to save the file under the name
AUGPL1.WK1 (AUGUST PROFIT/ LOSS
#1). You can locate a stored file more easily if
you give it a descriptive file name.

> **Note** *File Extensions* A file extension consists of a period followed by up to three characters and is placed after the file name. 1-2-3 automatically creates a file extension when you save your worksheet. Therefore, it is not necessary to type in a file extension when naming your files. The 1-2-3 extension is named .WK1.

■*Printing Your Worksheet*

After you have created your worksheet and saved it, you may want to print a copy of it. This section introduces you to the basics of printing your worksheet. Chapter 4 will show you how to use some of the more advanced print options available with 1-2-3.

Your AUGPL1 worksheet should still be displayed on your screen. Let's print a copy. Turn your printer on and line up the top edge of the paper with the print head.

■ *1* ⬜ and select Print.

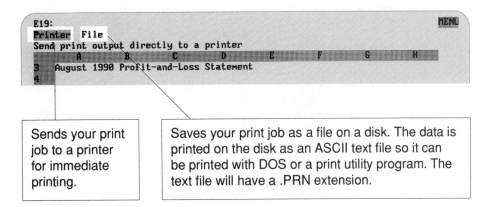

Sends your print job to a printer for immediate printing.

Saves your print job as a file on a disk. The data is printed on the disk as an ASCII text file so it can be printed with DOS or a print utility program. The text file will have a .PRN extension.

Be sure your printer is properly installed before you begin to print. See Appendix A.

■*2*   Select Printer.

```
E19:                                                              MENU
Range  Line  Page  Options  Clear  Align  Go  Quit
Specify a range to print
                            ┌─── Print Settings ───────────────
    Destination:  Printer

    Range:

    Header:
    Footer:

    Margins:
       Left 4      Right 76    Top 2    Bottom 2

    Borders:
       Columns
       Rows

    Setup string:

    Page length:  66

    Output:       As-Displayed (Formatted)

15-Aug-90  12:37 PM
```

You must always select the range of cells you want to print.

The default left and right margins are 4 spaces and 76 spaces respectively from the left edge of the paper. The top and bottom margins are 2 lines from the top and bottom of the page. The page length is 66 lines.

Print settings are the formatting commands that determine what your printed worksheet will look like.

2

■ *3*   Select Range.

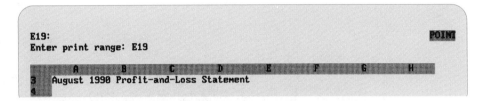

```
E19:                                                        POINT
Enter print range: E19

        A       B      C       D       E       F       G      H
3    August 1990 Profit-and-Loss Statement
4
```

■ *4*   HOME to move the pointer to cell A1.

```
A1: 'BRIARCLIFF AUIATION                                    POINT
Enter print range: A1

        A       B       C      D      E       F       G      H
1    BRIARCLIFF AUIATION
2    Santa Clarita, CA.
3    August 1990 Profit-and-Loss Statement
4
```

■ *5*   [.] (period) to anchor cell A1 in the range.

```
A1: 'BRIARCLIFF AUIATION                                    POINT
Enter print range: A1..A1

        A       B       C      D      E       F       G      H
1    BRIARCLIFF AUIATION
2    Santa Clarita, CA.
3    August 1990 Profit-and-Loss Statement
4
```

■6   Move the pointer to cell F21 to highlight the range of cells to be printed.

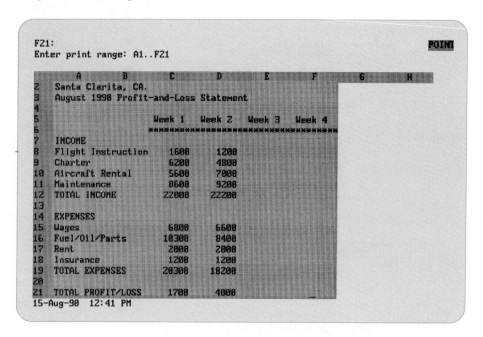

```
F21:                                                              POINT
Enter print range: A1..F21

         A       B        C       D       E       F        G       H
2   Santa Clarita, CA.
3   August 1990 Profit-and-Loss Statement
4
5                          Week 1  Week 2  Week 3  Week 4
6                          xxxxxxxxxxxxxxxxxxxxxxxxxxxxxxxxxxx
7   INCOME
8   Flight Instruction     1600    1200
9   Charter                6200    4800
10  Aircraft Rental        5600    7000
11  Maintenance            8600    9200
12  TOTAL INCOME           22000   22200
13
14  EXPENSES
15  Wages                  6800    6600
16  Fuel/Oil/Parts         10300   8400
17  Rent                   2000    2000
18  Insurance              1200    1200
19  TOTAL EXPENSES         20300   18200
20
21  TOTAL PROFIT/LOSS      1700    4000
15-Aug-90  12:41 PM
```

■7   ⏎ to return to the Printer menu. The selected range appears in the print settings.

```
E19:                                                             MENU
Range  Line  Page  Options  Clear  Align  Go  Quit
Specify a range to print
                          ── Print Settings ──────────────
   Destination:  Printer

   Range:        A1..F21

   Header:
   Footer:
```

■8 Select Align to tell 1-2-3 that the printer paper is aligned with the print head. If you use a LaserJet printer, see the Note "Printing with a LaserJet" on the next page before proceeding.

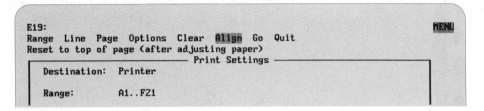

```
E19:                                                              MENU
Range  Line  Page  Options  Clear  Align  Go  Quit
Reset to top of page (after adjusting paper)
───────────────────────── Print Settings ─────────────────────────
   Destination:  Printer

   Range:       A1..F21
```

■9 Select Go to print the worksheet. If you use a LaserJet printer, you must select Page to advance the paper in the printer to the top of the next page. Your printout should look like this:

```
BRIARCLIFF AVIATION
Santa Clarita, CA.
August 1990 Profit-and-Loss Statement

                    Week 1   Week 2   Week 3   Week 4
**************************************
INCOME
Flight Instruction   1600     1200
Charter              6200     4800
Aircraft Rental      5600     7000
Maintenance          8600     9200
TOTAL INCOME        22000    22200

EXPENSES
Wages                6800     6600
Fuel/Oil/Parts      10300     8400
Rent                 2000     2000
Insurance            1200     1200
TOTAL EXPENSES      20300    18200

TOTAL PROFIT/LOSS    1700     4000
```

Note *Printing with a LaserJet* If the page length setting on the 1-2-3 Print Settings screen is greater than the page length defined from the LaserJet control panel (the FORM option), then information printed after the first page will be printed further down on the paper on subsequent pages. The FORM setting on the printer is often set at 60 lines, while the default setting for 1-2-3 is 66 lines. To prevent this "creep down" on pages after the first one, select /Print, Printer Options, Pg-Length and type **60** to change the 1-2-3 setting from 66 to 60 lines. Appendix E of your 1-2-3 documentation provides more information on using a LaserJet printer with 1-2-3.

■ *10* Select Quit to return to your worksheet.

```
E19:                                                                    READY

          A         B         C         D         E         F         G         H
 3   August 1990 Profit-and-Loss Statement
 4
 5                           Week 1    Week 2    Week 3    Week 4
 6                        xxxxxxxxxxxxxxxxxxxxxxxxxxxxxxxxxxxxx
 7   INCOME
 8   Flight Instruction     1600      1200
 9   Charter                6200      4800
10   Aircraft Rental        5600      7000
11   Maintenance            8600      9200
12   TOTAL INCOME          22000     22200
13
14   EXPENSES
15   Wages                  6800      6600
16   Fuel/Oil/Parts        10300      8400
17   Rent                   2000      2000
18   Insurance              1200      1200
19   TOTAL EXPENSES        20300     18200
20
21   TOTAL PROFIT/LOSS      1700      4000
22
15-Aug-90  12:44 PM              UNDO
```

Now that your worksheet is safely stored on a disk, please exit from the 1-2-3 program. This will be good practice, and will enable you to start Chapter 3 with a blank worksheet. Remember, to quit 1-2-3, first press the slash key (⌷) and select Quit from the Main menu. Follow the control panel prompts until you see the DOS prompt or the Access menu on your monitor screen.

■*Summary*

At this point, you should be able to begin developing your own worksheets. You can place labels and values on the worksheet. Remember, if a label starts with a number, place a label prefix in front of the number so 1-2-3 will not treat it as a value. When typing in a formula that begins with a cell address, be sure to place an operator in front of the cell address letter so 1-2-3 will not think you are creating a label.

You also have learned how to create simple formulas and to use the @SUM function to streamline formulas. Understanding the order of precedence of mathematical operators is important if you want to arrive at the correct answer in your calculations.

Finally, you learned how to save your worksheet. Remember, 1-2-3 automatically assigns the file extension .WK1 to a file name, so you do not have to type in an extension when you name your files.

Chapter 3 will round out your knowledge of developing a worksheet by showing you how to make changes to the data you place in the worksheet.

T H R E E

Editing Your Worksheet

Now that you have gained experience in constructing a worksheet, let's move on to some of the basic editing features of Lotus 1-2-3. Editing a worksheet involves any operation that changes the existing worksheet, such as correcting a value, adding a column, or deleting a row.

When you finish this chapter, you will have all the basic skills needed to design, create, and edit worksheets that meet all your spreadsheet requirements.

Retrieving a Saved File

■

Correcting Your Worksheet

■

Using 1-2-3's Help Feature

■

Working with Columns and Rows

■

Copying Data to Other Areas of the Worksheet

■

Saving an Existing Worksheet

■*Selecting Menu Items*

You will be using the Main menu and its submenus a great deal in the remaining exercises in this book, so let's briefly review the procedures for selecting menu items. In Chapter 2 you used two methods of selecting items from the menus displayed in the control panel: the "long" way of using the cursor keys to move the pointer to the menu item, then pressing ↵, and the shortcut of pressing the first letter of the item name. You are less likely to select the wrong menu item if you use the longer method, but typing the first letter of the menu item is much faster.

In the remaining exercises, I will instruct you to *select* a menu item and leave the method of selection up to you. For example, if you receive an instruction to select /File, Combine, you would simply press ⌐, then press the letters **FC** (lowercase letters also work) for File and Combine, or use the cursor keys to position the pointer on each menu item.

■*Retrieving a Saved File*

Once you have saved a worksheet, you will want to retrieve it for viewing or editing. To retrieve a file stored on a disk, you select /File, Retrieve. Let's retrieve the AUGPL1.WK1 file you created in Chapter 2.

■ *1* Start your computer, move to the 1-2-3 directory, and start 1-2-3. If you have a dual floppy-disk computer, place the disk containing the AUGPL1.WK1 file in drive B.

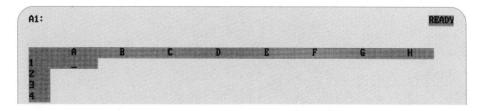

■*2* Select /File, Retrieve. A list of files are displayed in the control panel.

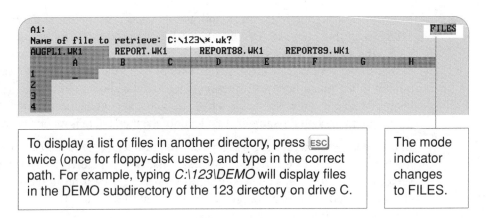

To display a list of files in another directory, press ESC
twice (once for floppy-disk users) and type in the correct
path. For example, typing *C:\123\DEMO* will display files
in the DEMO subdirectory of the 123 directory on drive C.

The mode
indicator
changes
to FILES.

■*3* Move the pointer to AUGPL1.WK1 and press
⏎. In the next exercise you'll make some
changes to the worksheet.

```
E19:                                                        READY

          A       B       C       D       E       F       G       H
 3  August 1990 Profit-and-Loss Statement
 4
 5                        Week 1  Week 2  Week 3  Week 4
 6                        xxxxxxxxxxxxxxxxxxxxxxxxxxxxxxxxxxx
 7  INCOME
 8  Flight Instruction    1600    1200
 9  Charter               6200    4800
10  Aircraft Rental       5600    7000
11  Maintenance           8600    9200
12  TOTAL INCOME         22000   22200
13
14  EXPENSES
15  Wages                 6800    6600
16  Fuel/Oil/Parts       10300    8400
17  Rent                  2000    2000
18  Insurance             1200    1200
19  TOTAL EXPENSES       20300   18200
20
21  TOTAL PROFIT/LOSS     1700    4000
22
16-Aug-90  12:03 PM            UNDO
```

> **Note** If you are working on one worksheet and want to retrieve another, save the current worksheet before retrieving the one stored on the disk. Otherwise, the retrieved worksheet will replace the worksheet you are working on without saving it, and all your current work will be lost.

Making Corrections
■*on Your Worksheet*

Earlier you used the Backspace key to correct labels and values *prior* to placing them into the worksheet. Now you will learn how to correct these items *after* they are placed in a cell. You'll also learn how to erase all or part of a worksheet and to use the Undo feature to restore your worksheet to the way it was before you made an incorrect edit.

Using the Edit Key for "What If" Analyses

Because 1-2-3 automatically recalculates whenever you change a value, you can play the "what if " game. What if you want to forecast profits if you increase the fees for maintenance or flight instruction? What if your rent is going to be raised in two months and your parts supplier has told you there will be an increase in parts prices? These questions can be answered simply by placing the anticipated changes into the appropriate cells on your worksheet; the results of these changes will automatically be computed by 1-2-3. Making these types of edits on a completed entry is as simple as pressing one key, the Edit (F2) key. Let's change an entry on the AUGPL1 worksheet.

■ *1* Move the pointer to cell C11.

```
4
5                            Week 1   Week 2   Week 3   Week 4
6                            ×××××××××××××××××××××××××××××××××
7    INCOME
8    Flight Instruction      1600     1200
9    Charter                 6200     4800
10   Aircraft Rental         5600     7000
11   Maintenance             8600     9200
12   TOTAL INCOME            22000    22200
13
```

■*2* F2

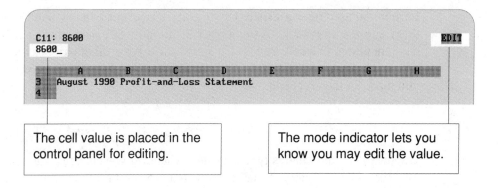

The cell value is placed in the control panel for editing.

The mode indicator lets you know you may edit the value.

■*3* ← four times to place the cursor on the *8* in *8600*. Press DEL, and type **6**.

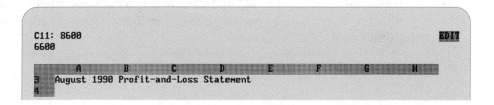

> **Note** *The Editing Keys* Use these keys to edit entries on the control panel:
>
> [→] Moves cursor to right
> [←] Moves cursor to left
> [↓] Completes edit and moves pointer down one cell
> [↑] Completes edit and moves pointer up one cell
> [BKSP ←] Erases character to left of cursor
> [DEL] Erases character at cursor location
> [END] Moves cursor to the right of the last character
> [ESC] Erases the entire entry
> [HOME] Moves cursor to first character
> [INS] Changes between Insert and Typeover modes

■ *4*   [←] The edit is complete and the new value is
now in cell Cll.

```
C11: 6600                                                        READY

          A         B         C         D         E         F         G         H
3   August 1990 Profit-and-Loss Statement
4
5                           Week 1    Week 2    Week 3    Week 4
6             xxxxxxxxxxxxxxxxxxxxxxxxxxxxxxxxxxxxxx
7   INCOME
8   Flight Instruction     1600      1200
9   Charter                6200      4800
10  Aircraft Rental        5600      7000
11  Maintenance            6600      9200
12  TOTAL INCOME          20000     22200
13
14  EXPENSES
15   Wages                 6800      6600
16   Fuel/Oil/Parts       10300      8400
17   Rent                  2000      2000
18   Insurance             1200      1200
19  TOTAL EXPENSES        20300     18200
20
21  TOTAL PROFIT/LOSS      -300      4000
22
16-Aug-90  12:07 PM           UNDO
```

The TOTAL INCOME and TOTAL PROFIT/LOSS entries are automatically updated.

■ *5*   Move the pointer to cell A3 and press F2.

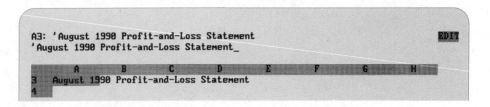

■ *6*   HOME to place the cursor on the *A* in *August*.

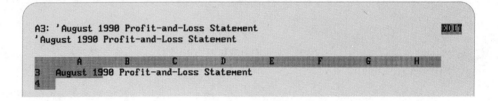

■ *7*   DEL six times and type **July**.

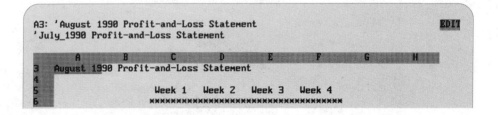

■*8*　↵ The edited label is now in cell A3.

```
A3: 'July 1990 Profit-and-Loss Statement                          READY

         A        B        C        D        E        F        G        H
3  July 1990 Profit-and-Loss Statement
4
```

> **Note** *Erasing Values and Labels* You cannot totally erase a value or label from a cell with F2. You must use the /Range, Erase command to delete a cell entry. (See "Erasing Part of the Worksheet below")

If you wish to take a break when you complete this or any other exercise, save the worksheet. See "Saving an Existing File" at the end of this chapter for instructions on how to save a file that has been previously saved.

Erasing Part of the Worksheet

You should be looking at the newly edited July 1990 Profit-and-Loss Statement worksheet. Now let's assume all the income values in Week 2 are incorrect and need changing. Instead of editing each cell, you can erase all the cells with the /Range, Erase commands and then place new values in each cell. Try it.

■*1*　Move the pointer to cell D8.

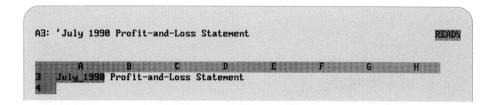

```
5                        Week 1   Week 2   Week 3   Week 4
6                        ****************************************
7  INCOME
8  Flight Instruction     1600     1200
9  Charter                6200     4800
10 Aircraft Rental        5600     7000
11 Maintenance            6600     9200
12 TOTAL INCOME          20000    22200
```

■*2*   Select /Range, Erase.

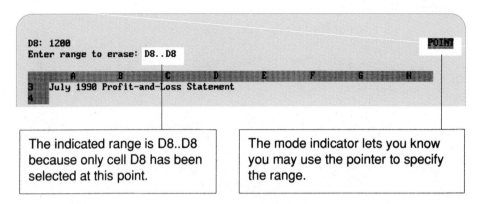

The indicated range is D8..D8 because only cell D8 has been selected at this point.

The mode indicator lets you know you may use the pointer to specify the range.

■*3*   ⬇ to move the pointer to cell D11.

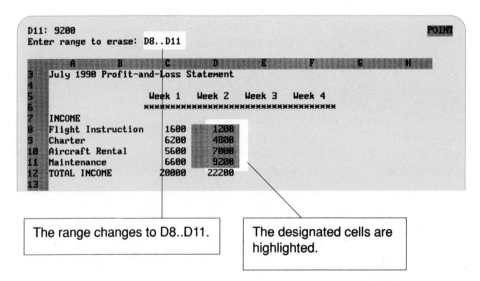

The range changes to D8..D11.

The designated cells are highlighted.

■4   ⏎ to delete the range.

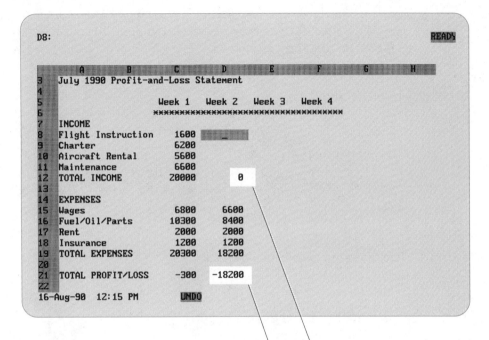

The TOTAL INCOME and TOTAL PROFIT/LOSS cells automatically change.

■5   Place the values shown in the screen below in cells D8 through D11 to update the worksheet.

		Week 1	Week 2	Week 3	Week 4
5					
6		××××××××××××××××××××××××××××××××××××			
7	INCOME				
8	Flight Instruction	1600	1300		
9	Charter	6200	5000		
10	Aircraft Rental	5600	6000		
11	Maintenance	6600	9000		
12	TOTAL INCOME	20000	21300		
13					

Erasing the Entire Worksheet

There will be times when a worksheet will need complete reorganization. When this happens, you need a way to erase the entire worksheet. To erase a worksheet, you use the /Worksheet, Erase commands.

■ *1*   Select /Worksheet, Erase.

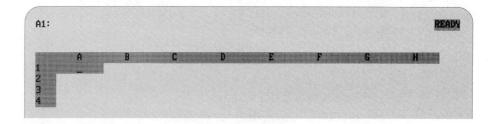

```
D12: +D8+D9+D10+D11                                              MENU
No  Yes
Do not erase the worksheet: return to READY mode
         A          B          C          D          E       F          G          H
3  July 1990 Profit-and-Loss Statement
4
```

You are asked to confirm the erasure.

■ *2*   [Y] or move the pointer to Yes and press [↵].

```
A1:                                                             READY


         A          B          C          D          E       F          G          H
1
2
3
4
```

You have erased the worksheet without saving it first. This was your intent, of course, but suppose you changed your mind, or decided you want to keep the worksheet on disk in case you need to refer to it later? The next exercise shows you how to recover the worksheet so you can then save it.

Using the Undo Feature

The Undo feature is used to recover the most recent changes to worksheet data since 1-2-3 was last in the Ready mode. Undo only works if *UNDO* is displayed on the bottom of the screen. Undo is automatically turned on when you start the program.

How does Undo work? Whenever you change from the Ready mode to a different mode, 1-2-3 creates a backup copy of your current worksheet. This backup is remembered by 1-2-3 after you return to the Ready mode. Therefore, if you edit the worksheet and make a mistake, you can use Undo to place the backup copy without the mistakes on the screen. Let's recover the worksheet that was erased in the last exercise and then save it properly.

3

■ *1*   ALT F4 (Be sure to hold ALT down while you press F4 .)

```
D12:  +D8+D9+D10+D11                                        READY

          A        B        C        D        E        F        G        H
  3  July 1990 Profit-and-Loss Statement
  4
  5                            Week 1   Week 2   Week 3   Week 4
  6                        xxxxxxxxxxxxxxxxxxxxxxxxxxxxxxxxxxx
  7  INCOME
  8  Flight Instruction       1600     1300
  9  Charter                  6200     5000
 10  Aircraft Rental          5600     6000
 11  Maintenance              6600     9000
 12  TOTAL INCOME            20000    21300
 13
 14  EXPENSES
 15  Wages                    6800     6600
 16  Fuel/Oil/Parts          10300     8400
 17  Rent                     2000     2000
 18  Insurance                1200     1200
 19  TOTAL EXPENSES          20300    18200
 20
 21  TOTAL PROFIT/LOSS        -300     3100
 22
 16-Aug-90  12:19 PM              UNDO
```

■*2*   Select /File, Save.

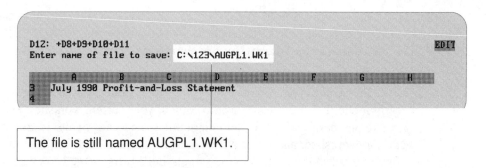

```
D12:  +D8+D9+D10+D11                                          EDIT
Enter name of file to save: C:\123\AUGPL1.WK1

        A        B        C        D        E        F        G        H
3    July 1990 Profit-and-Loss Statement
4
```

The file is still named AUGPL1.WK1.

■*3*   Type **JULYPL1** and press ⏎. The
worksheet is renamed and saved to the disk.

Note   *Some Limitations of Undo*   The Undo feature will not undo certain 1-2-3 commands. You cannot undo changes to a file that is stored on a disk. For example, if you delete a file from the disk, you cannot use Undo to recover the file. Refer to your 1-2-3 documentation for a detailed explanation of the limitations of Undo.

■*Using 1-2-3's Help Feature*

1-2-3 has an on-screen Help feature that gives you a brief description of each 1-2-3 command. You will find it useful as a quick reference when you cannot remember a command key sequence and don't have time to look it up in the manual. Let's take a look at how Help works.

■ *1*   F1 (the Help key)

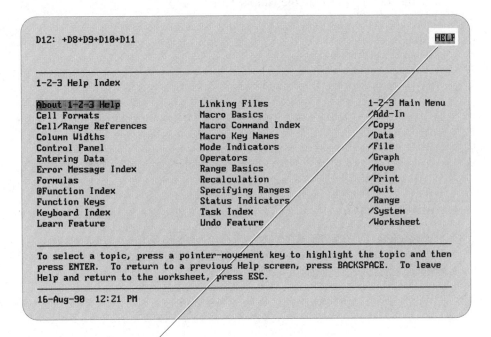

```
D12: +D8+D9+D10+D11                                              HELP


1-2-3 Help Index

About 1-2-3 Help          Linking Files              1-2-3 Main Menu
Cell Formats              Macro Basics               /Add-In
Cell/Range References     Macro Command Index        /Copy
Column Widths             Macro Key Names            /Data
Control Panel             Mode Indicators            /File
Entering Data             Operators                  /Graph
Error Message Index       Range Basics               /Move
Formulas                  Recalculation              /Print
@Function Index           Specifying Ranges          /Quit
Function Keys             Status Indicators          /Range
Keyboard Index            Task Index                 /System
Learn Feature             Undo Feature               /Worksheet


To select a topic, press a pointer-movement key to highlight the topic and then
press ENTER.  To return to a previous Help screen, press BACKSPACE.  To leave
Help and return to the worksheet, press ESC.

16-Aug-90  12:21 PM
```

The mode indicator indicates you are in the Help mode.

3

■*2* ⏎ for a brief description of how to move
the highlight around the Help screens.

```
D12:  +D8+D9+D10+D11                                              HELP

_____

About 1-2-3 Help

   The 1-2-3 Help system lets you pause at almost any time to view Help screens
   about the task you are trying to complete.  You can then continue your work
   where you left off.  To use Help, press HELP (F1).  The items on the Help
   screen that are displayed in color or a brighter intensity represent
   additional Help topics.  To get information on one of these topics, use the
   keys listed below to highlight the topic and then press ENTER.  1-2-3 displays
   the new Help screen and offers more Help topics.

   HOME or END    Moves highlight to the first or last Help topic.
   ← → ↑ or ↓      Moves highlight to the next topic in the direction indicated.

   You can also use these keys while you are in Help:

   HELP (F1)      Displays the first Help screen viewed.
   ESC            Returns you to the worksheet.
   BACKSPACE      Displays the previous Help screen you viewed.
_____
Press HOME to go here            Help Index            Press END to go here
16-Aug-90  12:22 PM
```

■*3* When you've read the explanation of 1-2-3
Help, press F1 to return to the first screen
you saw when activating Help.

```
D12:  +D8+D9+D10+D11                                              HELP

_____

1-2-3 Help Index

About 1-2-3 Help           Linking Files              1-2-3 Main Menu
Cell Formats               Macro Basics               /Add-In
Cell/Range References      Macro Command Index        /Copy
Column Widths              Macro Key Names            /Data
Control Panel              Mode Indicators            /File
```

You will be working with column widths in the next exercise, so let's use Help to get a preview of how to use this feature.

■4 ⬇ three times to move the pointer to
Column Widths, and then press ⏎.

```
D12: +D8+D9+D10+D11                                            HELP

───────────────────────────────────────────────────────────────

Column Widths

 /Worksheet Column Set-Width  sets the width of a single column (1-240
 characters).  Any column whose width you do not set in this way has the
 default column width (initially 9 characters).

 /Worksheet Global Column-Width changes the default column width setting.

 A column width that is too narrow never causes data to be lost, but it can
 cause problems with the way data appears in the worksheet.

 o If 1-2-3 cannot display a value accurately because the column width is too
   too narrow, it displays *** (asterisks) in the cell.

 o If a label is too long for its column, 1-2-3 attempts to display all
   of it.  It left-aligns the label and borrows space on the screen from
   empty cells to its right. If, however, the cells to the right are full,
   1-2-3 cuts off the label at the right edge of the column.

───────────────────────────────────────────────────────────────
Help Index
16-Aug-90  12:24 PM
```

3

See the book
covers for
reminders about
1-2-3 function
keys, and more.

■*5*   The pointer is on "/Worksheet Column Set-
Width." Press ⏎.

D12: +D8+D9+D10+D11   HELP

/Worksheet Column -- Sets or resets the width of one or more columns, and
 hides and redisplays columns.

  1. Select /Worksheet Column and select one of the following:

     Set-Width   Sets the width (1 to 240) of the current column.
     Reset-Width   Resets the width of the current column to the global
                    column width.
     Hide   Hides one or more columns to prevent them from being
                    displayed and printed.
     Display   Redisplays hidden columns.
     Column-Range   Sets and resets the width of a range of
                    columns.

  2. If you selected Set-Width, specify a width either by typing a number
     from 1 to 240, or by using ← or → to adjust column width and then
     pressing ENTER. If you selected Hide, specify the range of columns to hide.

Continued   /Worksheet Global Column-Width   Worksheet Commands   Help Index
16-Aug-90 12:25 PM

Continued   /Worksheet Global Column-Width   Worksheet Commands   Help Index
16-Aug-90 12:25 PM

To display more information   To get help with
about this subject   related subjects.

■*6* ESC to return to your worksheet.

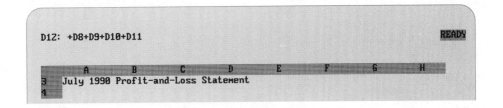

```
D12:  +D8+D9+D10+D11                                                   READY


        A       B       C       D       E       F       G       H
3  July 1990 Profit-and-Loss Statement
4
```

3

> **Note** If you are working with a particular feature of 1-2-3 and need help, press F1 and 1-2-3 will automatically display Help information about that feature. For example, if you select /File, Save from the menu and press F1, you will receive help with saving a file.

■*Editing Columns*

Columns are one of the major components of a worksheet. In order to allow you flexibility in determining what the columns will look like, 1-2-3 enables you to change the column widths, insert new columns among existing columns, delete columns that no longer serve your purpose, and even hide columns so they can't be seen or printed.

Changing Column Widths

The default width of 1-2-3 columns is nine characters. You will at times want smaller or larger column widths to accommodate more or less data. Let's change the width of column C from 9 to 12 characters.

■ *1* Move the pointer to Week 1 in cell C5. You
may place the pointer in any cell in the
column you want to modify.

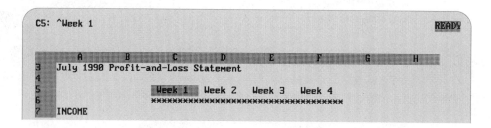

■ *2* Select /Worksheet, Column.

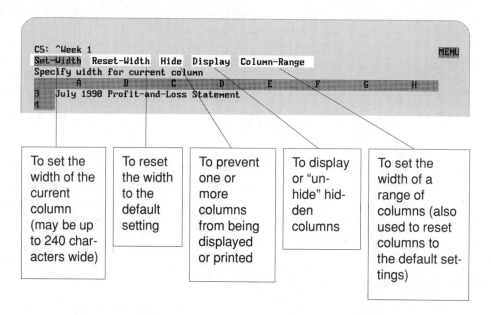

| To set the width of the current column (may be up to 240 characters wide) | To reset the width to the default setting | To prevent one or more columns from being displayed or printed | To display or "un-hide" hidden columns | To set the width of a range of columns (also used to reset columns to the default settings) |

■*3* The pointer is on "Set-Width." Press ⏎.

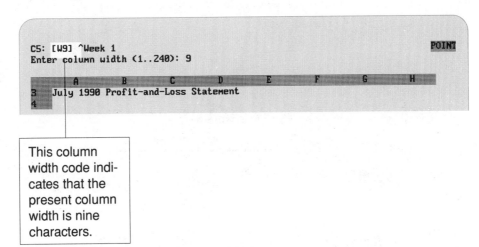

```
C5: [W9] ^Week 1                                                    POINT
Enter column width (1..240): 9

        A        B        C        D        E        F        G        H
 3  July 1990 Profit-and-Loss Statement
 4
```

This column width code indicates that the present column width is nine characters.

■*4* → three times and press ⏎. The column width code changes to 12 and the column C width adjusts to 12 characters.

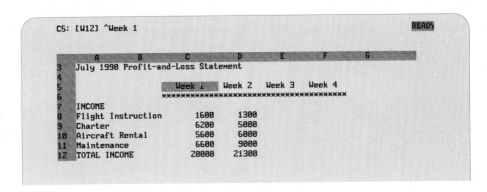

```
C5: [W12] ^Week 1                                                  READY

         A        B         C          D        E        F        G
 3  July 1990 Profit-and-Loss Statement
 4
 5                           Week 1    Week 2   Week 3   Week 4
 6                      xxxxxxxxxxxxxxxxxxxxxxxxxxxxxxxxxxxx
 7  INCOME
 8  Flight Instruction      1600      1300
 9  Charter                 6200      5000
10  Aircraft Rental         5600      6000
11  Maintenance             6600      9000
12  TOTAL INCOME           20000     21300
```

■*5*   Select /Worksheet, Column, Reset-Width.
This resets the column width to the default
setting of nine characters.

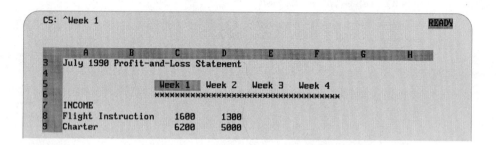

Changing a Range of Column Widths

This feature allows you to widen more than one adjacent column at a time. This
is a speedy method of changing column widths across a large worksheet.

■*1*   Position the pointer in the first column of the
group of columns you wish to change (in this
case, in cell C5). Select /Worksheet, Column,
Column-Range.

■*2*   ↵

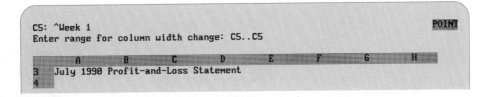

```
C5: ^Week 1                                                    POINT
Enter range for column width change: C5..C5

        A        B        C        D        E        F        G        H
3    July 1990 Profit-and-Loss Statement
4
```

■*3*   → three times to highlight columns C
through F.

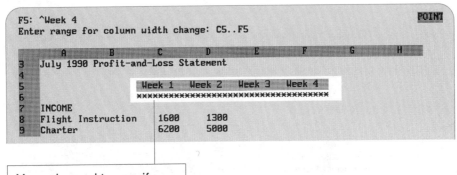

```
F5: ^Week 4                                                    POINT
Enter range for column width change: C5..F5

        A        B        C        D        E        F        G        H
3    July 1990 Profit-and-Loss Statement
4
5                         Week 1   Week 2   Week 3   Week 4
6                         ************************************
7    INCOME
8    Flight Instruction   1600     1300
9    Charter              6200     5000
```

You only need to specify
one cell in each column to
change the entire column.

■*4*   ↵

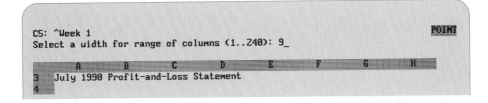

```
C5: ^Week 1                                                    POINT
Select a width for range of columns (1..240): 9_

        A        B        C        D        E        F        G        H
3    July 1990 Profit-and-Loss Statement
4
```

■5   Type **12** and press ⏎. Columns C through F
are adjusted to 12 characters in width.

```
C5: [W12] ^Week 1                                              READY

           A         B         C          D         E         F
 3   July 1990 Profit-and-Loss Statement
 4
 5                             Week 1    Week 2    Week 3    Week 4
 6                   *****************************************************
 7   INCOME
 8   Flight Instruction        1600      1300
 9   Charter                   6200      5000
10   Aircraft Rental           5600      6000
11   Maintenance               6600      9000
12   TOTAL INCOME             20000     21300
```

■6   To reset the columns to the default width of
nine characters, place the pointer in column C
and select /Worksheet, Column, Column-
Range, Reset-Width.

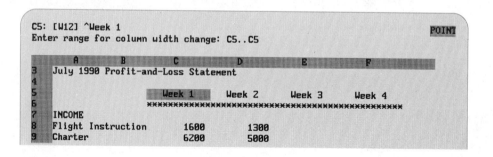

```
C5: [W12] ^Week 1                                              POINT
Enter range for column width change: C5..C5

           A         B         C          D         E         F
 3   July 1990 Profit-and-Loss Statement
 4
 5                             Week 1    Week 2    Week 3    Week 4
 6                   *****************************************************
 7   INCOME
 8   Flight Instruction        1600      1300
 9   Charter                   6200      5000
```

■ 7 ⬅ three times and press ⬅ . The columns
automatically readjust to nine
characters.

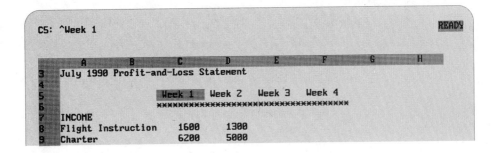

3

Hiding and Redisplaying Columns

If you work with sensitive data, there may be times when you do not want other
people to see information on your screen. With 1-2-3, you can hide one or more
columns. The hidden information will not print, but the worksheet formulas
that use data in the hidden columns will continue to work properly. Let's hide
columns D, E, and F on your worksheet.

■ 1 Place the cursor in cell D5 and select
/Worksheet, Column.

■*2*   Select Hide.

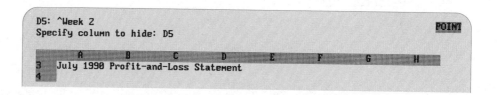

■*3*   ⌞.⌟ (period) to anchor column D as the left
edge of the range.

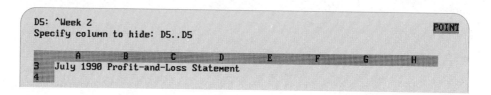

■*4*   ⌞→⌟ twice to enter the range.

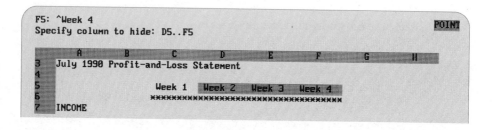

■5 ⏎ Columns D through F disappear from the display.

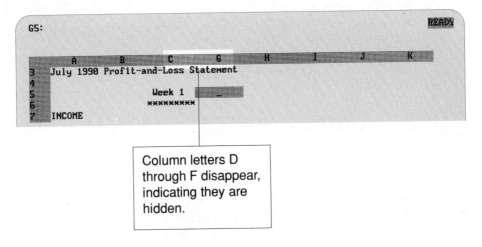

Column letters D through F disappear, indicating they are hidden.

Now let's redisplay the hidden columns.

■6 Select /Worksheet, Column.

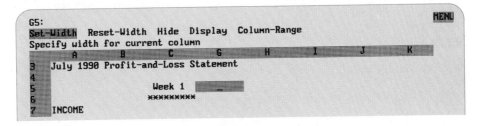

■7 Select Display.

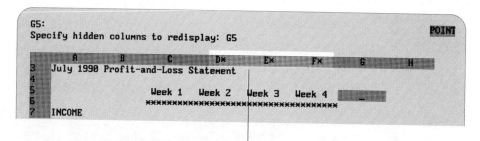

When 1-2-3 changes to Point mode, the columns that are hidden are displayed with an asterisk (*) next to the column letters.

■8 Type **d5 .. f5**. (You may type in the range as well as use the pointer to specify the range.)

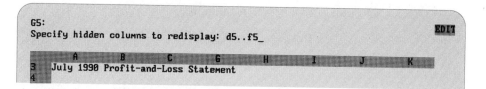

■9 ⏎ The columns are no longer hidden from view.

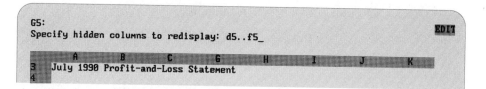

> **Note** *Using Undo with Hidden Columns* If you redisplay your columns and immediately realize you want them hidden again, press Undo ([ALT][F4]) before doing anything else. The columns will immediately return to the Hidden mode. Try it. Press [ALT][F4] once, and the columns disappear. Press [ALT][F4] again, and they reappear.

Inserting Columns

This is a handy feature to use whenever you need to add a column between existing columns. The new column can be used for data or just to alter the appearance of the worksheet. Let's add some space between the income and expenses labels and the Week 1 values. To do this, you'll add a blank new column, which will be in column C.

■ *1* Move the pointer to cell C5 and select
/Worksheet.

```
C5: ^Week 1                                                      MENU
Global  Insert  Delete  Column  Erase  Titles  Window  Status  Page  Learn
Format  Label-Prefix  Column-Width  Recalculation  Protection  Default  Zero
         A        B        C        D        E        F        G        H
 3   July 1990 Profit-and-Loss Statement
 4
 5                        Week 1   Week 2   Week 3   Week 4
 6                        xxxxxxxxxxxxxxxxxxxxxxxxxxxxxxxxxx
 7   INCOME
```

■ *2* Select Insert.

```
C5: ^Week 1                                                      MENU
Column  Row
Insert one or more blank columns to the left of the cell pointer
         A        B        C        D        E        F        G        H
 3   July 1990 Profit-and-Loss Statement
 4
```

■ *3* ⏎ to specify the range. You may insert one
or more adjacent columns.

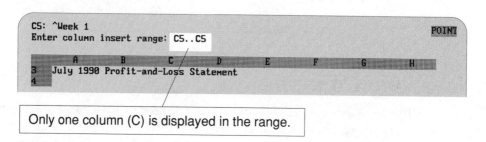

C5: ^Week 1   POINT
Enter column insert range: C5..C5

    A   B   C   D   E   F   G   H
3 July 1990 Profit-and-Loss Statement
4

Only one column (C) is displayed in the range.

■ *4* ⏎ to add the new column.

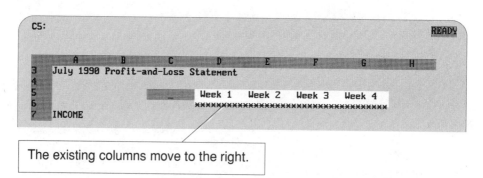

C5:   READY

    A   B   C   D   E   F   G   H
3 July 1990 Profit-and-Loss Statement
4
5   Week 1   Week 2   Week 3   Week 4
6   ***
7 INCOME

The existing columns move to the right.

Deleting Columns

When you discover a column or columns that are not needed on your worksheet, you can delete them as easily as 1-2-3. Let's delete the blank column you just placed in column C.

Before you begin this exercise be sure to save your worksheet. That way, if you should make an error that causes the worksheet to be unusable in future exercises, you can simply press Undo (ALT F4) immediately or retrieve the saved version of the file onto the screen.

■ *1* The pointer should still be located in cell C5.
Select /Worksheet.

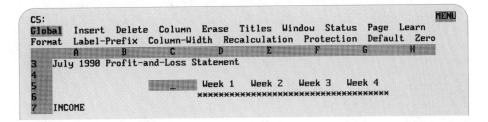

■ *2* Select Delete, Column.

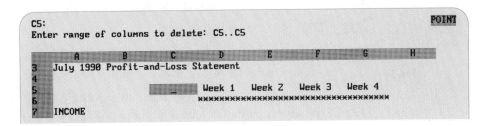

■ *3* ⏎ to delete column C. The column is
deleted totally and the remaining columns
move to the left to fill the empty space.

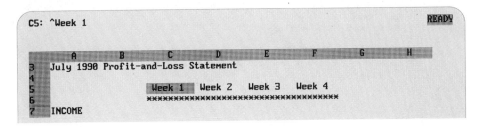

3

> **Note** *Deleting Columns and Rows* Keep these points in mind about column and row deletion:
>
> - You will not be able to delete columns if the Worksheet Global Protection setting is enabled. (See "Protecting Your Worksheet Data" in Chapter 5.)
> - Any data contained in a column or row is lost when the column (or row) is deleted.
> - A column or row is deleted in its entirety from the top (left) of the worksheet to the bottom (right).
> - When working on a larger worksheet, be careful not to delete data that is in the column or row but is not displayed on the screen.

Moving Columns

There may be times when you want to move data from one or more columns to another location on your worksheet. The Move command allows you to do this.

Let's try it using the JULYPL1 file. Remember to use Undo (ALT F4) if you make a mistake. Assume that the income data for Weeks 1 and 2 were actually the data for Weeks 3 and 4. Instead of deleting the values in columns C and D and retyping them in columns E and F, you can move them as a group.

■ *1*   Select / Move.

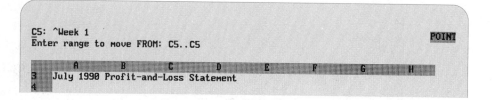

```
C5: ^Week 1                                          POINT
Enter range to move FROM: C5..C5

        A        B        C        D       E       F      G      H
3    July 1990 Profit-and-Loss Statement
4
```

■2 [ESC] The range is now unanchored.

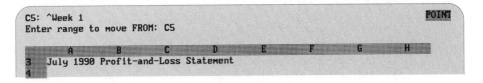

```
C5: ^Week 1                                                    POINT
Enter range to move FROM: C5

         A       B       C       D       E       F       G       H
3  July 1990 Profit-and-Loss Statement
4
```

■3 Move the pointer to cell C8 and press [.]
(period) to reanchor the cell.

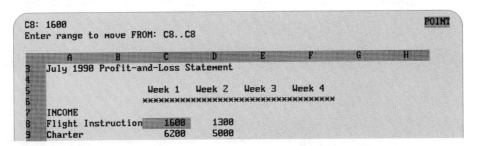

```
C8: 1600                                                       POINT
Enter range to move FROM: C8..C8

         A       B       C       D       E       F       G       H
3  July 1990 Profit-and-Loss Statement
4
5                       Week 1   Week 2   Week 3   Week 4
6                       xxxxxxxxxxxxxxxxxxxxxxxxxxxxxxxxx
7  INCOME
8  Flight Instruction    1600     1300
9  Charter               6200     5000
```

You may move any amount of worksheet data, from a single cell, to part of a
column, to an entire column.

■4 Move the pointer to cell D12.

```
D12: +D8+D9+D10+D11                                            POINT
Enter range to move FROM: C8..D12

         A       B       C       D       E       F       G       H
3  July 1990 Profit-and-Loss Statement
4
5                       Week 1   Week 2   Week 3   Week 4
6                       xxxxxxxxxxxxxxxxxxxxxxxxxxxxxxxxx
7  INCOME
8  Flight Instruction    1600     1300
9  Charter               6200     5000
10 Aircraft Rental       5600     6000
11 Maintenance           6600     9000
12 TOTAL INCOME         20000    21300
13
```

■*5*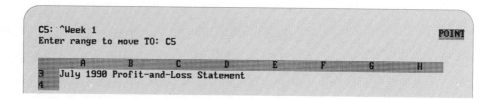

```
C5: ^Week 1                                                    POINT
Enter range to move TO: C5

        A       B       C       D       E       F       G       H
3    July 1990 Profit-and-Loss Statement
4
```

You are asked to specify the location where you wish to move the data. The Move command will overwrite existing data, so you could lose important information if you aren't careful. Make sure there are enough blank cells (or unimportant data) to move the data into.

■*6*   Move the pointer to E8 and press ⏎ .

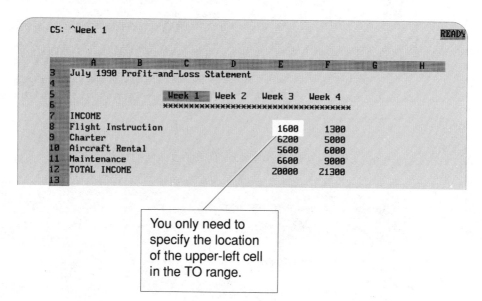

```
C5: ^Week 1                                                    READY

        A       B       C       D       E       F       G       H
3    July 1990 Profit-and-Loss Statement
4
5                              Week 1   Week 2   Week 3   Week 4
6                              *****************************************
7    INCOME
8    Flight Instruction                 1600     1300
9    Charter                            6200     5000
10   Aircraft Rental                    5600     6000
11   Maintenance                        6600     9000
12   TOTAL INCOME                      20000    21300
13
```

You only need to
specify the location
of the upper-left cell
in the TO range.

■ 7   Press ⌈ALT⌉⌈F4⌉ (Undo) to return the data in
columns E and F to columns C and D.

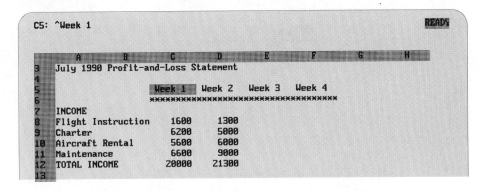

■*Editing Rows*

As you saw in the previous exercises, 1-2-3 provides you with some powerful
tools that enable you to edit columns of data. Well, you can use these same features to edit rows of data. This section shows you how to insert, delete, and move
rows in your worksheet.

Inserting Rows

Let's insert a blank row to put some space between the weekly column headings
and the income data.

■ 1   Select /Worksheet, Insert, Row.

■*2* ⌷ESC⌷ to unanchor the range.

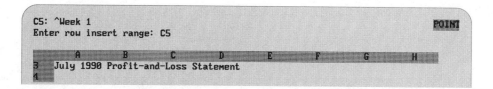

■*3* Move the pointer to the row where you want
to insert the blank row (in this case, cell A7)
and press ⌷←⌷.

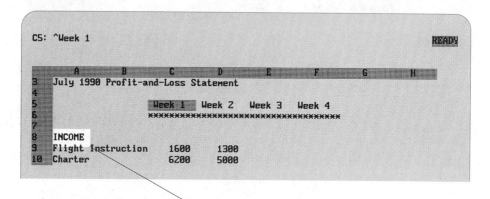

> The INCOME label is now located in row 8
> and a blank row is placed above it.

Deleting Rows

Deleting an unwanted row of data is as easy as inserting a new row. Let's delete
the asterisks under the weekly column headings. After you delete the asterisks,
you'll place them back on the worksheet with the Undo key.

1 Move the pointer to cell C6, the first cell the
asterisks appear in. You may place the pointer
on any cell in the row, however.

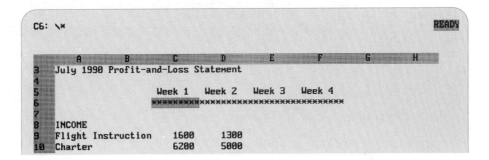

2 Select /Worksheet, Delete, Row.

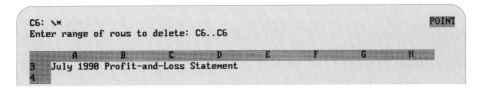

3 ⏎

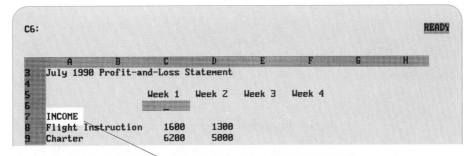

The row containing the asterisks is deleted. Notice that
the INCOME label moved from cell A8 to A7.

■4   ⟨ALT⟩⟨F4⟩ to restore the asterisks to the
worksheet.

```
C6: \*                                                              READY



        A        B        C        D        E        F        G        H
3  July 1990 Profit-and-Loss Statement
4
5                            Week 1   Week 2   Week 3   Week 4
6                          ×××××××××××××××××××××××××××××××××××××××××
7
8  INCOME
9  Flight Instruction       1600     1300
10 Charter                  6200     5000
```

Moving Rows

Use this feature whenever you want to move a row of data to a different row on
the worksheet. For example, in this exercise, let's move row 13 (TOTAL IN-
COME) to row 14.

■1   Move the pointer to cell A13.

```
8  INCOME
9  Flight Instruction      1600     1300
10 Charter                 6200     5000
11 Aircraft Rental         5600     6000
12 Maintenance             6600     9000
13 TOTAL INCOME           20000    21300
14
15 EXPENSES
16 Wages                   6800     6600
17 Fuel/Oil/Parts         10300     8400
```

■2   Select /Move.

```
A13: 'TOTAL INCOME                                                   POINT
Enter range to move FROM: A13..A13


        A        B        C        D        E        F        G        H
3  July 1990 Profit-and-Loss Statement
4
```

You may move any amount of worksheet data, from a single cell, to part of a row, to an entire row.

■*3*   ⎘ three times to highlight the cells you want to move.

```
 8  INCOME
 9  Flight Instruction    1600    1300
10  Charter               6200    5000
11  Aircraft Rental       5600    6000
12  Maintenance           6600    9000
13  TOTAL INCOME         20000   21300
14
15  EXPENSES
16  Wages                 6800    6600
17  Fuel/Oil/Parts       10300    8400
```

■*4*   ⏎

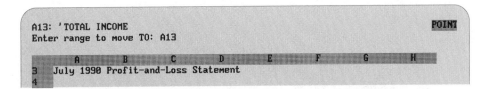

```
A13: 'TOTAL INCOME                                          POINT
Enter range to move TO: A13

        A       B       C       D       E       F       G       H
 3  July 1990 Profit-and-Loss Statement
 4
```

You are asked to specify the location where you wish to move the row data. The Move command will overwrite existing data, so you could lose important information if you aren't careful. Make sure there are enough blank cells (or unimportant data) to move the data into.

■5   Move the pointer to cell A14 and press ⏎ .

```
8    INCOME
9    Flight Instruction    1600    1300
10   Charter               6200    5000
11   Aircraft Rental       5600    6000
12   Maintenance           6600    9000
13
14   TOTAL INCOME          20000   21300
15   EXPENSES
16   Wages                 6800    6600
17   Fuel/Oil/Parts        10300   8400
```

You only need to specify the location of the upper-left cell (if moving more than one row) in the TO range. In this case (one row), the furthest left cell sufficed.

■6   ALT F4 to restore the previous display.

```
8    INCOME
9    Flight Instruction    1600    1300
10   Charter               6200    5000
11   Aircraft Rental       5600    6000
12   Maintenance           6600    9000
13   TOTAL INCOME          20000   21300
14
15   EXPENSES
16   Wages                 6800    6600
17   Fuel/Oil/Parts        10300   8400
```

Copying Data to
■*Other Areas of the Worksheet*

3

When you construct your worksheets, you will often use the same data and formulas in more than one cell. The Copy feature makes it possible for you to create the initial data or formula once, and then place copies of this information in the appropriate cells. You do not have to go to each cell and enter the same data.

Using the JULYPL1 file, let's copy some data from one location to another, restoring the original worksheet with the Undo key when you are finished.

Copying One Cell to Another Cell

■*1*   Select /Copy.

```
A13: 'TOTAL INCOME                                            POINT
Enter range to copy FROM: A13..A13

         A        B        C        D        E        F        G        H
3   July 1990 Profit-and-Loss Statement
4
```

■*2*   ESC to unanchor cell A13.

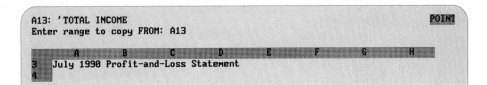

```
A13: 'TOTAL INCOME                                            POINT
Enter range to copy FROM: A13

         A        B        C        D        E        F        G        H
3   July 1990 Profit-and-Loss Statement
4
```

■*3* Move the pointer to C13. The formula total-
ing cells C9 through C12 appears. You will be
copying this formula to cell E13.

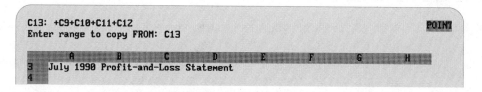

```
C13: +C9+C10+C11+C12                                            POINT
Enter range to copy FROM: C13

      A       B       C       D       E       F       G       H
3   July 1990 Profit-and-Loss Statement
4
```

■*4* ⏎

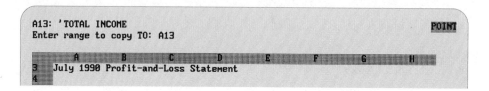

```
A13: 'TOTAL INCOME                                              POINT
Enter range to copy TO: A13

      A       B       C       D       E       F       G       H
3   July 1990 Profit-and-Loss Statement
4
```

■*5* Move the pointer to cell E13 and press ⏎.

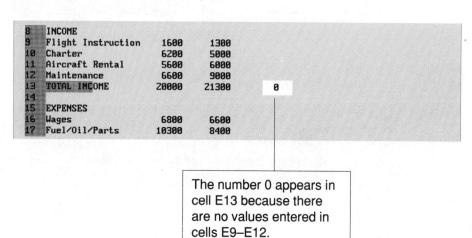

```
8    INCOME
9    Flight Instruction   1600    1300
10   Charter              6200    5000
11   Aircraft Rental      5600    6000
12   Maintenance          6600    9000
13   TOTAL INCOME        20000   21300            0
14
15   EXPENSES
16   Wages                6800    6600
17   Fuel/Oil/Parts      10300    8400
```

The number 0 appears in
cell E13 because there
are no values entered in
cells E9–E12.

■ *6*   Move the pointer to cell E13.

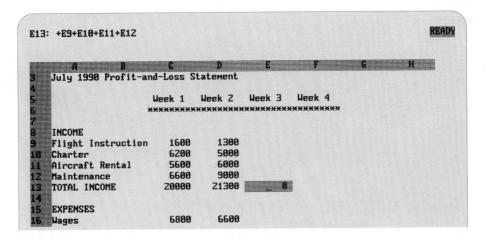

The cell addresses in the formula have changed automatically from +C9+C10+C11+C12 to +E9+E10+E11+E12. This happens because the formula contains *relative* cell addresses, which means that the cell addresses in the formula change relative to the cell the formula is placed in, in this case, cell E13.

■ *7*   ALT F4 to restore the worksheet.

Copying One Cell to a Range of Cells

■ *1*   Move the pointer to cell C20.

15	EXPENSES		
16	Wages	6800	6600
17	Fuel/Oil/Parts	10300	8400
18	Rent	2000	2000
19	Insurance	1200	1200
20	TOTAL EXPENSES	20300	18200
21			
22	TOTAL PROFIT/LOSS	-300	3100

16-Aug-90   13:25 PM   UNDO

■ *2*   Select /Copy, and press ⏎ to copy the value
in cell C20.

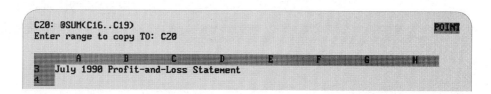

■ *3*   Type **E20..F20** and press ⏎. (You may also
use the pointer to select the range.) The formula from cell C20, @SUM(C16..C19), is
copied into cells E20 and F20.

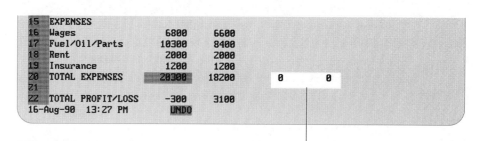

The 0 indicates no values have been entered in the cells above E20 and F20.

■ *4*   Move the pointer to cell E20.

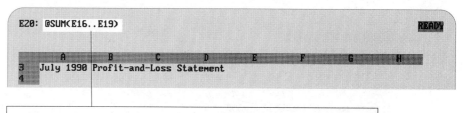

The formula has changed to reflect column E. Moving the
pointer to cell F20 would show the formula @SUM(F16..F19).

■5 `ALT` `F4` to restore the worksheet.

Copying a Range of Cells to Another Range of Cells

■ 1 With the pointer in cell C20, select /Copy.

```
C20: @SUM(C16..C19)                                          POINT
Enter range to copy FROM: C20..C20

          A         B         C         D         E         F         G         H
3  July 1990 Profit-and-Loss Statement
4
```

■2 Move the pointer to cell D16.

```
15  EXPENSES
16  Wages                         6800      6600
17  Fuel/Oil/Parts               10300      8400
18  Rent                          2000      2000
19  Insurance                     1200      1200
20  TOTAL EXPENSES               20300     18200
21
22  TOTAL PROFIT/LOSS             -300      3100
16-Aug-90  13:30 PM
```

■3 ↵, move the pointer to cell E16,
and press ↵ again.

```
15  EXPENSES
16  Wages                 6800      6600      6800      6600
17  Fuel/Oil/Parts       10300      8400     10300      8400
18  Rent                  2000      2000      2000      2000
19  Insurance             1200      1200      1200      1200
20  TOTAL EXPENSES       20300     18200     20300     18200
21
22  TOTAL PROFIT/LOSS     -300      3100
16-Aug-90  13:31 PM             UNDO
```

3

■4 [ALT][F4] to restore the worksheet.

■*A Word About Cell References*

Cell references are the individual entries that make up the formulas you create to analyze your worksheet data. These entries are called cell references because they refer to the values found in specific cells. For example, the formula you created in cell C20 reads @SUM(C16..C19). The C16..C19 are the formula entries that refer to the values in cells C16, C17, C18, and C19.

There are three types of cell references: relative, absolute, and mixed. The type of cell reference you use in a formula will determine how the formula is affected when you use the Copy command to copy the formula into a different cell.

Relative References

The formulas you have created thus far contain relative references. This means that when you copy a formula from one cell to another, the cell references in the formula change to reflect the cells at the new location of the formula. You saw an example of a relative reference formula in the exercise in the section "Copying One Cell to Another Cell."

Absolute References

An absolute reference is an entry in a formula that does not refer to a new cell when the formula is copied to a new cell. There are certain formulas that you will create wherein you will want an entry to always refer to one specific cell value.

An example of this is calculating the interest on several different principle amounts. The interest percentage remains unchanged, or absolute, so the entry in the formula that refers to the interest percentage should be designated as an absolute reference. However, the principle amounts change, so they should have relative reference entries in the formula. Consequently, no matter which cells you might copy this formula into, the interest cell reference will always refer to the one cell that contains the interest percentage.

To designate a formula entry as absolute, you type a dollar sign ($) in front of the column designator and row designator. For example, typing +C3+$C$4 in cell C5 would make cell C4 an absolute reference. If you then copied this formula to cell D5, the formula would change to +D3+$C$4. The C3 entry changes to D3 because it is a relative reference, and the $C$4 entry continues to refer to the original cell location because it is an absolute reference. (You'll learn more about absolute references in Chapter 4.)

Mixed References

A mixed reference is a single cell entry in a formula that contains both a relative and an absolute reference. All formula entries contain a column reference and a row reference, and you can designate one of them as an absolute reference. For example, if you type the cell entry $E5, the column E portion of the entry is absolute and will not change when the entry is copied to a new cell. However, the row 5 entry will change. Typing the entry as E$5 works the opposite way; the column designator would change to reflect a new location, but the row designator would continue to refer to row 5. A mixed reference is helpful when you need a formula that always refers to the values in a specific column, but the values in the rows must change, and vice versa.

■Saving an Existing File

Saving a file that has been previously saved is slightly different than saving a newly created worksheet. Let's end this chapter by saving JULYPL1 once again. If you have a dual floppy-disk computer, remember to place your data disk in drive B.

■ *1*   Select /File, Save.

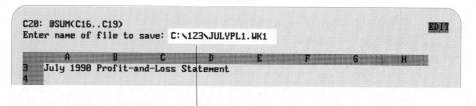

You are shown the current file name. If you want to rename the file, type in a new file name. If you want to save it to another directory or disk, press ᴇꜱᴄ three times (twice for a dual floppy setup) and type in the new path and file name.

■ *2*   ⏎ to accept the current path and file name.

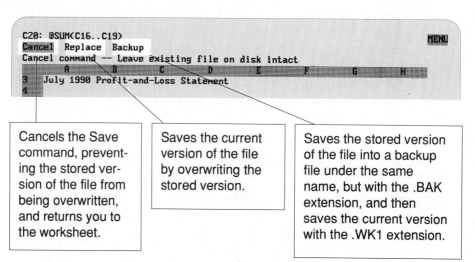

Cancels the Save command, preventing the stored version of the file from being overwritten, and returns you to the worksheet.

Saves the current version of the file by overwriting the stored version.

Saves the stored version of the file into a backup file under the same name, but with the .BAK extension, and then saves the current version with the .WK1 extension.

■*3*   Select Replace to save the file.

■*4*   Select /Quit, Yes to end this work session.

■*Summary*

3

You now have been introduced to all the basic tools necessary to create, edit, and print worksheets. Remember to use 1-2-3's Help feature for a quick fix when you can't remember the commands you need. You have learned how to work with columns and rows. You also know how to copy and move data from one location to another. Don't hesitate to refer back to these exercises when working on your own documents. Just follow the steps, substituting your worksheet data in place of the given examples.

Formatting
■ *Your Worksheet*

In this chapter you'll learn how to use 1-2-3's formatting tools to format your worksheets. Formatting changes the appearance of a worksheet. For example, you may want the contents of certain cells to be displayed with currency signs and decimal points or in scientific notation. Or, the columns may need to be wider to accommodate more characters or to achieve a more pleasing look. Labels might look better centered rather than left- or right-aligned. These are only a few of the many ways you can format your worksheets.

Adjusting Worksheet Column Widths

■

Formatting Cell Values

■

Assigning Names to Worksheet Data

■

Creating Fixed Titles

■

Positioning Labels within Columns

■

Creating Worksheet Comments

Adjusting All Your
■ *Worksheet Column Widths*

In Chapter 3, you learned how to widen a single column. But what if you need to widen all the worksheet columns? Widening columns becomes necessary when you want to include currency signs, decimal points, and commas in your values, or if you are dealing with numbers that contain more than nine characters. By the way, when the size of a value exceeds the cell width, 1-2-3 displays asterisks across the width of the cell.

Let's widen all the columns on the AUGPL1 worksheet you created in Chapter 2. Remember, the default column width is nine characters. Let's expand all the worksheet columns to 12 characters.

4

■ *1* Retrieve the file AUGPL1.WK1 using the
/File, Retrieve command.

```
E19:                                                                    READY

        A        B        C        D        E        F        G        H
 3  August 1990 Profit-and-Loss Statement
 4
 5                            Week 1   Week 2   Week 3   Week 4
 6                         xxxxxxxxxxxxxxxxxxxxxxxxxxxxxxxxxxxxxx
 7  INCOME
 8  Flight Instruction       1600     1200
 9  Charter                  6200     4800
10  Aircraft Rental          5600     7000
11  Maintenance              8600     9200
12  TOTAL INCOME            22000    22200
13
14  EXPENSES
15  Wages                    6800     6600
16  Fuel/Oil/Parts          10300     8400
17  Rent                     2000     2000
18  Insurance                1200     1200
19  TOTAL EXPENSES          20300    18200
20
21  TOTAL PROFIT/LOSS        1700     4000
22
17 Aug-90  12:01 PM        UNDO
```

■*2* Select /Worksheet, Global.

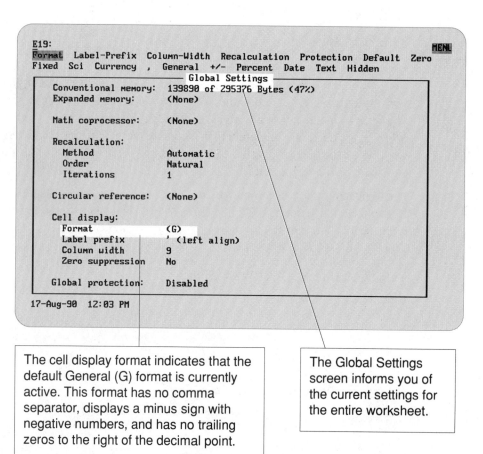

The cell display format indicates that the default General (G) format is currently active. This format has no comma separator, displays a minus sign with negative numbers, and has no trailing zeros to the right of the decimal point.

The Global Settings screen informs you of the current settings for the entire worksheet.

■*3* Select Column-Width.

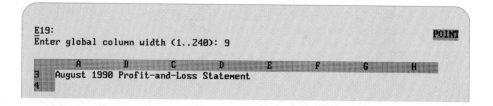

■*4* Type **12** and press ⏎, or use → to expand
the cell width to 12 characters and press ⏎.

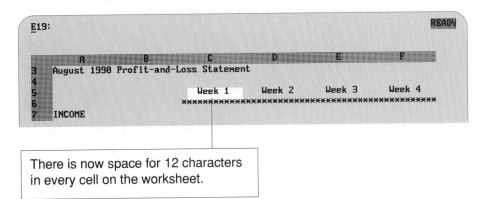

E19:   READY

	A	B	C	D	E	F
3	August 1990 Profit-and-Loss Statement					
4						
5			Week 1	Week 2	Week 3	Week 4
6			xxxxxxxxxxxxxxxxxxxxxxxxxxxxxxxxxxxxxxxxxxxxxx			
7	INCOME					

There is now space for 12 characters
in every cell on the worksheet.

4

■*Formatting Cell Values*

When you format a cell value, you determine how the value will be displayed on
the screen. For example, the currency values you worked with in Chapters 1–3
can be displayed with dollar signs and decimal points, which they presently do
not contain.

There are ten cell formatting options available: General, Currency, Commas,
Percent, Fixed, Scientific, + and −, Date, Text, and Hidden. The cell format
you've used so far is the General format—no commas, dollar signs, trailing
zeros, or decimal points.

The exercises in this section will demonstrate how to place commas and dollar
signs in the values in your AUGPL1.WK1 worksheet. Be sure you've increased
all the column widths to 12 characters. When you place values into a cell that
isn't wide enough to hold them, 1-2-3 places asterisks across the full width of the
cell. 1-2-3 will still accept and work with the values, but you won't see them
displayed on your screen.

Formatting Your Entire Worksheet

With your AUGPL1.WK1 worksheet on the screen, let's place commas and decimal points in all the values in the entire worksheet.

■ *1*   Select /Worksheet, Global.

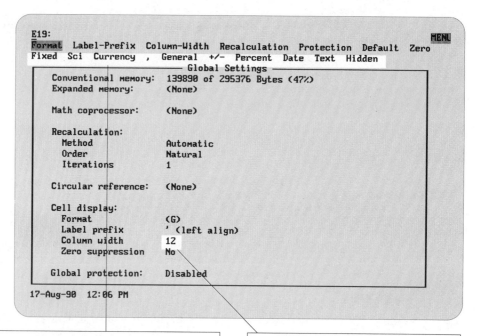

```
E19:                                                              MENU
Format  Label-Prefix  Column-Width  Recalculation  Protection  Default  Zero
Fixed  Sci  Currency  ,  General  +/-  Percent  Date  Text  Hidden
                        ──── Global Settings ────
    Conventional memory:    139890 of 295376 Bytes (47%)
    Expanded memory:        (None)

    Math coprocessor:       (None)

    Recalculation:
      Method                Automatic
      Order                 Natural
      Iterations            1

    Circular reference:     (None)

    Cell display:
      Format                (G)
      Label prefix          ' (left align)
      Column width          12
      Zero suppression      No

    Global protection:      Disabled

17-Aug-90  12:06 PM
```

These ten cell formatting selections are described inside the covers of this book.

The column width is recorded on the Global Settings screen.

■ *2*   Select Format.

```
E19:                                                              MENU
Fixed  Sci  Currency  ,  General  +/-  Percent  Date  Text  Hidden
Fixed number of decimal places (x.xx)
                        ──── Global Settings ────
    Conventional memory:    139890 of 295376 Bytes (47%)
    Expanded memory:        (None)
```

■*3* Select , (comma) to set the number of decimal
places displayed and to include commas.

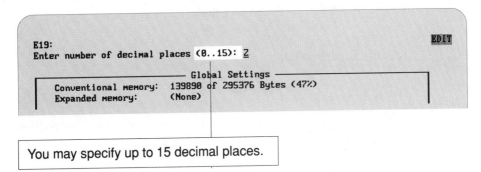

```
E19:                                                              EDIT
Enter number of decimal places (0..15): 2

                        ── Global Settings ──
    Conventional memory:   139890 of 295376 Bytes (47%)
    Expanded memory:       (None)
```

> You may specify up to 15 decimal places.

■*4* ⏎ to accept two decimal places.

```
E19:                                                             READY


         A          B           C          D          E          F
3   August 1990 Profit-and-Loss Statement
4
5                               Week 1      Week 2     Week 3     Week 4
6                           ×××××××××××××××××××××××××××××××××××××××××××
7   INCOME
8   Flight Instruction      1,600.00     1,200.00
9   Charter                 6,200.00     4,800.00
10  Aircraft Rental         5,600.00     7,000.00
11  Maintenance             8,600.00     9,200.00
12  TOTAL INCOME           22,000.00    22,200.00
13
14  EXPENSES
15  Wages                   6,800.00     6,600.00
16  Fuel/Oil/Parts         10,300.00     8,400.00
17  Rent                    2,000.00     2,000.00
18  Insurance               1,200.00     1,200.00
19  TOTAL EXPENSES         20,300.00    18,200.00
20
21  TOTAL PROFIT/LOSS       1,700.00     4,000.00
22
18-Aug-90  12:09 PM       UNDO
```

Formatting Part of Your Worksheet

Working with the AUGPL1.WK1 worksheet again, let's place dollar signs in the TOTAL PROFIT/LOSS row of values.

■*1*   Select /Range, Format.

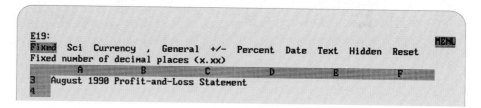

■*2*   Select Currency.

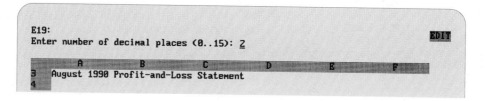

■*3*   [↵] to accept two decimal places.

```
E19:
Enter range to format: E19..E19                              POINT

       A            B            C          D          E          F
3  August 1990 Profit-and-Loss Statement
4
```

■*4*   ESC to unanchor the range and move the
pointer to cell C21.

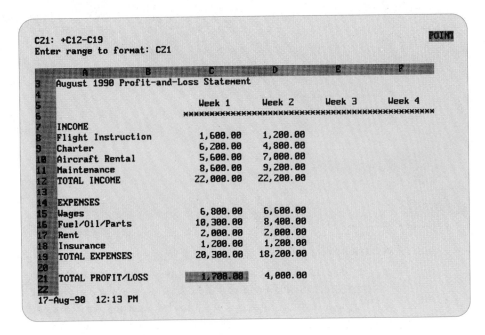

```
C21: +C12-C19                                              POINT
Enter range to format: C21
          A         B         C         D         E         F
   3  August 1990 Profit-and-Loss Statement
   4
   5                                Week 1    Week 2    Week 3    Week 4
   6              xxxxxxxxxxxxxxxxxxxxxxxxxxxxxxxxxxxxxxxxxxxxxxxxxxx
   7  INCOME
   8  Flight Instruction           1,600.00  1,200.00
   9  Charter                      6,200.00  4,800.00
  10  Aircraft Rental              5,600.00  7,000.00
  11  Maintenance                  8,600.00  9,200.00
  12  TOTAL INCOME                22,000.00 22,200.00
  13
  14  EXPENSES
  15  Wages                        6,800.00  6,600.00
  16  Fuel/Oil/Parts              10,300.00  8,400.00
  17  Rent                         2,000.00  2,000.00
  18  Insurance                    1,200.00  1,200.00
  19  TOTAL EXPENSES              20,300.00 18,200.00
  20
  21  TOTAL PROFIT/LOSS            1,700.00  4,000.00
  22
  17-Aug-90  12:13 PM
```

■*5*   . (period) to anchor cell C21 and move the
pointer to cell D21.

```
  17  Rent                         2,000.00  2,000.00
  18  Insurance                    1,200.00  1,200.00
  19  TOTAL EXPENSES              20,300.00 18,200.00
  20
  21  TOTAL PROFIT/LOSS            1,700.00  4,000.00
  22
  17-Aug-90  12:14 PM
```

■6   ↵

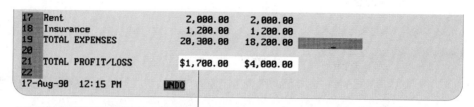

The range of cells C21 through D21 now display dollar signs.

Assigning Names
■*to Worksheet Data*

1-2-3 enables you to assign a name to a value or formula in a single cell or a range of cells. This allows you to treat a range of cells as a unit. You can then use the assigned name instead of the cell addresses when specifying a cell or range of cells for use in printing, copying, moving, erasing, or formatting. You can even specify the range name when using the GoTo (F5) key.

For example, in your AUGPL1.WK1 worksheet, the formula in cell C21 is +C12–C19. You could assign the name INC1 to cell C12 and EXP1 to cell C19 and then rewrite the formula in C21 as +INC1–EXP1.

Let's assign a range name to cells C5 through D12, the INCOME portion of the AUGPL1 worksheet, and then print a copy of that range of data.

■1   Move the pointer to cell A5.

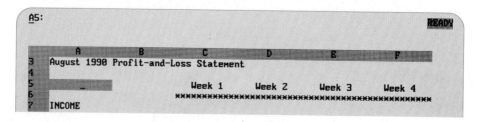

■2 Select /Range, Name. You see five options for
naming and working with ranges.

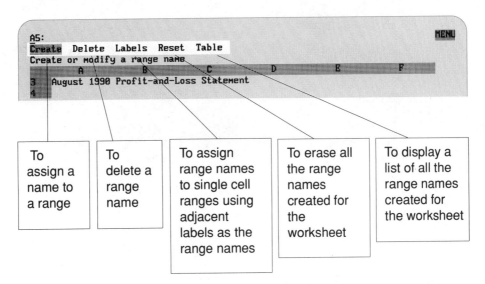

A5:   MENU
█Create█ Delete Labels Reset Table
Create or modify a range name
      A   B   C   D   E   F
3 August 1990 Profit-and-Loss Statement
4

| To assign a name to a range | To delete a range name | To assign range names to single cell ranges using adjacent labels as the range names | To erase all the range names created for the worksheet | To display a list of all the range names created for the worksheet |

■3 Select Create, type **INCOME**, and press ⏎.

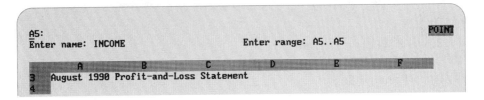

A5:   POINT
Enter name: INCOME   Enter range: A5..A5

      A   B   C   D   E   F
3 August 1990 Profit-and-Loss Statement
4

■4   Move the pointer to cell D12.

```
D12:  +D8+D9+D10+D11                                                    POINT
Enter name: INCOME                    Enter range: A5..D12

         A          B           C          D         E          F
 3  August 1990 Profit-and-Loss Statement
 4
 5                              Week 1      Week 2    Week 3     Week 4
 6  ******************************************************************
 7  INCOME
 8  Flight Instruction       1,600.00    1,200.00
 9  Charter                  6,200.00    4,800.00
10  Aircraft Rental          5,500.00    7,000.00
11  Maintenance              8,600.00    9,200.00
12  TOTAL INCOME            22,000.00   22,200.00
13
14  EXPENSES
```

■5   ⏎ to complete naming the range.

```
A5:                                                                    READY

         A          B           C          D         E          F
 3  August 1990 Profit-and-Loss Statement
 4
 5                              Week 1      Week 2    Week 3     Week 4
 6  ******************************************************************
 7  INCOME
```

■6   Turn your printer on and select /Print,
Printer, Range.

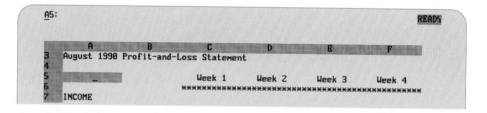

```
A5:                                                                    POINT
Enter print range: A5

         A          B           C          D         E          F
 3  August 1990 Profit-and-Loss Statement
 4
```

■ 7   F3 (the Name key)

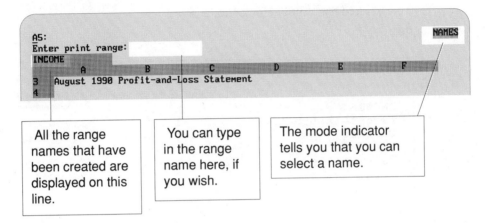

All the range names that have been created are displayed on this line.

You can type in the range name here, if you wish.

The mode indicator tells you that you can select a name.

■ 8   With the pointer on INCOME, press ⏎.

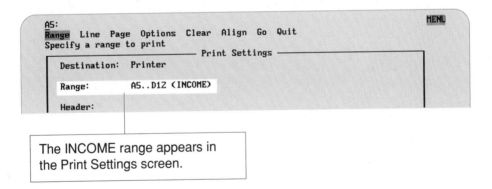

The INCOME range appears in the Print Settings screen.

4

■ *9*   Select Align, Go, Page to print the range.
Your printed page should look similar to
this:

```
                            Week 1      Week 2
                       ************************
           INCOME
           Flight Instruction   1,600.00    1,200.00
           Charter              6,200.00    4,800.00
           Aircraft Rental      5,600.00    7,000.00
           Maintenance          8,600.00    9,200.00
           TOTAL INCOME        22,000.00   22,200.00
```

■ *10*   Select Quit to return to your worksheet.

∎*Creating Fixed Titles*

As you know, when you move the pointer beyond the columns and rows currently displayed, the upper-left columns and rows scroll off the screen, out of sight. This can cause difficulties when you wish to refer to the column and row labels as you place values in cells, but you can't see the labels. 1-2-3's Worksheet Titles feature allows you to fix labels (or values) so they remain displayed at all times.

You may fix any number of row and column titles as long as they border the top and/or left edges of your worksheet. You may fix titles horizontally, across the top of the worksheet, or vertically, down the left edge of the worksheet, or both horizontally and vertically at the same time. Let's try each of these methods. Use your AUGPL1.WK1 worksheet.

Fixing Horizontal Titles

∎*1*   Always place the pointer one cell below the rows you want to fix into place. In this case, move the pointer to any cell in row 6 (the row containing asterisks); I chose cell A6.

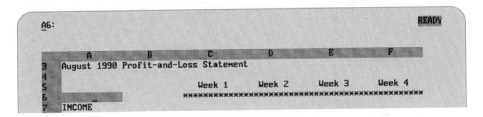

■2   Select /Worksheet, Titles.

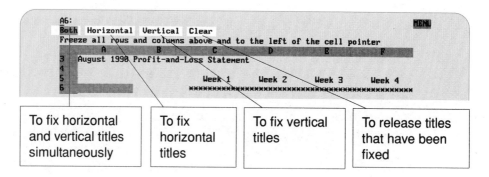

| To fix horizontal and vertical titles simultaneously | To fix horizontal titles | To fix vertical titles | To release titles that have been fixed |

■3   Select Horizontal, then press ⬇ to move the
       pointer to cell A30.

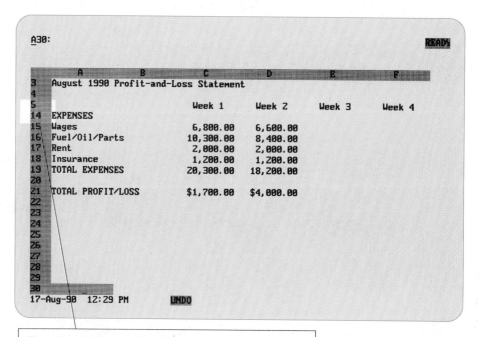

The titles from row 5 and above remain fixed in
place. Rows 6 through 13 disappear from view.

■ *4*   ALT F4 (Undo) to restore the worksheet.

Fixing Vertical Titles

■ *1*   Always place the pointer one column to the
right of the columns you want to fix. In this
case, move the pointer to any cell in column B;
I chose cell B6.

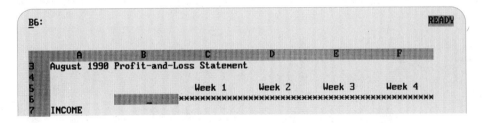

■ *2*   Select /Worksheet, Titles, Vertical, then move
the pointer to column H.

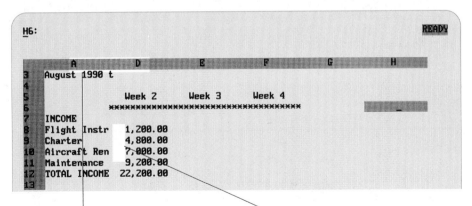

The titles in column A remain fixed
in place as columns B and C disappear off the screen.

Notice that the labels that spilled over the edge
of column A into column B have been chopped
off as column B scrolls off the screen.

■ *3*   [ALT] [F4] (Undo) to restore the worksheet.

Fixing Horizontal and Vertical Titles Simultaneously

■ *1*   Move the pointer to cell E13 to fix all the titles
(rows and columns) above row 13 and to the
left of column E.

```
E13:                                                              READY

          A          B          C          D          E          F
3     August 1990 Profit-and-Loss Statement
4
5                              Week 1     Week 2     Week 3     Week 4
6                   ××××××××××××××××××××××××××××××××××××××××××××××××××
7     INCOME
8     Flight Instruction     1,600.00   1,200.00
9     Charter                6,200.00   4,800.00
10    Aircraft Rental        5,600.00   7,000.00
11    Maintenance            8,600.00   9,200.00
12    TOTAL INCOME          22,000.00  22,200.00
13
```

■2   Select /Worksheet, Titles, Both. Use the
Arrow keys to move the pointer to cell I29.

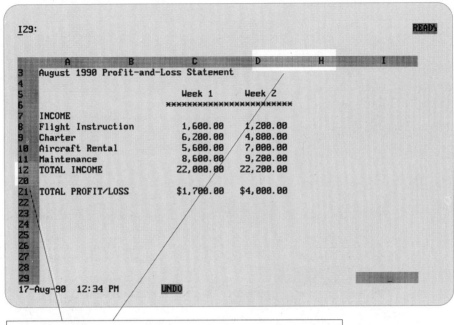

Rows 13–19 and columns E–G scroll off the screen.

Editing a Worksheet with Fixed Titles

You cannot move the pointer into an area of fixed titles except with the Go To key. Let's suppose you want to edit cell A6 in the fixed area of the worksheet.

■1   [F5] (GoTo key)

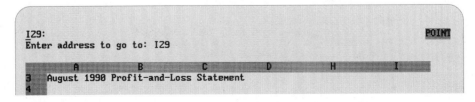

■2   Type **A6** and press ⏎ . A copy of the
worksheet is placed outside the fixed titles
range so it can be edited.

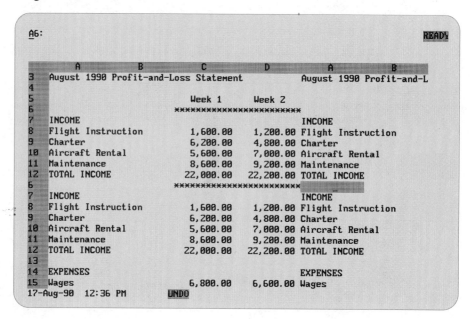

To remove the second copy of the worksheet, you would press PG UP until all
extra rows disappear, then press PG DN until 1-2-3 beeps. Then, press CTRL→ until
the extra columns disappear, then press CTRL← until 1-2-3 beeps.

Clearing Fixed Titles

■1   Select /Worksheet, Titles.

■*2*   Select Clear.

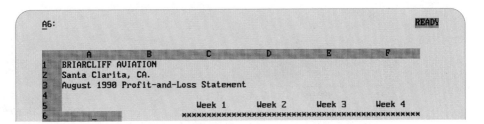

Positioning
■*Labels within Columns*

You may decide that you don't like the location of your worksheet labels within their respective cells. You know how to edit them one at a time, but with the /Range, Label command, you can shift an entire range of labels.

Let's shift the Week 1 through Week 4 labels from the center position to the right-aligned position. Use your AUGPL1.WK1 worksheet.

■*1*   With the pointer in cell A6, select /Range,
Label, Right.

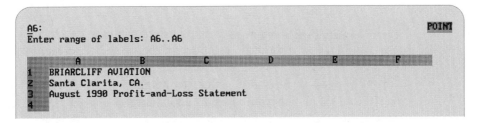

■2   ESC to unanchor the range.

A6:
Enter range of labels: A6   POINT

	A	B	C	D	E	F
1	BRIARCLIFF AVIATION
2	Santa Clarita, CA.
3	August 1990 Profit-and-Loss Statement
4

■3   Type **C5 . . F5** and press ⏎ .

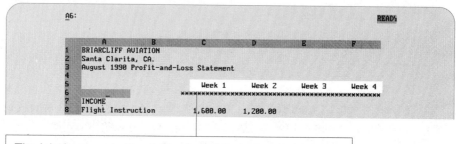

The labels move to the right edge of their respective cells.

■*Creating Worksheet Comments*

Worksheet comments can be very helpful in managing your documents. Comments can range from brief descriptions of the worksheet contents to personal notes and reminders. The Range Justify feature allows you to place text comments on your worksheet and then create margins within which the text will be placed. Your comments can be up to 256 characters in length (the number of characters that will fit in a single cell).

Let's add a short comment to your AUGPL1.WK1 worksheet.

■ *1*   ⬇ to move the pointer to the cell you want
the comment to appear in (in this case, cell
A23). Type the following text: **'Submit to
Audits Unlimited by September 3, 1990.**

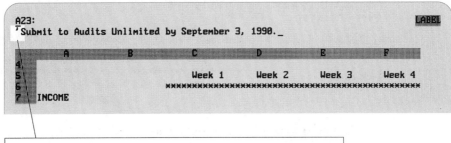

The apostrophe aligns the comment at the left margin.

■ *2*   ⬅ to place the text on the worksheet.

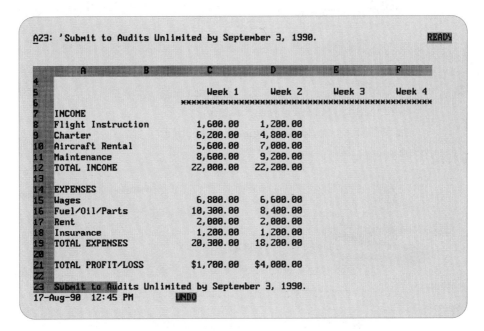

4

Now specify the margins you want for the comment.

■3 Select /Range, Justify.

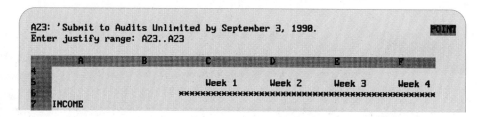

```
A23: 'Submit to Audits Unlimited by September 3, 1990.          POINT
Enter justify range: A23..A23
        A           B           C           D           E           F
  4
  5                                 Week 1      Week 2      Week 3      Week 4
  6                             **************************************************
  7   INCOME
```

■4 Move the pointer to cell B23 (the right margin) and press ⏎.

```
 19  TOTAL EXPENSES              20,300.00   18,200.00
 20
 21  TOTAL PROFIT/LOSS           $1,700.00   $4,000.00
 22
 23  Submit to Audits
 17-Aug-90  12:47 PM      UNDO
```

■5 Move the pointer to cell A26 to see the comment justified between margins defined by the left edge of column A and the right edge of column B.

```
 22
 23  Submit to Audits
 24  Unlimited by September
 25  3, 1990.
 26
 17-Aug-90  12:48 PM      UNDO
```

■ *6*   Select /File, Save, press ⏎, and select
Replace to save the AUGPL1 worksheet.

■*Summary*

Chapter 4 has presented some of the features that allow you to change the appearance of your worksheets. You've learned how to change the look of your cell values, shift labels within their cells, and fix titles so they won't disappear off the screen when you scroll the worksheet. You used 1-2-3 as a simple word processor to include comments in your worksheets, and to give names to ranges of data for ease of editing.

4

Working with 1-2-3's Advanced Features

You should now feel confident in creating your own worksheets. This chapter introduces you to some advanced features of Lotus 1-2-3. Once you've added these tools to your bag of skills you'll be able to take full advantage of 1-2-3's ability to create and edit professional-quality spreadsheets.

Creating Windows

Protecting Your Worksheet Data

Working with Automatic and Manual Recalculation

Understanding Global and Default Settings

Creating Absolute Formulas

Printing Options

■*Creating Windows*

When working with a large worksheet, all your data may not be visible on your screen. When you need to compare visible data with data in an area of the worksheet that has scrolled off the screen, it is disconcerting and time consuming to have to move the pointer back and forth between the two worksheet areas. 1-2-3 has a helpful command called Worksheet Window that places two areas of a worksheet on the screen at the same time.

Let's use your AUGPL1.WK1 worksheet to experiment with 1-2-3's windows.

Dividing the Screen Horizontally

■*1* [HOME] to move the pointer to cell A1.

```
A1: 'BRIARCLIFF AVIATION                                              READY

            A          B          C          D          E          F
1    BRIARCLIFF AVIATION
2    Santa Clarita, CA.
3    August 1990 Profit-and-Loss Statement
4
```

■*2* Move the pointer to cell A10, which is the row where you'll split the screen.

```
7    INCOME
8    Flight Instruction      1,600.00    1,200.00
9    Charter                 6,200.00    4,800.00
10   Aircraft Rental         5,600.00    7,000.00
11   Maintenance             8,600.00    9,200.00
12   TOTAL INCOME           22,000.00   22,200.00
13
14   EXPENSES
```

■*3*   Select /Worksheet, Window.

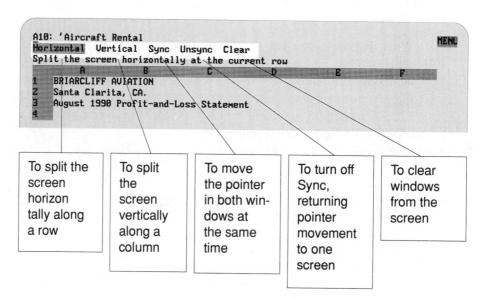

```
A10: 'Aircraft Rental                                          MENU
Horizontal  Vertical  Sync  Unsync  Clear
Split the screen horizontally at the current row
         A          B          C          D          E       F
1    BRIARCLIFF AVIATION
2    Santa Clarita, CA.
3    August 1990 Profit-and-Loss Statement
4
```

| To split the screen horizon tally along a row | To split the screen vertically along a column | To move the pointer in both win- dows at the same time | To turn off Sync, returning pointer movement to one screen | To clear windows from the screen |

Use Worksheet Window to divide your screen horizontally or vertically.

■*4*   Select Horizontal.

```
A9: 'Charter                                                        READY

          A          B          C          D          E          F
1    BRIARCLIFF AVIATION
2    Santa Clarita, CA.
3    August 1990 Profit-and-Loss Statement
4
5                            Week 1     Week 2     Week 3     Week 4
6    xxxxxxxxxxxxxxxxxxxxxxxxxxxxxxxxxxxxxxxxxxxxxxxxxxxxxxxx
7    INCOME
8    Flight Instruction     1,600.00   1,200.00
9    Charter                6,200.00   4,800.00
          A          B          C          D          E          F
10   Aircraft Rental        5,600.00   7,000.00
11   Maintenance            8,600.00   9,200.00
12   TOTAL INCOME          22,000.00  22,200.00
13
14   EXPENSES
15   Wages                  6,800.00   6,600.00
16   Fuel/Oil/Parts        10,300.00   8,400.00
17   Rent                   2,000.00   2,000.00
18   Insurance              1,200.00   1,200.00
19   TOTAL EXPENSES        20,300.00  18,200.00
17-Aug-90  12:52 PM         UNDO
```

Two column heads are displayed to indicate
that two windows have been created.

■*5*   F6 (Windows key) to move the pointer to
       the lower screen. (F6 moves the pointer be-
       tween windows.)

```
5                            Week 1     Week 2     Week 3     Week 4
6    xxxxxxxxxxxxxxxxxxxxxxxxxxxxxxxxxxxxxxxxxxxxxxxxxxxxxxxx
7    INCOME
8    Flight Instruction     1,600.00   1,200.00
9    Charter                6,200.00   4,800.00
          A          B          C          D          E          F
10   Aircraft Rental        5,600.00   7,000.00
11   Maintenance            8,600.00   9,200.00
12   TOTAL INCOME          22,000.00  22,200.00
13
14   EXPENSES
```

5

■6 $\downarrow$ to move the pointer to cell A25. Only the data in the bottom window scrolls.

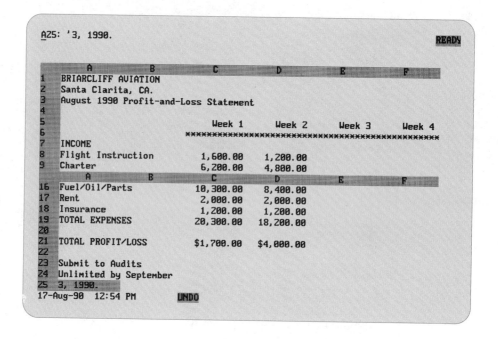

```
A25: '3, 1990.                                                  READY

         A          B         C         D         E         F
1   BRIARCLIFF AVIATION
2   Santa Clarita, CA.
3   August 1990 Profit-and-Loss Statement
4
5                             Week 1    Week 2    Week 3    Week 4
6              *****************************************************
7   INCOME
8   Flight Instruction        1,600.00  1,200.00
9   Charter                   6,200.00  4,800.00
         A          B         C         D         E         F
16  Fuel/Oil/Parts           10,300.00  8,400.00
17  Rent                      2,000.00  2,000.00
18  Insurance                 1,200.00  1,200.00
19  TOTAL EXPENSES           20,300.00 18,200.00
20
21  TOTAL PROFIT/LOSS        $1,700.00 $4,000.00
22
23  Submit to Audits
24  Unlimited by September
25  3, 1990.
17-Aug-90  12:54 PM          UNDO
```

Keep this worksheet on the screen for the next exercise.

Turning Synchronized Scrolling On and Off

Synchronized scrolling allows you to scroll through both windows at the same time.

■ *1*   Select /Worksheet, Window, Sync. Then press
[→] to move the pointer to column J. Both
worksheets scroll off the screen to the left
(they will not scroll together vertically).

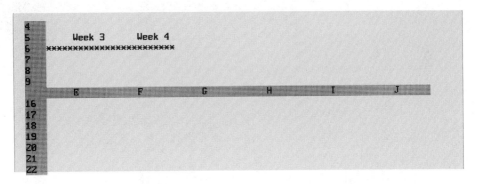

■ *2*   Select /Worksheet, Window, Unsync to turn
synchronized scrolling off.

Keep this worksheet on the screen for the next exercise.

5

Clearing Windows

■ *1*   ⬅ to move the pointer back to cell A25 in
the lower window.

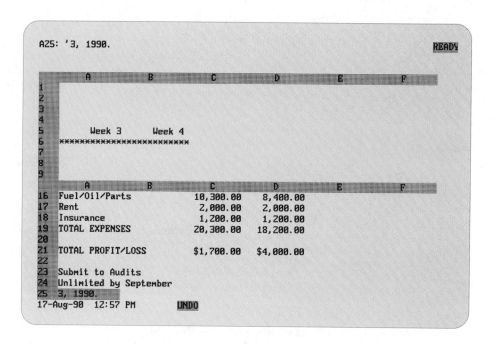

■*2* Select /Worksheet, Window, Clear. Then
press HOME to return to cell A1 with only one
window displayed.

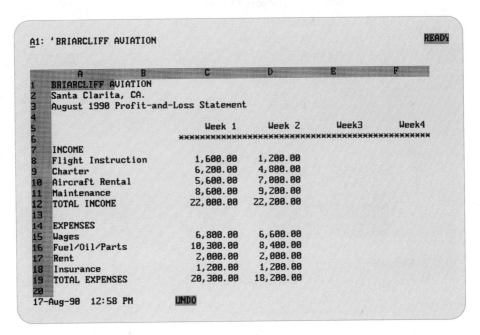

```
A1: 'BRIARCLIFF AVIATION                                          READY

         A         B          C          D          E          F
 1  BRIARCLIFF AVIATION
 2  Santa Clarita, CA.
 3  August 1990 Profit-and-Loss Statement
 4
 5                            Week 1     Week 2     Week3      Week4
 6                        ************************************************
 7  INCOME
 8  Flight Instruction     1,600.00   1,200.00
 9  Charter                6,200.00   4,800.00
10  Aircraft Rental        5,600.00   7,000.00
11  Maintenance            8,600.00   9,200.00
12  TOTAL INCOME          22,000.00  22,200.00
13
14  EXPENSES
15  Wages                  6,800.00   6,600.00
16  Fuel/Oil/Parts        10,300.00   8,400.00
17  Rent                   2,000.00   2,000.00
18  Insurance              1,200.00   1,200.00
19  TOTAL EXPENSES        20,300.00  18,200.00
20
17-Aug-90  12:58 PM           UNDO
```

5

Dividing the Screen Vertically

■ *1*   Move the pointer to column D, which is the
column where the screen will be split.

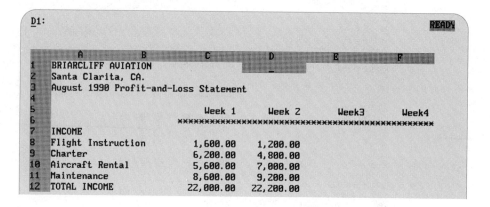

F6 (Window
key) moves
the pointer
between
windows.

■*2*   Select /Worksheet, Window, Vertical.

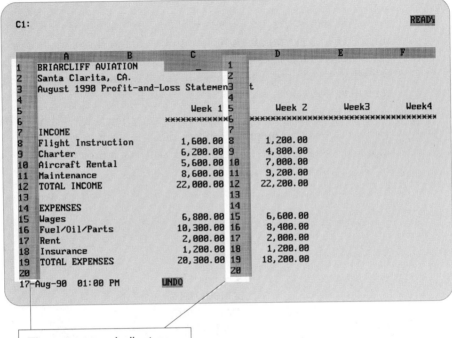

These two row indicators
show where the screen is
split vertically.

When you divide the screen vertically, you can scroll through both screens from
top to bottom (but not horizontally) when Sync is turned on.

■*3*   Select /Worksheet, Window, Clear to clear the
windows from the screen.

■*Protecting Your Worksheet Data*

Protecting worksheet data prevents all, or a portion of, the worksheet from being edited. This is an important feature when data is crucial and other individuals have access to the worksheet. It can also prevent you from accidentally editing cells that you do not want changed. You'll certainly want to protect cells that contain valuable formulas.

There are two ways of protecting and unprotecting data. You can protect the entire worksheet, then unprotect those cells you want to work with. Or, you can unprotect those cells you want to work with, then protect the entire worksheet. For these exercises, we'll use the first method.

Be sure to protect cells that contain valuable formulas.

Protecting the Entire Worksheet

■ *1*   With your AUGPL1.WK1 worksheet on the
screen (the cell pointer should be in cell C1),
Select /Worksheet, Global, Protection.

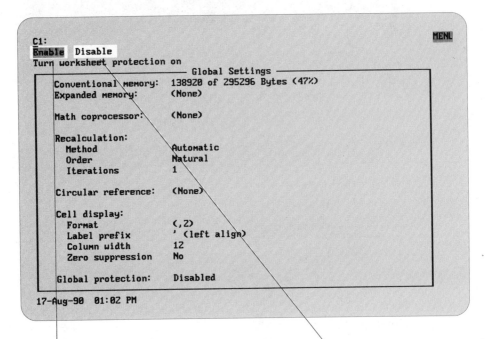

```
C1:                                                    MENU
Enable  Disable
Turn worksheet protection on
                        ┌──────── Global Settings ────────┐
Conventional memory:    138920 of 295296 Bytes (47%)
Expanded memory:        (None)

Math coprocessor:       (None)

Recalculation:
  Method                Automatic
  Order                 Natural
  Iterations            1

Circular reference:     (None)

Cell display:
  Format                (,2)
  Label prefix          ' (left align)
  Column width          12
  Zero suppression      No

Global protection:      Disabled

17-Aug-90  01:02 PM
```

Turns protection on to
prevent entering or
editing data in the
worksheet except in
unprotected cells.

Turns protection off, allowing you
to edit or enter data anywhere in
the worksheet.

5

■2   Select Enable.

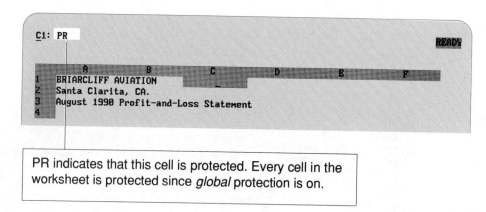

C1: PR   READY

	A	B	C	D	E	F
1	BRIARCLIFF AVIATION					
2	Santa Clarita, CA.					
3	August 1990 Profit-and-Loss Statement					
4						

PR indicates that this cell is protected. Every cell in the worksheet is protected since *global* protection is on.

Note To check the status of worksheet protection, select /Worksheet, Status and look for the status displayed on the bottom of the screen where it says *Global protection:*.

Protecting and Unprotecting a Range of Cells

When you need to work on data that has been protected, use the /Range, Unprot command. When you want to protect only a certain group of cells, as opposed to the entire worksheet, use the /Range, Prot command.

Using the protected worksheet from the previous exercise, let's unprotect a range of cells. This procedure can also be used to protect a range of cells.

■ *1*   Move the pointer to cell C8, the first cell in
the range we want to unprotect.

```
5
6                                 Week 1      Week 2      Week 3      Week 4
                          xxxxxxxxxxxxxxxxxxxxxxxxxxxxxxxxxxxxxxxxxxxxxxxxx
7    INCOME
8    Flight Instruction   1,600.00    1,200.00
9    Charter              6,200.00    4,800.00
10   Aircraft Rental      5,600.00    7,000.00
11   Maintenance          8,600.00    9,200.00
12   TOTAL INCOME        22,000.00   22,200.00
```

■ *2*   Select /Range, Unprot. This same procedure
is followed when protecting a range of cells,
except you select Prot.

5

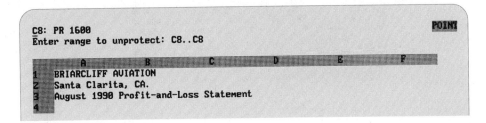

```
C8: PR 1600                                                        POINT
Enter range to unprotect: C8..C8

        A          B          C          D          E          F
1    BRIARCLIFF AVIATION
2    Santa Clarita, CA.
3    August 1990 Profit-and-Loss Statement
4
```

■ *3*   Move the pointer to cell D11 to highlight
the range.

```
4
5                                 Week 1      Week 2      Week 3      Week 4
6                          xxxxxxxxxxxxxxxxxxxxxxxxxxxxxxxxxxxxxxxxxxxxxxxxx
7    INCOME
8    Flight Instruction   1,600.00    1,200.00
9    Charter              6,200.00    4,800.00
10   Aircraft Rental      5,600.00    7,000.00
11   Maintenance          8,600.00    9,200.00
12   TOTAL INCOME        22,000.00   22,200.00
```

Note It is sometimes helpful in locating certain areas of worksheet data if you highlight the data with the /Range, Unprotect command so it stands out from the surrounding data.

■*4* ⏎

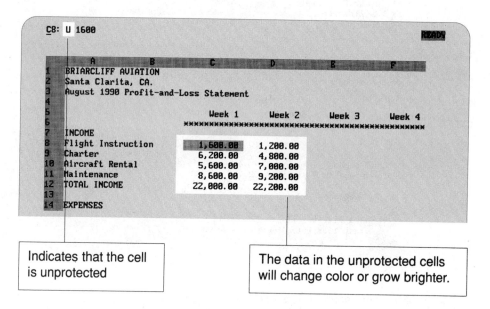

Indicates that the cell is unprotected

The data in the unprotected cells will change color or grow brighter.

■*5* ALT F4 to restore the worksheet.

Unprotecting the Entire Worksheet

The worksheet from the last exercise is still protected. Let's disable the protection.

■ *1*   Select /Worksheet, Global, Protection.

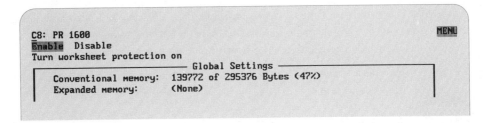

■ *2*   Select Disable.

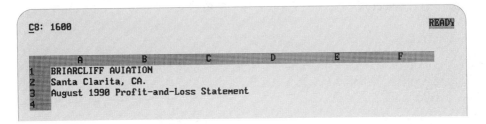

Notice that "PR" has disappeared from the control panel, indicating that the worksheet is no longer protected.

Working With Automatic
■and Manual Recalculation

Whenever you enter or edit a cell value that is part of a formula, or if you edit the formula itself, 1-2-3 automatically recalculates the formula and gives you updated results. Versions of 1-2-3 prior to release 2.2 recalculate every formula in the worksheet, even if only one formula was affected by a change. If you have a large worksheet with many formulas, this recalculation process is very time consuming. Release 2.2 has improved this feature by only recalculating the formulas involved in a change of data. This is known as *minimal recalculation*.

There will be times when you'll want to turn automatic recalculation off (by turning manual recalculation on), especially when you want to manually control when 1-2-3 recalculates the formulas in your worksheets.

Let's use the AUGPL1.WK1 worksheet to demonstrate how to turn manual recalculation on.

Turning On Manual Recalculation

■ *1*   Select /Worksheet, Global, Recalculation.

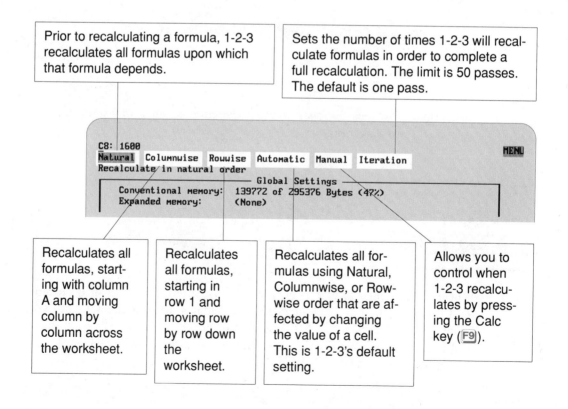

Prior to recalculating a formula, 1-2-3 recalculates all formulas upon which that formula depends.

Sets the number of times 1-2-3 will recalculate formulas in order to complete a full recalculation. The limit is 50 passes. The default is one pass.

Recalculates all formulas, starting with column A and moving column by column across the worksheet.

Recalculates all formulas, starting in row 1 and moving row by row down the worksheet.

Recalculates all formulas using Natural, Columnwise, or Rowwise order that are affected by changing the value of a cell. This is 1-2-3's default setting.

Allows you to control when 1-2-3 recalculates by pressing the Calc key (F9).

■*2*   Select Manual. Notice that the Week 1
TOTAL INCOME is 22,000.00.

```
 4
 5                                 Week 1     Week 2     Week 3     Week 4
 6                              XXXXXXXXXXXXXXXXXXXXXXXXXXXXXXXXXXXXXXXXXX
 7     INCOME
 8     Flight Instruction         1,600.00   1,200.00
 9     Charter                    6,200.00   4,800.00
10     Aircraft Rental            5,600.00   7,000.00
11     Maintenance                8,600.00   9,200.00
12     TOTAL INCOME              22,000.00  22,200.00
13
```

■*3*   [F2] Use [BKSP ←] to delete 1600 from the control
panel, then type **2600** and press [←].

```
 4
 5                                 Week 1     Week 2     Week 3     Week 4
 6                              XXXXXXXXXXXXXXXXXXXXXXXXXXXXXXXXXXXXXXXXXX
 7     INCOME
 8     Flight Instruction         2,600.00   1,200.00
 9     Charter                    6,200.00   4,800.00
10     Aircraft Rental            5,600.00   7,000.00
11     Maintenance                8,600.00   9,200.00
12     TOTAL INCOME              22,000.00  22,200.00
13
```

Notice that the Week1 TOTAL INCOME value did not automatically recalculate. Also, the CALC indicator appears on the status line, alerting you that you're in the Manual Recalculation mode and that a change has been made to the worksheet.

5

■4 [F9] (Calc key)

```
4
5                                Week 1      Week 2      Week 3      Week 4
6                              xxxxxxxxxxxxxxxxxxxxxxxxxxxxxxxxxxxxxxxxxxxxxxx
7   INCOME
8   Flight Instruction          2,600.00    1,200.00
9   Charter                     6,200.00    4,800.00
10  Aircraft Rental             5,600.00    7,000.00
11  Maintenance                 8,600.00    9,200.00
12  TOTAL INCOME               23,000.00   22,200.00
13
```

The formula in cell
C12 is recalculated
and updated.

Turning Automatic Recalculation On

■1 Select /Worksheet, Global, Recalculation,
Automatic.

```
4
5                                Week 1      Week 2      Week 3      Week 4
6                              xxxxxxxxxxxxxxxxxxxxxxxxxxxxxxxxxxxxxxxxxxxxxxx
7   INCOME
8   Flight Instruction          2,600.00    1,200.00
9   Charter                     6,200.00    4,800.00
10  Aircraft Rental             5,600.00    7,000.00
11  Maintenance                 8,600.00    9,200.00
12  TOTAL INCOME               23,000.00   22,200.00
13
```

■2   With the pointer in cell C8, type **1600** and
press ⏎.

		Week 1	Week 2	Week 3	Week 4
4					
5		Week 1	Week 2	Week 3	Week 4
6		xxxxxxxxxxxxxxxxxxxxxxxxxxxxxxxxxxxxxxxxxxxxxxxxxxx			
7	INCOME				
8	Flight Instruction	1,600.00	1,200.00		
9	Charter	6,200.00	4,800.00		
10	Aircraft Rental	5,600.00	7,000.00		
11	Maintenance	8,600.00	9,200.00		
12	TOTAL INCOME	22,000.00	22,200.00		
13					

The formula is automatically recalculated and the data is updated.

5

Understanding
■ *Global and Default Settings*

As you know, the 1-2-3 *default settings* are those settings that are in place when
you start the 1-2-3 program. Default settings should not be confused with global
settings. *Global settings*, some of which you've worked with in this chapter,
only affect the worksheet you are currently working on. These settings are saved
with the worksheet when it is saved and become the current settings when the
worksheet is retrieved. Default settings are saved into a specific file of their own
and are activated automatically when you start 1-2-3, initially affecting each
new worksheet you create. There are some default settings that can be overrid-
den by other 1-2-3 commands, but they only apply to the current worksheet in
which you're working.

Let's take a look at the global and default setting options.

■ *1*   Select /Worksheet, Global to display the
global settings.

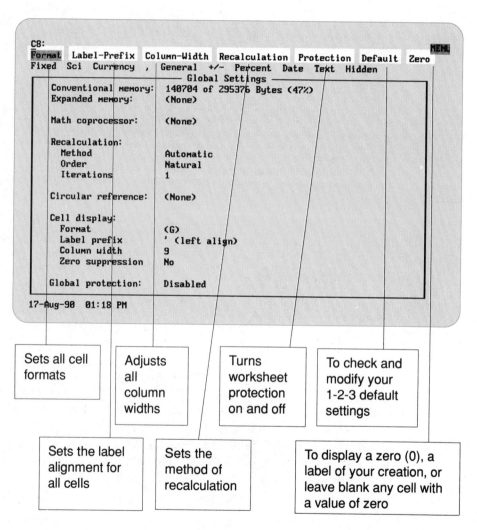

Sets all cell formats

Adjusts all column widths

Turns worksheet protection on and off

To check and modify your 1-2-3 default settings

Sets the label alignment for all cells

Sets the method of recalculation

To display a zero (0), a label of your creation, or leave blank any cell with a value of zero

■*2* Select Default.

Sets the directory where your 1-2-3 files are saved

Turns UNDO on and off, sets clock displays, turns the beep signal on and off, determines the Help access method for floppy-disk users, changes the format of numbers, currency, dates, and times, and runs Add-In programs (see NOTE on next page).

5

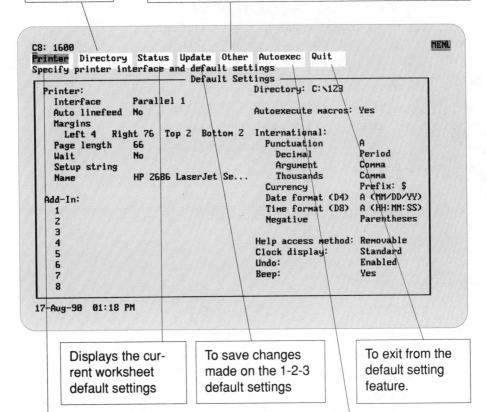

```
C8: 1600                                                          MENU
Printer  Directory  Status  Update  Other  Autoexec  Quit
Specify printer interface and default settings
                        ─── Default Settings ───
┌──────────────────────────────────────────────────────────────────┐
│ Printer:                          Directory: C:\123               │
│   Interface      Parallel 1                                       │
│   Auto linefeed  No               Autoexecute macros: Yes         │
│   Margins                                                         │
│     Left 4   Right 76  Top 2  Bottom 2  International:            │
│   Page length    66                Punctuation      A             │
│   Wait           No                  Decimal        Period        │
│   Setup string                       Argument       Comma         │
│   Name           HP 2686 LaserJet Se...  Thousands  Comma         │
│                                      Currency       Prefix: $      │
│ Add-In:                              Date format (D4) A (MM/DD/YY) │
│   1                                  Time format (D8) A (HH:MM:SS) │
│   2                                  Negative       Parentheses    │
│   3                                                               │
│   4                                Help access method: Removable   │
│   5                                Clock display:   Standard       │
│   6                                Undo:            Enabled        │
│   7                                Beep:            Yes            │
│   8                                                               │
└──────────────────────────────────────────────────────────────────┘
17-Aug-90  01:18 PM
```

Displays the current worksheet default settings

To save changes made on the 1-2-3 default settings

To exit from the default setting feature.

Sets all the parameters for your printer. Some settings may also be changed for an individual worksheet with the /Print, Printer, Options command.

Enables and disables the running of autoexecute macros when retrieving a worksheet that contains them.

> **Note** *Add-In Programs* Add-In programs are additional programs that you may wish to run simultaneously with 1-2-3. Allways Spreadsheet Publishing, which is included with 1-2-3 release 2.2, is an Add-In program.

■ *3*   Experiment with changing some of the default settings. As long as you don't update (save) the changes, they will not be in effect the next time you start 1-2-3. If you change default settings and save them (using /Worksheet, Global, Default, Update), and you have a dual-floppy disk computer, be sure there is no write-protect tab on your System disk.

■ *4*   To exit Default Settings, select Quit.

■ *Creating Absolute Formulas*

In Chapter 3, you read about the three types of cell references: relative, absolute, and mixed. In this section, I'll guide you through an example of how to create an absolute formula. Using the JULYPL1 worksheet, let's compute the percentage of the total income for each INCOME item for Week 1 and Week 2.

■ *1* Retrieve your JULYPL1.WK1 file to the
screen and press HOME .

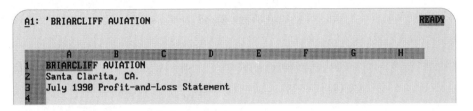

■ *2* Move the pointer to cell G5, type ^**TOTAL**,
and press ↓ .

5

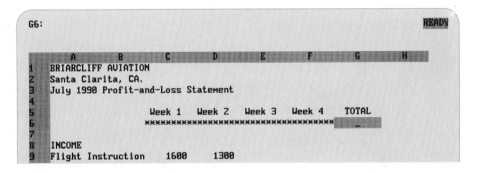

■ *3* Type * and press ↓ .

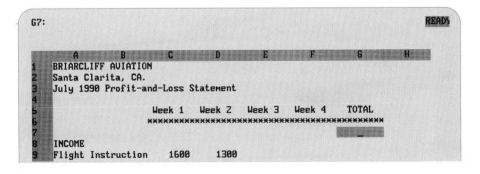

■ *4* Move the pointer to cell G13 and type
@SUM(C13 .. F13) and press ⏎. (Cells
E13 and F13 are included in the formula
range for future totals of Week 3 and Week 4.)

```
8   INCOME
9   Flight Instruction   1600   1300
10  Charter              6200   5000
11  Aircraft Rental      5600   6000
12  Maintenance          6600   9000
13  TOTAL INCOME        20000  21300                    41300
14
15  EXPENSES
16  Wages                6800   6600
17  Fuel/Oil/Parts      10300   8400
```

■ *5* Move the pointer to cell H5, type **^% of
TOTAL**, and press ↓ .

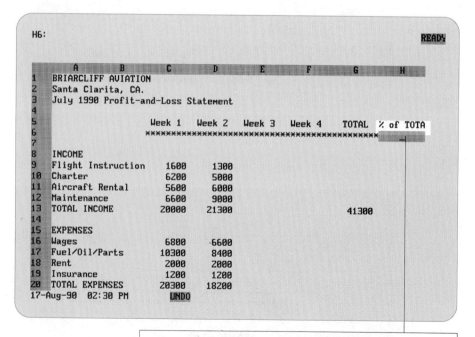

```
H6:                                                          READY

      A        B          C        D        E       F       G       H
1  BRIARCLIFF AVIATION
2  Santa Clarita, CA.
3  July 1990 Profit-and-Loss Statement
4
5               Week 1   Week 2   Week 3  Week 4   TOTAL  % of TOTA
6  ****************************************************************
7
8  INCOME
9  Flight Instruction   1600   1300
10 Charter              6200   5000
11 Aircraft Rental      5600   6000
12 Maintenance          6600   9000
13 TOTAL INCOME        20000  21300                    41300
14
15 EXPENSES
16 Wages                6800   6600
17 Fuel/Oil/Parts      10300   8400
18 Rent                 2000   2000
19 Insurance            1200   1200
20 TOTAL EXPENSES      20300  18200
17-Aug-90  02:30 PM        UNDO
```

The " L" in TOTAL disappears off the screen because
the label is longer than the nine-character cell.

■ *6* Type * and press ⬇ three times to move the
pointer to cell H9.

```
H9:                                                                    READY

        A        B        C        D        E        F        G        H
1  BRIARCLIFF AVIATION
2  Santa Clarita, CA.
3  July 1990 Profit-and-Loss Statement
4
5                       Week 1   Week 2   Week 3   Week 4    TOTAL  % of TOTA
6           xxxxxxxxxxxxxxxxxxxxxxxxxxxxxxxxxxxxxxxxxxxxxxxxxxxxxxxxx
7
8  INCOME
9  Flight Instruction   1600     1300
10 Charter              6200     5000
11 Aircraft Rental      5600     6000
12 Maintenance          6600     9000
13 TOTAL INCOME        20000    21300                       41300
14
15 EXPENSES
16 Wages                6800     6600
17 Fuel/Oil/Parts      10300     8400
18 Rent                 2000     2000
19 Insurance            1200     1200
20 TOTAL EXPENSES      20300    18200
17-Aug-90  02:31 PM            UNDO
```

■ *7* Type **@SUM(C9..F9)/$G$13**.

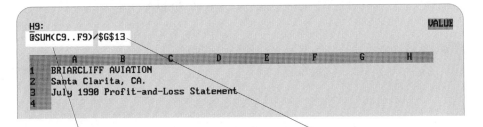

```
H9:                                                                    VALUE
@SUM(C9..F9)/$G$13

        A        B        C        D        E        F        G        H
1  BRIARCLIFF AVIATION
2  Santa Clarita, CA.
3  July 1990 Profit-and-Loss Statement
4
```

This part of the formula totals the weekly values for Flight Instruction. Cells E9 and F9 are included for future totals for Week 3 and Week 4. It is a relative reference.

This part of the formula refers to the cell containing the TOTAL INCOME value. It is an absolute reference.

■ 8 ⏎

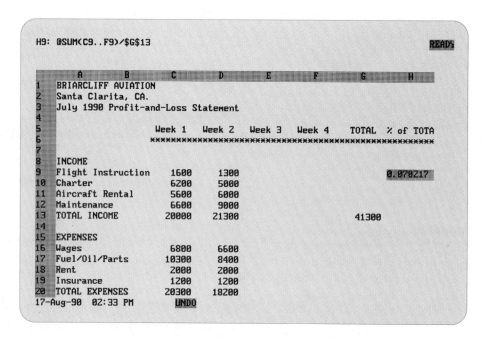

The percentage value is computed and placed in the cell. There are too many decimal places for a percentage value because the cell format is set to General (the default). You'll change it to Percent in just a moment.

■ 9 To copy the formula in cell H9 to cells H10, H11, and H12, select /Copy.

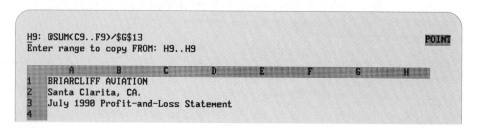

■ *10* ⏎ to accept cell H9 as the range to copy FROM.

```
H9: @SUM(C9..F9)/$G$13                                    POINT
Enter range to copy TO: H9

       A        B        C      D      E      F      G      H
1   BRIARCLIFF AVIATION
2   Santa Clarita, CA.
3   July 1990 Profit-and-Loss Statement
4
```

■ *11* Type **H10 .. H12** and press ⏎.

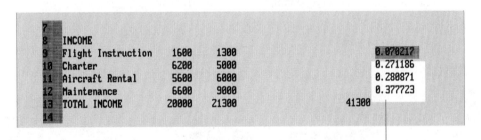

```
7
8   INCOME
9   Flight Instruction   1600    1300                       0.070217
10  Charter              6200    5000                       0.271186
11  Aircraft Rental      5600    6000                       0.280871
12  Maintenance          6600    9000                       0.377723
13  TOTAL INCOME        20000   21300              41300
14
```

The formula is copied into the appropriate cells and the TOTAL INCOME percentage is computed for each income item.

Moving the pointer through cells H10, H11, and H12 will show the relative reference portion of the formula changes to refer to the new rows, but the absolute reference portion of the formula continues to refer specifically to cell G13.

5

■ *12*   To change the decimals to percentages, place
the pointer in cell H9 and select /Range, Format, Percent. Type **0** and press ⏎.

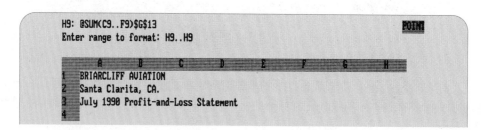

```
H9: @SUM(C9..F9)$G$13                                    POINT
Enter range to format: H9..H9

        A        B        C        D        E        F        G        H
1   BRIARCLIFF AVIATION
2   Santa Clarita, CA.
3   July 1990 Profit-and-Loss Statement
4
```

■ *13*   Move the pointer to cell H12 to highlight the
range and press ⏎. The decimals change the
percentages.

```
7
8    INCOME
9    Flight Instruction   1600    1300                              27%
10   Charter              6200    5000                              27%
11   Aircraft Rental      5600    6000                              28%
12   Maintenance          6600    9000                              38%
13   TOTAL INCOME        20000   21300              41300
14
```

■ *14*   Select /File, Save, press ⏎, and select
Replace to save the worksheet.

■*Advanced Printing Options*

In this section you'll learn about some of the advanced printing options available
with 1-2-3. You'll be able to change margins and choose printing sizes, create

headers and footers, print labels for data columns that run over onto a second page, and print the formulas used to compute worksheet values.

Printing with Borders

The Borders option lets you select labels and titles that are located on the top edge and left side of your worksheet and print them on every page of the printout. This option is useful when a worksheet is too wide to print on a single page. The extra columns will be printed on subsequent pages without any descriptive information unless you use borders. Let's print the JULYPL1.WK1 worksheet with borders.

■ *1*   Retrieve the JULYPL1.WK1 file to the screen. If you have not modified the file since you last worked on it, it should look like this:

5

```
H9: (P0) @SUM(C9..F9)/$G$13                                    READY


         A        B         C       D       E       F       G       H
 1  BRIARCLIFF AVIATION
 2  Santa Clarita, CA.
 3  July 1990 Profit-and-Loss Statement
 4
 5                        Week 1  Week 2  Week 3  Week 4   TOTAL  % of TOTA
 6             xxxxxxxxxxxxxxxxxxxxxxxxxxxxxxxxxxxxxxxxxxxxxxxxxxxxxxxxxxx
 7
 8  INCOME
 9  Flight Instruction     1600    1300                              7%
10  Charter                6200    5000                             27%
11  Aircraft Rental        5600    6000                             28%
12  Maintenance            6600    9000                             38%
13  TOTAL INCOME          20000   21300                    41300
14
15  EXPENSES
16  Wages                  6800    6600
17  Fuel/Oil/Parts        10300    8400
18  Rent                   2000    2000
19  Insurance              1200    1200
20  TOTAL EXPENSES        20300   18200
    17-Aug-90  02:39 PM        UNDO
```

■*2*   Select /Worksheet, Global, Column-Width
so you can widen the worksheet columns to
12 characters.

```
H9: (P0) @SUM(C9..F9)/$G$13                                    POINT
Enter global column width (1..240): 9

        A        B        C        D        E        F        G        H
1   BRIARCLIFF AVIATION
2   Santa Clarita, CA.
3   July 1990 Profit-and-Loss Statement
4
```

■*3*   Type **12** and press ⏎. This widens the
worksheet columns to 12 characters.

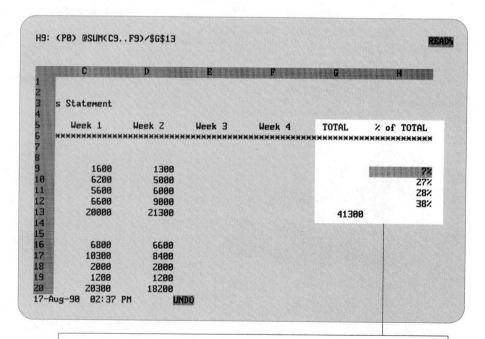

Columns G and H will not print on the first page of an 8½ by 11-inch sheet of paper. They will be split onto a second page.

■*4* Select /Print, Printer. You are already familiar
with some of these menu items from Chapter 2.

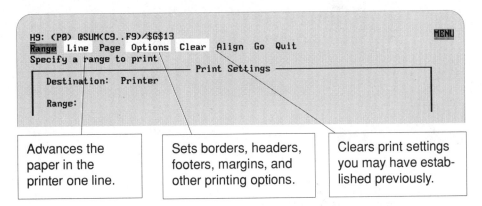

Advances the paper in the printer one line.

Sets borders, headers, footers, margins, and other printing options.

Clears print settings you may have established previously.

■*5* Select Options.

Places a line of text, page number, date, or time on the top of each page.

Sets the top, bottom, left, and right margins.

Sends print commands to the printer that affect the size and style of type.

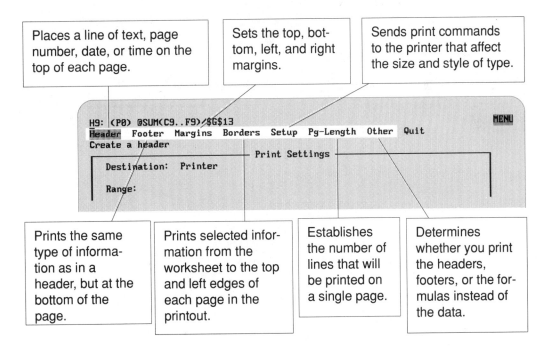

Prints the same type of information as in a header, but at the bottom of the page.

Prints selected information from the worksheet to the top and left edges of each page in the printout.

Establishes the number of lines that will be printed on a single page.

Determines whether you print the headers, footers, or the formulas instead of the data.

5

■*6*   Select Borders.

```
H9: <P0> @SUM(C9..F9)/$G$13                                    MENU
Columns  Rows
Print border columns to the left of each print range
─────────────────────── Print Settings ───────────────────────
│  Destination:  Printer                                       │
│                                                              │
│  Range:                                                      │
```

■*7*   Select Columns.

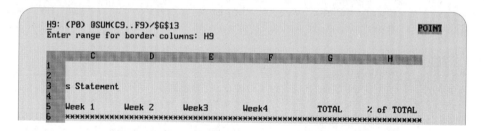

```
H9: <P0> @SUM(C9..F9)/$G$13                                   POINT
Enter range for border columns: H9
```

Borders add a
professional
touch to your
worksheets.

■ *8*   [HOME] [.] (period). Move the pointer to B22.
This designates the labels in columns A and B
as borders.

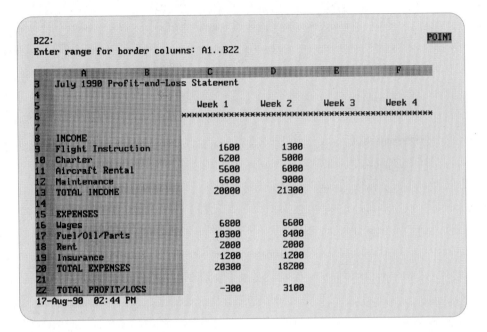

```
B22:                                                           POINT
Enter range for border columns: A1..B22

           A          B          C          D          E          F
 3     July 1990 Profit-and-Loss Statement
 4
 5                               Week 1     Week 2     Week 3     Week 4
 6     xxxxxxxxxxxxxxxxxxxxxxxxxxxxxxxxxxxxxxxxxxxxxxxxxxxxxx
 7
 8     INCOME
 9     Flight Instruction        1600       1300
10     Charter                   6200       5000
11     Aircraft Rental           5600       6000
12     Maintenance               6600       9000
13     TOTAL INCOME             20000      21300
14
15     EXPENSES
16     Wages                     6800       6600
17     Fuel/Oil/Parts           10300       8400
18     Rent                      2000       2000
19     Insurance                 1200       1200
20     TOTAL EXPENSES           20300      18200
21
22     TOTAL PROFIT/LOSS         -300       3100
17-Aug-90  02:44 PM
```

> **Note**   *Page Length*   If your printer is set up for 60 lines per page, as is the case
> for many laser printers, use the Pg-Length option to change the page length on the
> Print Settings sheet to 60 lines. Do this before proceeding with step 10.

■*9*   ⊟ The column borders are displayed on the
Print Settings screen.

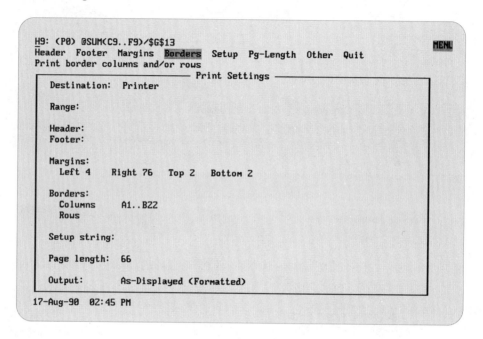

```
H9: (P0) @SUM(C9..F9)/$G$13                              MENU
Header  Footer  Margins  Borders  Setup  Pg-Length  Other  Quit
Print border columns and/or rows
                        ————— Print Settings —————
    Destination:  Printer

    Range:

    Header:
    Footer:

    Margins:
      Left 4     Right 76    Top 2   Bottom 2

    Borders:
      Columns    A1..B22
      Rows

    Setup string:

    Page length:  66

    Output:       As-Displayed (Formatted)

17-Aug-90   02:45 PM
```

■*10* ESC and select Range to enter the range of
data to be printed. Type **C1..H22**. Do not include the border range (column A and B in
this example) or 1-2-3 will print them twice.

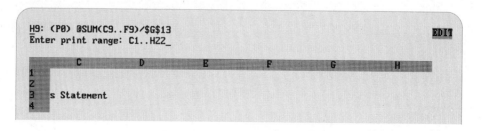

```
H9: (P0) @SUM(C9..F9)/$G$13                              EDIT
Enter print range: C1..H22_

        C         D         E         F         G         H
1
2
3   s Statement
4
```

■ *11* ⏎ and select Align, Go, Page to print the worksheet.

```
BRIARCLIFF AVIATION
Santa Clarita, CA.
July 1990 Profit-and-Loss Statement
                        Week 1      Week 2      Week 3      Week 4
               ***************************************************

INCOME
Flight Instruction       1600        1300
Charter                  6200        5000
Aircraft Rental          5600        6000
Maintenance              6600        9000
TOTAL INCOME            20000       21300

EXPENSES
Wages                    6800        6600
Fuel/Oil/Parts          10300        8400
Rent                     2000        2000
Insurance                1200        1200
TOTAL EXPENSES          20300       18200

TOTAL PROFIT/LOSS        -300        3100
```

5

```
BRIARCLIFF AVIATION
Santa Clarita, CA.
July 1990 Profit-and-Los
                         TOTAL      % of TOTAL
               *************************
INCOME
Flight Instruction                     7%
Charter                               27%
Aircraft Rental                       28%
Maintenance                           38%
TOTAL INCOME             41300

EXPENSES
Wages
Fuel/Oil/Parts
Rent
Insurance
TOTAL EXPENSES

TOTAL PROFIT/LOSS
```

■ *12* Select Quit to return to the worksheet.

Creating Headers and Footers

Headers and footers are lines of text that are printed at the top and bottom of every page in a print job: headers at the top, footers at the bottom. Let's create a header for the JULYPL1.WK1 worksheet.

■ *1* Select /Print, Printer, Options.

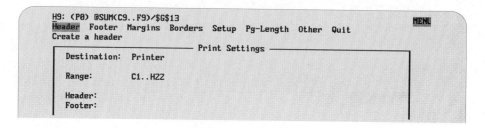

■ *2* Select Header. (If you wanted to create a footer, you'd select Footer and follow the same steps below.)

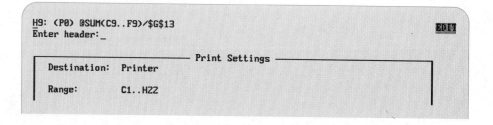

> **Note** *Formatting Headers and Footers* There are several guidelines to follow when creating headers and footers.
>
> - Place the # symbol after the text to automatically place the correct page number on every page of the print job.
> - Use the @ symbol after the text to automatically place the current date on every page of the print job.
> - Use the | symbol to align the text with the left margin, right margin, or centered on the page. Text typed in *front* of the | symbol or without the symbol is left aligned. Text typed *after one* | symbol is centered. Text typed *after two* | symbols is right aligned.
> - You can use up to 240 characters, including spaces, to accommodate wide printouts.

5

■*3*   Type **Prepared by: J.W.|Page #|Date @**

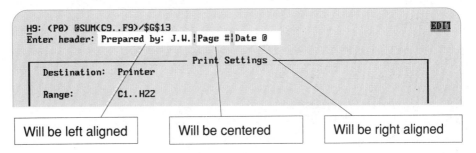

■*4*   ⏎ The header text is displayed on the Print
Settings screen.

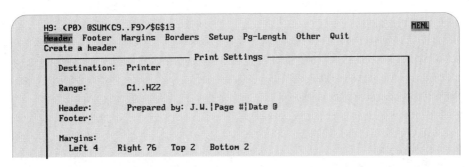

■ *5* ESC Select Align, Go, Page to print the
worksheet.

```
Prepared by: J.W.              Page 1              Date 17-Aug-90


BRIARCLIFF AVIATION
Santa Clarita, CA.
July 1990 Profit-and-Loss Statement

                         Week 1      Week 2      Week 3      Week 4
                  **************************************************

INCOME
Flight Instruction        1600        1300
Charter                   6200        5000
Aircraft Rental           5600        6000
Maintenance               6600        9000
TOTAL INCOME             20000       21300


EXPENSES
Wages                     6800        6600
Fuel/Oil/Parts           10300        8400
Rent                      2000        2000
Insurance                 1200        1200
TOTAL EXPENSES           20300       18200


TOTAL PROFIT/LOSS         -300        3100
```

```
Prepared by: J.W.              Page 2              Date 17-Aug-90


BRIARCLIFF AVIATION
Santa Clarita, CA.
July 1990 Profit-and-Los

                         TOTAL       % of TOTAL
                  **************************

INCOME
Flight Instruction                       7%
Charter                                 27%
Aircraft Rental                         28%
Maintenance                             38%
TOTAL INCOME             41300

EXPENSES
Wages
Fuel/Oil/Parts
Rent
Insurance
TOTAL EXPENSES

TOTAL PROFIT/LOSS
```

■ *6*   Select Quit to return to the worksheet.

Printing Cell Formulas

Sometimes you'll need to check the formulas used to compute your worksheet data. Printing the formulas makes this task much easier than displaying them on the monitor. Let's print the formulas used on the JULYPL.WK1 worksheet.

■ *1*   Select /Print, Printer, Options, Other.

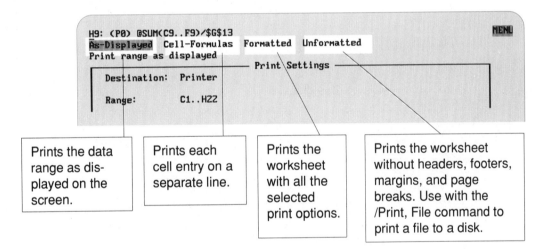

```
H9: (P0) @SUM(C9..F9)/$G$13                              MENU
As-Displayed  Cell-Formulas  Formatted  Unformatted
Print range as displayed
                              ─── Print Settings ───
   Destination:  Printer

   Range:        C1..H22
```

| Prints the data range as displayed on the screen. | Prints each cell entry on a separate line. | Prints the worksheet with all the selected print options. | Prints the worksheet without headers, footers, margins, and page breaks. Use with the /Print, File command to print a file to a disk. |

■ *2*   Select Cell-Formulas. Cell-Formulas is recorded as the output mode on the Print Settings sheet.

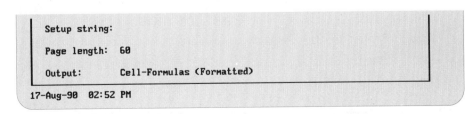

```
   Setup string:

   Page length:  60

   Output:       Cell-Formulas (Formatted)

17-Aug-90  02:52 PM
```

■*3*   ESC Select Align, Go, Page to print all the
worksheet cell entries.

```
Prepared by: J.W.           Page 1              Date 17-Aug-90


C5:  ^Week 1
D5:  ^Week 2
E5:  ^Week 3
F5:  ^Week 4
G5:  ^TOTAL
H5:  ^% of TOTAL
C6:  \*
D6:  \*
E6:  \*
F6:  \*
G6:  \*
H6:  \*
C9:  1600
D9:  1300
H9:  (P0) @SUM(C9..F9)/$G$13
C10: 6200
D10: 5000
H10: (P0) @SUM(C10..F10)/$G$13
C11: 5600
D11: 6000
H11: (P0) @SUM(C11..F11)/$G$13
C12: 6600
D12: 9000
H12: (P0) @SUM(C12..F12)/$G$13
C13: +C9+C10+C11+C12
D13: +D9+D10+D11+D12
G13: @SUM(C13..F13)
C16: 6800
D16: 6600
C17: 10300
D17: 8400
C18: 2000
D18: 2000
C19: 1200
D19: 1200
C20: @SUM(C16..C19)
D20: @SUM(D16..D19)
C22: +C13-C20
D22: +D13-D20
```

■*4*   Select Options, Other, As-Displayed to return
to the normal print mode.

```
Setup string:

Page length:   60

Output:        As-Displayed (Formatted)

17-Aug-90  02:53 PM
```

■*5*   Select Quit twice to return to the worksheet.

Changing Print Size with a Setup String

You can use *printer setup strings* (a three-digit code) to change the type or size
of print. You can do such things as compress, bold, italicize, and underline print,
or change the print font. Your printer manual contains printer control codes that
can be translated into setup string codes using the Setup Strings Table in Appendix B of your 1-2-3 documentation.

Let's print the JULYPL1.WK1 worksheet in a smaller print size.

■ *1*   Select /Print, Printer, Options, Setup and type
the setup string for your printer. My printer
uses this string: \027(s16.66H.

```
H9: (P0) @SUM(C9..F9)/$G$13                              EDIT
Enter setup string: \027(s16.66H_
    ┌─────────────────── Print Settings ───────────────────
    │  Destination:   Printer
    │
    │  Range:         C1..H22
```

■ *2*   [↵] and select Quit. The setup string is displayed in the Print Settings screen.

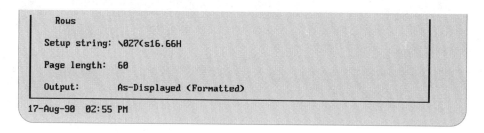

```
    │   Rows
    │
    │   Setup string: \027(s16.66H
    │
    │   Page length:  60
    │
    │   Output:       As-Displayed (Formatted)
    │  17-Aug-90  02:55 PM
```

■*3* Select Align, Go, Page to print the worksheet.
You'll see that the size and style of print has
changed.

```
Prepared by: J.W.            Page 1              Date 17-Aug-90


BRIARCLIFF AVIATION
Santa Clarita, CA.
July 1990 Profit-and-Loss Statement

                        Week 1    Week 2    Week 3    Week 4
                   **************************************************

INCOME
Flight Instruction       1600      1300
Charter                  6200      5000
Aircraft Rental          5600      6000
Maintenance              6600      9000
TOTAL INCOME            20000     21300


EXPENSES
Wages                    6800      6600
Fuel/Oil/Parts          10300      8400
Rent                     2000      2000
Insurance                1200      1200
TOTAL EXPENSES          20300     18200


TOTAL PROFIT/LOSS        -300      3100
```

```
Prepared by: J.W.            Page 2              Date 17-Aug-90


BRIARCLIFF AVIATION
Santa Clarita, CA.
July 1990 Profit-and-Los

                        TOTAL     % of TOTAL
                   ************************

INCOME
Flight Instruction                  7%
Charter                            27%
Aircraft Rental                    28%
Maintenance                        38%
TOTAL INCOME            41300

EXPENSES
Wages
Fuel/Oil/Parts
Rent
Insurance
TOTAL EXPENSES


TOTAL PROFIT/LOSS
```

5

■*4*   Select Quit to return to the worksheet.

Changing the Print Margins

You can easily modify the top and bottom margins to change the vertical position of the worksheet on the printed page. You can change the left and right margins in order to print more columns than will fit across an 8½-inch sheet of paper. You will, however, need a printer that accommodates wider sheets of paper.

The following steps show you how to change the current margin settings. We'll use the JULYPL1.WK1 file currently in use.

■*1*   Select /Print, Printer, Options, Margins.

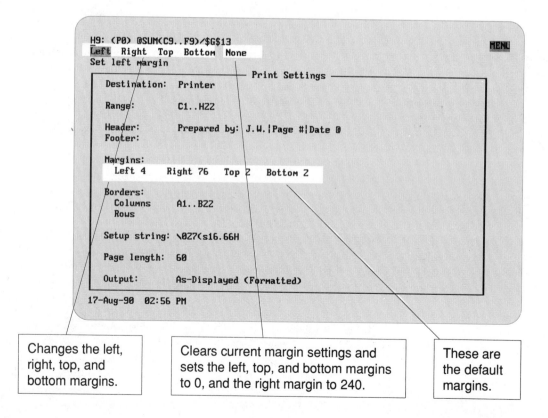

| Changes the left, right, top, and bottom margins. | Clears current margin settings and sets the left, top, and bottom margins to 0, and the right margin to 240. | These are the default margins. |

■*2* Select Right and type **100**. This means you'll
have a right margin located 100 characters
from the left edge of the page.

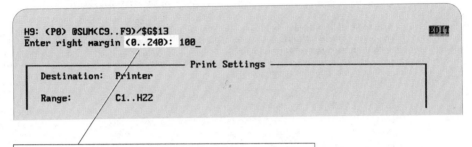

```
H9: (P0) @SUM(C9..F9)/$G$13                                    EDIT
Enter right margin (0..240): 100_
                              ───────── Print Settings ─────────
     │ Destination:  Printer
     │
     │ Range:       C1..H22
```

There is a 240-character limit for placing the left
or right margin. Be sure the left margin is always
smaller than the right margin, since both are
measured from the left edge of the page.

■*3* ⏎ and select Margins, Top.

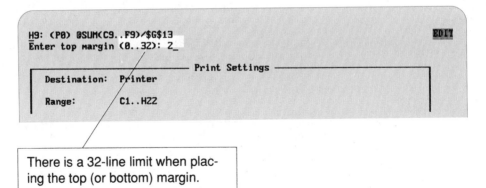

```
H9: (P0) @SUM(C9..F9)/$G$13                                    EDIT
Enter top margin (0..32): 2_
                              ───────── Print Settings ─────────
     │ Destination:  Printer
     │
     │ Range:       C1..H22
```

There is a 32-line limit when placing the top (or bottom) margin.

■4 Type **15** and press ⏎. The new right and
top margin settings are recorded on the
Print Settings sheet.

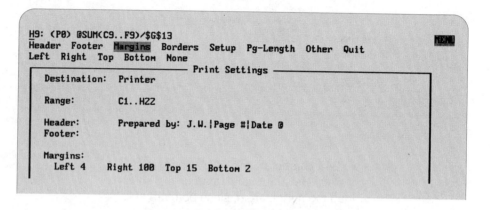

```
H9: (P0) @SUM(C9..F9)/$G$13
Header  Footer  Margins  Borders  Setup  Pg-Length  Other  Quit
Left  Right  Top  Bottom  None
                          ─── Print Settings ───
    Destination:  Printer

    Range:        C1..H22

    Header:       Prepared by: J.W.|Page #|Date @
    Footer:

    Margins:
      Left 4     Right 100  Top 15  Bottom 2
```

Some margin
settings require
a printer that
handles wide
paper.

■*5*   Select Quit, Align, Go, Page to print the
worksheet. Notice the entire worksheet prints
in a more centered position on the page. (This
printout was done on an HP LaserJet printer.
Your printout may look different.)

```
Prepared by: J.W.                    Page 1                    Date 17-Aug-90


BRIARCLIFF AVIATION
Santa Clarita, CA.
July 1990 Profit-and-Loss Statement

                      Week 1    Week 2    Week 3    Week 4    TOTAL    % of TOTAL
                      ***********************************************************

INCOME
Flight Instruction     1600      1300                                     7%
Charter                6200      5000                                    27%
Aircraft Rental        5600      6000                                    28%
Maintenance            6600      9000                                    38%
TOTAL INCOME          20000     21300                          41300

EXPENSES
Wages                  6800      6600
Fuel/Oil/Parts        10300      8400
Rent                   2000      2000
Insurance              1200      1200
TOTAL EXPENSES        20300     18200


TOTAL PROFIT/LOSS      -300      3100
```

5

■*6*   Select Quit to return to the worksheet.

Clearing Print Options

If you make changes to your print settings, and then want to reset some or all of the changes to the default settings, you can use the /Print, Printer (or File), Clear command. Using the print settings created in the previous exercises, let's clear all the changes and reset them to the default settings.

■ *1*   Select /Print, Printer, Clear.

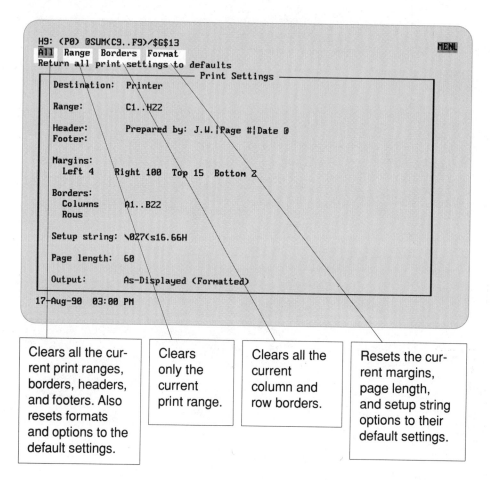

```
H9: (P0) @SUM(C9..F9)/$G$13                                          MENU
All   Range  Borders  Format
Return all print settings to defaults
                              ─── Print Settings ───
      Destination:  Printer

      Range:        C1..H22

      Header:       Prepared by: J.W.|Page #|Date @
      Footer:

      Margins:
        Left 4     Right 100  Top 15  Bottom 2

      Borders:
        Columns    A1..B22
        Rows

      Setup string: \027(s16.66H

      Page length:  60

      Output:       As-Displayed (Formatted)

  17-Aug-90  03:00 PM
```

Clears all the current print ranges, borders, headers, and footers. Also resets formats and options to the default settings.

Clears only the current print range.

Clears all the current column and row borders.

Resets the current margins, page length, and setup string options to their default settings.

■*2*   Select All. All the print settings return to their
default settings.

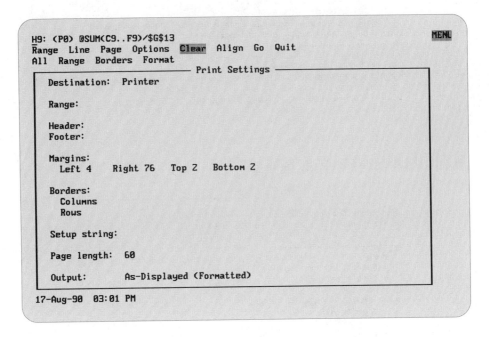

```
H9: <P0> @SUM(C9..F9)/$G$13                                    MENU
Range  Line  Page  Options  Clear  Align  Go  Quit
All  Range  Borders  Format
─────────────────────────── Print Settings ───────────────────────
  Destination:  Printer

  Range:

  Header:
  Footer:

  Margins:
    Left 4      Right 76    Top 2    Bottom 2

  Borders:
    Columns
    Rows

  Setup string:

  Page length:  60

  Output:       As-Displayed (Formatted)

17-Aug-90  03:01 PM
```

■*3*   Select Quit to return to the worksheet.

Changing the Print Default Settings

If there are certain print settings that you use on a daily basis, you can make them
permanent by changing the default settings with the /Worksheet, Global, Default
command. As an example, let's change the page length so it is always 60 lines
whenever you start 1-2-3.

■ *1* Select /Worksheet, Global, Default.

```
H9: <P0> @SUM(C9..F9)/$G$13                                    MENU
Printer  Directory  Status  Update  Other  Autoexec  Quit
Specify printer interface and default settings
                         ──── Default Settings ────
  Printer:                                  Directory: C:\123
    Interface      Parallel 1
    Auto linefeed  No
    Margins                                 Autoexecute macros: Yes
      Left 4   Right 76  Top 2  Bottom 2  International:
    Page length    66                        Punctuation      A
```

■ *2* Select Printer, Pg-Length.

```
H9: <P0> @SUM(C9..F9)/$G$13                                    EDIT
Enter lines per page (1..100): 66

                         ──── Default Settings ────
  Printer:                                  Directory: C:\123
    Interface      Parallel 1
    Auto linefeed  No
    Margins                                 Autoexecute macros: Yes
      Left 4   Right 76  Top 2  Bottom 2  International:
    Page length    66                        Punctuation      A
```

■ *3* Type **60** and press ⏎.

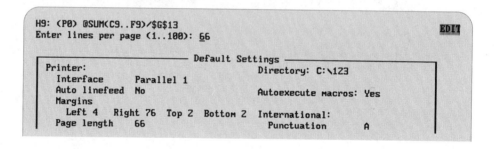

```
H9: <P0> @SUM(C9..F9)/$G$13                                    MENU
Interface  AutoLF  Left  Right  Top  Bot  Pg-Length  Wait  Setup  Name  Quit
Set default number of lines per page
                         ──── Default Settings ────
  Printer:                                  Directory: C:\123
    Interface      Parallel 1
    Auto linefeed  No
    Margins                                 Autoexecute macros: Yes
      Left 4   Right 76  Top 2  Bottom 2  International:
    Page length    60                        Punctuation      A
    Wait           No                        Decimal          Period
```

The page length is recorded as 60 lines.

■4 Select Quit to return to the Default menu. If you have a dual floppy-disk computer, be sure the 1-2-3 System disk, located in drive A, does not have a write-protect tab on it.

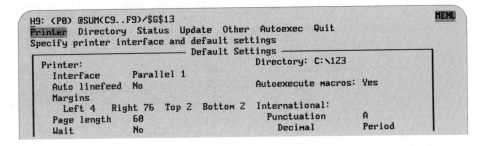

■5 Select Update to record the change permanently on the disk.

■6 Select Quit and press HOME . Then select /File, Save, press ⏎, and select Replace to save the worksheet.

■*Summary*

This chapter presented some of the advanced features available with 1-2-3. You can now work with two different areas of a worksheet at the same time using the Windows feature. You can use worksheet protection to safeguard sensitive information. You can also change between manual and automatic recalculation when you want more control over the calculation of data.

If you need to revamp your worksheet settings, you know how to use the global settings for the worksheet you are currently working in, and the default settings for each new worksheet you create when you start 1-2-3. Remember to refer to the global and default setting sheets whenever you aren't sure exactly what settings are in operation.

You also were introduced to absolute formulas. As your requirements for working with worksheets become more complex, so will your experience with formulas increase.

Finally, you learned about some advanced printing options. Setup strings are difficult to understand at first, but with some experimentation, practice, and a good printer manual, you will be able to create some very interesting print results.

SIX

Sharing Data with Other Programs and between Worksheets

Because of the diversity of data processing programs in the business world, it is increasingly important to be able to process files with one program that were produced in a different program. This chapter will introduce you to two methods of sharing the worksheets you create in 1-2-3 with associates that use a different data processing program. You'll also learn how to move data between worksheets. Finally, you'll learn how to link files so that when you change data in one worksheet, other worksheets that are affected by that change are automatically updated.

Sharing Data with Other Programs

Moving Data between Worksheets

Linking Your Worksheets

Sharing Data
■with Other Programs

There are times when your 1-2-3 worksheets will be needed in documents prepared in a different database or spreadsheet program or with an earlier version of 1-2-3. Also, you may want to import spreadsheets or database data from another program into your 1-2-3 documents.

You have two methods available for sharing data between 1-2-3 and other programs. First, you can create an ASCII text file to transfer data to another program, or to import an ASCII text file into 1-2-3. Second, you may use 1-2-3's Translate utility to convert files from programs such as dBASE II and III, Multiplan, Visi-Calc, Symphony, and previous releases of 1-2-3, and vice versa. Let's take a look at how to use these two methods.

6

Creating an ASCII Text File

To create an ASCII text file, you use the /Print, File command after you create a worksheet and are ready to save or print it.

■ *1*   Start 1-2-3's Access System by typing
LOTUS at a DOS prompt.

```
1-2-3  PrintGraph  Translate  Install  Exit
Use 1-2-3


             1-2-3 Access System
           Copyright  1986, 1989
         Lotus Development Corporation
              All Rights Reserved
                 Release 2.2
```

■2   Select 1-2-3 and retrieve your
JULYPL1.WK1 worksheet.

```
A1: 'BRIARCLIFF AVIATION                                              READY

          A          B          C          D          E          F
 1  BRIARCLIFF AVIATION
 2  Santa Clarita, CA.
 3  July 1990 Profit-and-Loss Statement
 4
 5                             Week 1     Week 2     Week 3     Week 4
 6              ****************************************************
 7
 8  INCOME
 9  Flight Instruction          1600       1300
10  Charter                     6200       5000
11  Aircraft Rental             5600       6000
12  Maintenance                 6600       9000
13  TOTAL INCOME               20000      21300
14
15  EXPENSES
16  Wages                       6800       6600
17  Fuel/Oil/Parts             10300       8400
18  Rent                        2000       2000
19  Insurance                   1200       1200
20  TOTAL EXPENSES             20300      18200
17-Aug-90  01:20 PM          UNDO
```

■3   Select /Print, File. (You do not need your
printer for this exercise.)

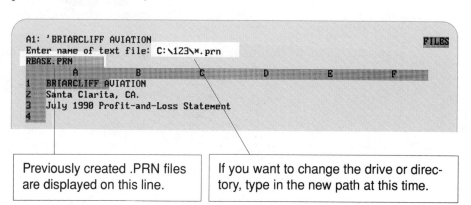

```
A1: 'BRIARCLIFF AVIATION                                              FILES
Enter name of text file: C:\123\*.prn
RBASE.PRN
          A          B          C          D          E          F
 1  BRIARCLIFF AVIATION
 2  Santa Clarita, CA.
 3  July 1990 Profit-and-Loss Statement
 4
```

Previously created .PRN files
are displayed on this line.

If you want to change the drive or directory, type in the new path at this time.

■*4*   Type in a new name for the text file:
TESTFILE. 1-2-3 will automatically assign
a .PRN extension to the new file name.

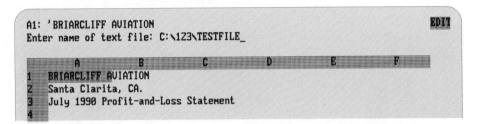

■*5*   ⏎

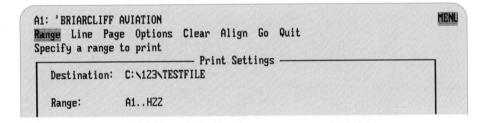

■*6*   Select Range.

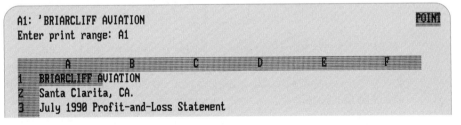

6

■7 Press ⌐⌐ (period) to anchor the range. Move
the pointer to cell H22 to specify the data to
be printed to the file. If you want to print
more than one range, select them before
proceeding with the Go command.

```
H22:                                                          POINT
Enter print range: A1..H22

        C           D           E           F           G           H
3   s Statement
4
5       Week 1      Week 2      Week 3      Week 4      TOTAL    % of TOTAL
6   ********************************************************************************
7
8
9          1600        1300                                              7%
10         6200        5000                                             27%
11         5600        6000                                             28%
12         6600        9000                                             38%
13        20000       21300                              41300
14
15
16         6800        6600
17        10300        8400
18         2000        2000
19         1200        1200
20        20300       18200
21
22         -300        3100
17-Aug-90   01:24 PM
```

Now, before printing the range to a file, you will probably want to eliminate the
header and footer information from the worksheet. You may also want to change
the left margin to zero (0). I suggest you do this so that the worksheet will conform to the margins of the program into which you will retrieve the worksheet.

■ *8*   ⏎ and select Options, Other, Unformatted.

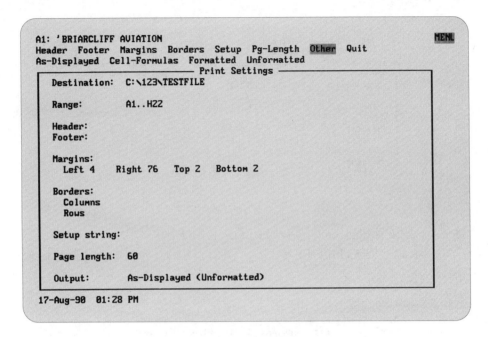

```
A1: 'BRIARCLIFF AVIATION                                         MENU
Header  Footer  Margins  Borders  Setup  Pg-Length  Other  Quit
As-Displayed  Cell-Formulas  Formatted  Unformatted
┌──────────────────────── Print Settings ─────────────────────────┐
│   Destination:   C:\123\TESTFILE                                 │
│                                                                  │
│   Range:         A1..H22                                         │
│                                                                  │
│   Header:                                                        │
│   Footer:                                                        │
│                                                                  │
│   Margins:                                                       │
│     Left 4     Right 76    Top 2    Bottom 2                     │
│                                                                  │
│   Borders:                                                       │
│     Columns                                                      │
│     Rows                                                         │
│                                                                  │
│   Setup string:                                                  │
│                                                                  │
│   Page length:   60                                             │
│                                                                  │
│   Output:        As-Displayed (Unformatted)                     │
└──────────────────────────────────────────────────────────────────┘
17-Aug-90  01:28 PM
```

■ *9*   Select Margins, Left and type **0** (zero). The
right margin should already be set at 76.

```
A1: 'BRIARCLIFF AVIATION                                         EDIT
Enter left margin (0..240): 0_
┌──────────────────────── Print Settings ─────────────────────────┐
│   Destination:   C:\123\TESTFILE                                 │
│                                                                  │
│   Range:         A1..H22                                         │
```

6

■ *10* ⏎ ⎋

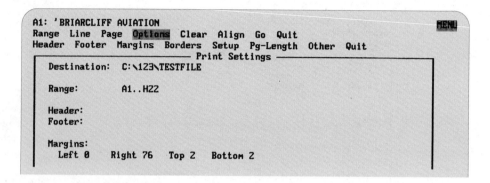

■ *11* Select Align, Go to print the range to a file
called TESTFILE.PRN.

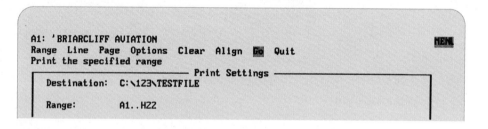

■ *12* Select Quit to return to your worksheet.

Note *Printing Wide Worksheets* If your worksheet is wider than the margins of
the page it will be printed on, the columns that extend beyond the margins will be
printed below the columns that fit within the margins.

Importing an ASCII Text File Into 1-2-3

There are two types of ASCII text files that you can import into 1-2-3: non-delimited and delimited. *Delimited* text files contain punctuation characters called delimiters that separate pieces of discrete data. In this type of file, labels must be enclosed in quotation marks. Values and labels must be separated by a comma, space, semicolon, or colon. When typing in numbers, be careful not to use a comma because the number will be split apart at the comma.

A *nondelimited* text file does not have the punctuation marks that a delimited text file must have. 1-2-3 saves ASCII text files in the nondelimited format. Nondelimited files must have a carriage return at the end of each line of data.

Let's retrieve the nondelimited text file TESTFILE.PRN, which you created in the previous exercise.

■ *1*   Select /File, Import.

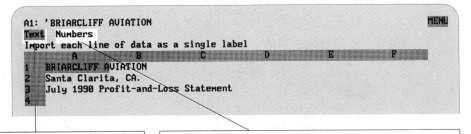

6

```
A1: 'BRIARCLIFF AVIATION                                          MENU
Text  Numbers
Import each line of data as a single label
        A          B          C          D          E          F
1  BRIARCLIFF AVIATION
2  Santa Clarita, CA.
3  July 1990 Profit-and-Loss Statement
4
```

To import text and numbers from nondelimited files.

To import only numbers from nondelimited text files. The numbers may not contain commas.

> **Note** *Using the Text and Numbers Options* When you use the Text option, each line of imported data (up to 240 characters) is placed in a single cell. You must use the /Data, Parse command to place values in individual cells so they may be calculated by 1-2-3. The Numbers option is also used to import delimited text files that contain numbers and labels that are separated by a colon, semicolon, space, or comma. Labels must be enclosed in quotation marks. Each entry is placed in a separate cell.

■*2*   Select Text.

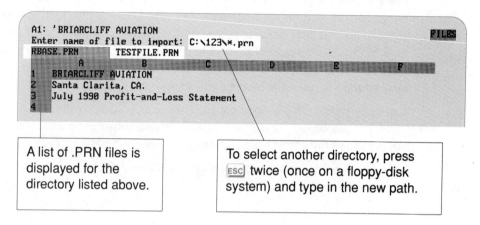

A list of .PRN files is displayed for the directory listed above.

To select another directory, press ESC twice (once on a floppy-disk system) and type in the new path.

■*3*   Select TESTFILE.PRN.

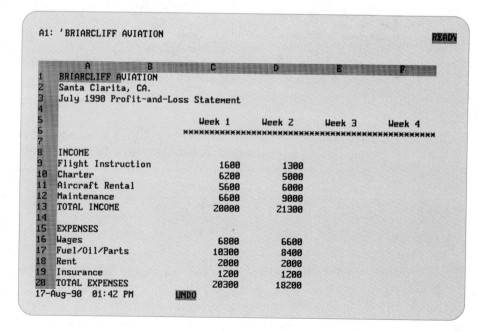

This worksheet looks normal, but it's not. Move the pointer down column A and you'll see on the control panel that all the data in each row is contained in one cell. Move the pointer down column B and you'll find there is no data displayed on the control panel for any cell in column B. Also, there are no formulas in any cell on the worksheet. The next exercise explains how to format the imported text file.

Formatting an Imported ASCII Text File

After you've imported a nondelimited ASCII text file, you will need to format the data into cells so you can use 1-2-3's analytical powers. Let's do this with the nondelimited TESTFILE.PRN file that you imported into 1-2-3 in the previous exercise.

6

Once your text file is formatted, you can edit, create formulas, replace data— and more.

■*1* Move the pointer to cell A9, the first row that
contains values.

```
7
8    INCOME
9    Flight Instruction        1600        1300
10   Charter                   6200        5000
11   Aircraft Rental           5600        6000
12   Maintenance               6600        9000
13   TOTAL INCOME             20000       21300
14
15   EXPENSES
16   Wages                     6800        6600
17   Fuel/Oil/Parts           10300        8400
```

■*2* Select /Data, Parse.

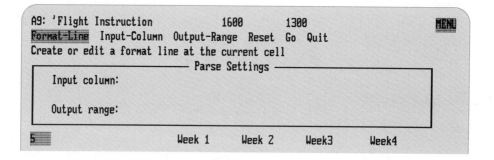

■*3* Select Format-Line.

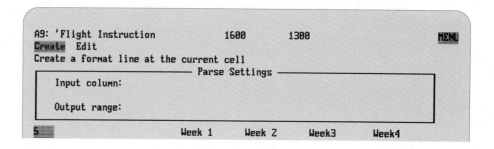

■ *4* Select Create to insert a format line based on
the type of data contained in row 9.

```
 8   INCOME
 9   L>>>>>*L>>>>>>>>>>>>>×××××××××××××U>>>×××××××U>>>
10   Flight Instruction          1600          1300
11   Charter                     6200          5000
12   Aircraft Rental             5600          6000
13   Maintenance                 6600          9000
14   TOTAL INCOME               20000         21300
15
16   EXPENSES
```

> The L and V represent the
> first letter in the labels and
> values. You might also see a
> D or T, which represent
> dates and times.

■ *5* Select Format-Line, Edit to make a change to
the format line. The format line changes color.

```
 8   INCOME
 9   L>>>>>*L>>>>>>>>>>>>>×××××××××××××U>>>×××××××U>>>
10   Flight Instruction          1600          1300
11   Charter                     6200          5000
12   Aircraft Rental             5600          6000
13   Maintenance                 6600          9000
14   TOTAL INCOME               20000         21300
15
16   EXPENSES
17   Wages                       6800          6600
```

6

■ 6   ⟶ to move the cursor to the first asterisk
(*). Press ⟩ ⟩ (greater than).

```
7
8  INCOME
9  L>>>>>>>>>>>>>>>>>************U>>>********U>>>
10 Flight Instruction         1600        1300
11 Charter                    6200        5000
12 Aircraft Rental            5600        6000
13 Maintenance                6600        9000
14 TOTAL INCOME              20000       21300
15
```

The * and L characters are over written by
the two >'s. This prevents the long labels
from being split into two cells.

■ 7   ⏎ and select Input-Column.

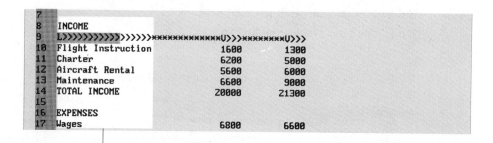

```
7
8  INCOME
9  L>>>>>>>>>>>>>>>>>************U>>>********U>>>
10 Flight Instruction         1600        1300
11 Charter                    6200        5000
12 Aircraft Rental            5600        6000
13 Maintenance                6600        9000
14 TOTAL INCOME              20000       21300
15
16 EXPENSES
17 Wages                      6800        6600
```

You need only
designate column
A because all the
data is located in
the A column.

■*8*   ⌴ (period) to anchor cell A9. Move the
pointer to cell A23.

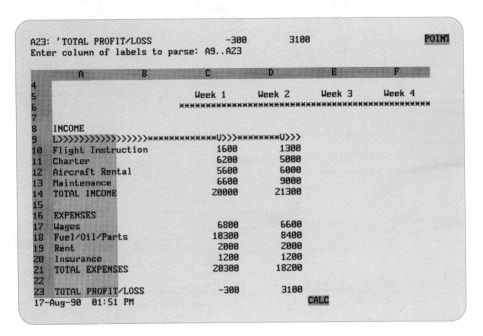

```
A23: 'TOTAL PROFIT/LOSS          -300      3100                    POINT
Enter column of labels to parse: A9..A23

         A          B          C          D          E          F
 4
 5                              Week 1     Week 2     Week 3     Week 4
 6                              ××××××××××××××××××××××××××××××××××××××××
 7
 8   INCOME
 9   L>>>>>>>>>>>>>>>>>>××××××××××××××U>>>××××××××U>>>
10   Flight Instruction         1600       1300
11   Charter                    6200       5000
12   Aircraft Rental            5600       6000
13   Maintenance                6600       9000
14   TOTAL INCOME              20000      21300
15
16   EXPENSES
17   Wages                      6800       6600
18   Fuel/Oil/Parts            10300       8400
19   Rent                       2000       2000
20   Insurance                  1200       1200
21   TOTAL EXPENSES            20300      18200
22
23   TOTAL PROFIT/LOSS          -300       3100
17-Aug-90  01:51 PM                                              CALC
```

■*9*   ⏎ and select Output-Range.

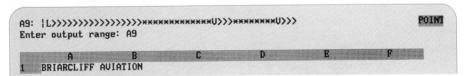

```
A9: |L>>>>>>>>>>>>>>>>>>××××××××××××××U>>>××××××××U>>>              POINT
Enter output range: A9

         A          B          C          D          E          F
 1   BRIARCLIFF AVIATION
```

You now must move the pointer to an empty area of the worksheet that is large
enough to contain the entire Input-Range.

■ *10*   Move the pointer to cell A25 and press ⏎.

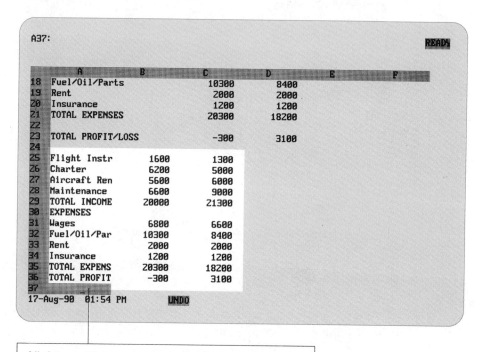

A9: |L>>>>>>>>>>>>>>>>>>×××××××××××U>>>×××××××U>>>   MENU

Format-Line   Input-Column   Output-Range   Reset   Go   Quit
Specify the range in which parsed data is placed
────────────────── Parse Settings ──────────────────

   Input column: A9..A23

   Output range: A25..A25

5   Week 1   Week 2   Week3   Week4

■ *11*   Select Go to place the parsed data at cell A25.

Move the pointer to cell A37.

A37:   READY

	A	B	C	D	E	F
18	Fuel/Oil/Parts		10300	8400		
19	Rent		2000	2000		
20	Insurance		1200	1200		
21	TOTAL EXPENSES		20300	18200		
22						
23	TOTAL PROFIT/LOSS		-300	3100		
24						
25	Flight Instr	1600	1300			
26	Charter	6200	5000			
27	Aircraft Ren	5600	6000			
28	Maintenance	6600	9000			
29	TOTAL INCOME	20000	21300			
30	EXPENSES					
31	Wages	6800	6600			
32	Fuel/Oil/Par	10300	8400			
33	Rent	2000	2000			
34	Insurance	1200	1200			
35	TOTAL EXPENS	20300	18200			
36	TOTAL PROFIT	-300	3100			
37						

17-Aug-90   01:54 PM   UNDO

All data entries are now placed in individual cells.

If you move the pointer through columns A, B, and C, you'll see entries on the control panel for each label and value. You may now use 1-2-3's editing features to make the necessary changes to widen the label columns to display all the long labels, replace blank rows that were deleted, create formulas in the appropriate cells, delete the imported data, and copy the edited worksheet into the cells below the worksheet title labels.

■ *12* Select /Quit, Yes, Yes to exit 1-2-3 without saving this worksheet. You should return to the Access System screen.

Using 1-2-3's Translate Utility

Let's translate your JULYPL1.WK1 file into a 1-2-3 1A file format.

■ *1* If you do not have the Access System screen displayed, type **LOTUS** at a DOS prompt and press ⏎ .

```
1-2-3  PrintGraph  Translate  Install  Exit
Use 1-2-3

                    1-2-3 Access System
                   Copyright  1986, 1989
```

6

■*2*   Select Translate. (If you are using a dual floppy system, you will be prompted to switch
your System disk with your Translate disk in
drive A.)

```
                 Lotus  1-2-3  Release 2.2 Translate Utility
         Copr. 1985, 1989  Lotus Development Corporation  All Rights Reserved

      What do you want to translate FROM?

            1-2-3  1A
            1-2-3  2, 2.01 or 2.2
            dBase II
            dBase III
            DIF
            Multiplan (SYLK)
            Symphony  1.0
            Symphony  1.1, 1.2 or 2.0
            VisiCalc




                    Highlight your selection and press ENTER
                    Press ESC to end the Translate utility
                     Press HELP (F1) for more information
```

This is the list of programs
from which you can choose
to select the *source* program, or the program that
contains the data you want
to translate.

■3   Select 1-2-3 2, 2.01, or 2.2.

```
Translate FROM: 1-2-3 2.2          What do you want to translate TO?

                                       1-2-3  1A
                                       1-2-3  3
                                       dBase II
                                       dBase III
                                       DIF
                                       Symphony  1.0
                                       Symphony  1.1, 1.2 or 2.0
```

■4   Select 1-2-3 1A and read the message screens
      that appear. ⏎ to see subsequent pages.

■5   ESC to continue with the translation.

```
Translate FROM: 1-2-3 2.2          Translate TO: 1-2-3  1A

Source file: C:\123\*.WK1

 AUGPL1   WK1   8/17/90  01:30 p     2414

           AUGPL1    WK1
           JULYPL1   WK1
           REPORT    WK1
           REPORT88  WK1
           REPORT89  WK1
```

6

■6   Highlight JULYPL1.WK1 and press ⏎.

```
Translate FROM: 1-2-3 2.2          Translate TO: 1-2-3  1A

Source file: C:\123\JULYPL1.WK1

Target file: C:\123\JULYPL1.WKS
```

The new file (the *target* file) has a .WKS extension.

■7   ⏎

```
Translate FROM: 1-2-3 2.2          Translate TO: 1-2-3  1A

Source file: C:\123\JULYPL1.WK1

Target file: C:\123\JULYPL1.WKS


    Proceed with translation
    Yes  No  Quit
```

■8   Select Yes.

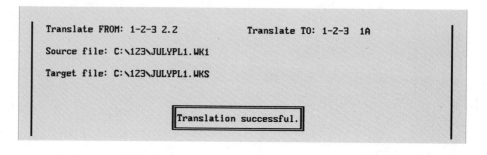

```
Translate FROM: 1-2-3 2.2          Translate TO: 1-2-3  1A

Source file: C:\123\JULYPL1.WK1

Target file: C:\123\JULYPL1.WKS


                    Translation successful.
```

■*9*   [ESC] [ESC] and select Yes to exit to the Access
System.

You can import files into 1-2-3 Release 2.2 by using the above method to translate a different file format into the 1-2-3 Release 2.2 format.

Moving Data
■between Worksheets

There are two methods you can employ when you want to move some information from one worksheet into another: /File, Combine and /File, Xtract. There may be data that exists in exactly the form you wish to use in another file. Or, you may wish to pull values into a worksheet and add or subtract them to or from similar data to achieve new values.

Using /File, Combine

You can retrieve a range of data or an entire file into a worksheet you're currently working on. Let's move two columns of values from your AUGPL1.WK1 worksheet into the JULYPL1.WK1 worksheet. You must first know the range of data in AUGPL1 that you want to move to the JULYPL1 worksheet.

6

■ *1*   Start 1-2-3 and retrieve the AUGPL1.WK1 worksheet.

```
A26:                                                          READY

          A         B         C          D          E        F
 7   INCOME
 8   Flight Instruction      1,600.00   1,200.00
 9   Charter                 6,200.00   4,800.00
10   Aircraft Rental         5,600.00   7,000.00
11   Maintenance             8,600.00   9,200.00
12   TOTAL INCOME           22,000.00  22,200.00
13
14   EXPENSES
15   Wages                   6,800.00   6,600.00
16   Fuel/Oil/Parts         10,300.00   8,400.00
17   Rent                    2,000.00   2,000.00
18   Insurance               1,200.00   1,200.00
19   TOTAL EXPENSES         20,300.00  18,200.00
20
21   TOTAL PROFIT/LOSS      $1,700.00  $4,000.00
22
23   Submit to Audits
24   Unlimited by September
25   3, 1990.
26
17-Aug-90  01:55 PM         UNDO
```

We will move only the values in columns C and D. Jot down on a piece of paper that the range is from cell C8 to D23.

■ *2*   Select /File, Retrieve JULYPL1.WK1.

```
A1: 'BRIARCLIFF AVIATION                                          READY

           A        B          C          D          E          F
1    BRIARCLIFF AVIATION
2    Santa Clarita, CA.
3    July 1990 Profit-and-Loss Statement
4
5                            Week 1     Week 2     Week 3     Week 4
6                     xxxxxxxxxxxxxxxxxxxxxxxxxxxxxxxxxxxxxxxxxxxxxxxx
7
8    INCOME
9    Flight Instruction       1600       1300
10   Charter                  6200       5000
11   Aircraft Rental          5600       6000
12   Maintenance              6600       9000
13   TOTAL INCOME            20000      21300
14
15   EXPENSES
16   Wages                    6800       6600
17   Fuel/Oil/Parts          10300       8400
18   Rent                     2000       2000
19   Insurance                1200       1200
20   TOTAL EXPENSES          20300      18200
17-Aug-90  01:56 PM          UNDO
```

■ *3*   Move the pointer to cell E9, the location
where the data from AUGPL1 will be placed,
and select /File, Combine.

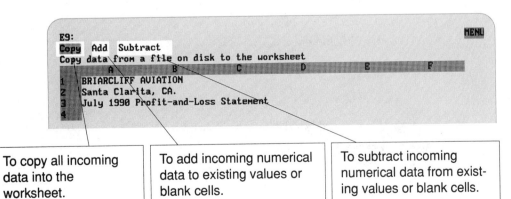

```
E9:                                                              MENU
Copy  Add  Subtract
Copy data from a file on disk to the worksheet
           A        B          C          D          E          F
1    BRIARCLIFF AVIATION
2    Santa Clarita, CA.
3    July 1990 Profit-and-Loss Statement
4
```

| To copy all incoming data into the worksheet. | To add incoming numerical data to existing values or blank cells. | To subtract incoming numerical data from existing values or blank cells. |

■ *4*   Select Copy.

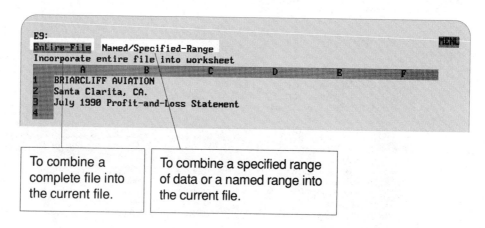

To combine a complete file into the current file.

To combine a specified range of data or a named range into the current file.

■ *5*   Select Named/Specified-Range.

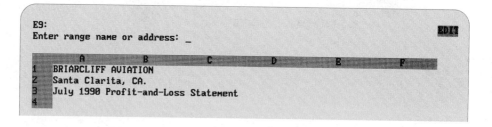

■ *6*   Type **C8..D23** (the range of data located in the AUGPL1 file) and press ⏎.

■ 7   Select AUGPL1.WK1.

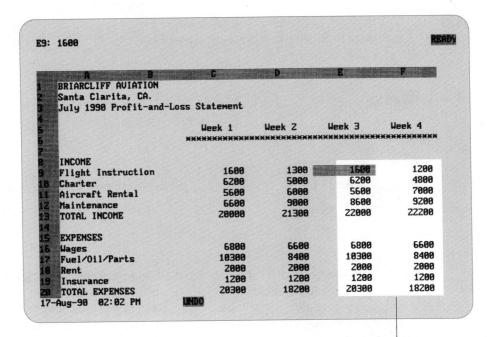

E9: 1600   READY

```
              A           B           C           D           E           F
1   BRIARCLIFF AVIATION
2   Santa Clarita, CA.
3   July 1990 Profit-and-Loss Statement
4
5                                Week 1      Week 2      Week 3      Week 4
6                          xxxxxxxxxxxxxxxxxxxxxxxxxxxxxxxxxxxxxxxxxxxxxx
7
8   INCOME
9   Flight Instruction          1600        1300        1600        1200
10  Charter                     6200        5000        6200        4800
11  Aircraft Rental             5600        6000        5600        7000
12  Maintenance                 6600        9000        8600        9200
13  TOTAL INCOME               20000       21300       22000       22200
14
15  EXPENSES
16  Wages                       6800        6600        6800        6600
17  Fuel/Oil/Parts             10300        8400       10300        8400
18  Rent                        2000        2000        2000        2000
19  Insurance                   1200        1200        1200        1200
20  TOTAL EXPENSES             20300       18200       20300       18200
17-Aug-90  02:02 PM         UNDO
```

The specified range of data is placed into the JULYPL1 worksheet at the pointer location.

■ 8   Select /File, Save, press ⏎, and select Replace to save the edited version of JULYPL1.WK1.

Using /File, Xtract

The /File, Xtract command is useful when you want to move a small section of a larger worksheet into another worksheet. Let's use the JULYPL1 worksheet created in the last exercise.

■ *1*   With the pointer in cell E9, select /File, Xtract.

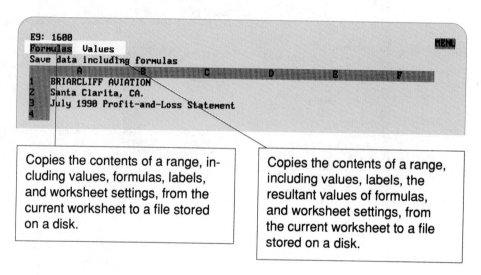

Copies the contents of a range, including values, formulas, labels, and worksheet settings, from the current worksheet to a file stored on a disk.

Copies the contents of a range, including values, labels, the resultant values of formulas, and worksheet settings, from the current worksheet to a file stored on a disk.

■ *2*   Select Formulas.

```
E9: 1600                                                          FILES
Enter name of file to extract to: C:\123\*.wk1
AUGPL1.WK1       JULYPL1.WK1       JULYPL1.WK1     REPORT.WK1    REPORT88.WK1
        A               B               C             D            E          F
1   BRIARCLIFF AVIATION
2   Santa Clarita, CA.
3   July 1990 Profit-and-Loss Statement
4
```

■ *3* Type **EXTRACT** and press ⏎ to save the
range into a new file with the name
EXTRACT.

```
E9: 1600                                                    POINT
Enter extract range: E9..E9

            A         B         C         D         E         F
 1  BRIARCLIFF AVIATION
 2  Santa Clarita, CA.
 3  July 1990 Profit-and-Loss Statement
 4
```

■ *4* Move the pointer to cell F22 to designate the
range of data to be saved.

```
F22: (C2) +F13-F20                                          POINT
Enter extract range: E9..F22

            A         B         C         D         E         F
 3  July 1990 Profit-and-Loss Statement
 4
 5                          Week 1     Week 2     Week 3     Week 4
 6          xxxxxxxxxxxxxxxxxxxxxxxxxxxxxxxxxxxxxxxxxxxxxxxxx
 7
 8  INCOME
 9  Flight Instruction        1600       1300       1600       1200
10  Charter                   6200       5000       6200       4800
11  Aircraft Rental           5600       6000       5600       7000
12  Maintenance               6600       9000       8600       9200
13  TOTAL INCOME             20000      21300      22000      22200
14
15  EXPENSES
16  Wages                     6800       6600       6800       6600
17  Fuel/Oil/Parts           10300       8400      10300       8400
18  Rent                      2000       2000       2000       2000
19  Insurance                 1200       1200       1200       1200
20  TOTAL EXPENSES           20300      18200      20300      18200
21
22  TOTAL PROFIT/LOSS         -300       3100  $1,700.00  $4,000.00
    17-Aug-90  02:07 PM
```

6

■5 ⏎ to extract the data.

■6 Select /File, Retrieve.

```
E9: 1600                                                              FILES
Name of file to retrieve: C:\123\*.wk?
AUGPL1.WK1      EXTRACT.WK1     JULYPL1.WK1     JULYPL1.WKS    REPORT.WK1
         A              B              C             D           E          F
1    BRIARCLIFF AUIATION
2    Santa Clarita, CA.
3    July 1990 Profit-and-Loss Statement
4
```

■7 Select AUGPL1.WK1.

```
A26:                                                                 READY


         A              B              C             D           E          F
7    INCOME
8    Flight Instruction       1,600.00    1,200.00
9    Charter                  6,200.00    4,800.00
10   Aircraft Rental          5,600.00    7,000.00
11   Maintenance              8,600.00    9,200.00
12   TOTAL INCOME            22,000.00   22,200.00
```

■8 Move the pointer to cell E8, which is where
you will place the extracted data. Select /File,
Combine, Copy, Entire-File.

```
E8:                                                                  READY
Enter name of file to combine: C:\123\*.wk?
AUGPL1.WK1      EXTRACT.WK1     JULYPL1.WK1     JULYPL1.WKS    REPORT.WK1
         A              B              C             D           E          F
7    INCOME
8    Flight Instruction       1,600.00    1,200.00
9    Charter                  6,200.00    4,800.00
10   Aircraft Rental          5,600.00    7,000.00
11   Maintenance              8,600.00    9,200.00
12   TOTAL INCOME            22,000.00   22,200.00
```

■ *9* Select EXTRACT.WK1.

```
E8: 1600                                                      READY

         A         B          C          D          E          F
 7  INCOME
 8  Flight Instruction    1,600.00    1,200.00    1,600.00    1,200.00
 9  Charter               6,200.00    4,800.00    6,200.00    4,800.00
10  Aircraft Rental       5,600.00    7,000.00    5,600.00    7,000.00
11  Maintenance           8,600.00    9,200.00    8,600.00    9,200.00
12  TOTAL INCOME         22,000.00   22,200.00   22,000.00   22,200.00
13
14  EXPENSES
15  Wages                 6,800.00    6,600.00    6,800.00    6,600.00
16  Fuel/Oil/Parts       10,300.00    8,400.00   10,300.00    8,400.00
17  Rent                  2,000.00    2,000.00    2,000.00    2,000.00
18  Insurance             1,200.00    1,200.00    1,200.00    1,200.00
19  TOTAL EXPENSES       20,300.00   18,200.00   20,300.00   18,200.00
20
21  TOTAL PROFIT/LOSS    $1,700.00   $4,000.00   $1,700.00   $4,000.00
22
23  Submit to Audits
24  Unlimited by September
25  3, 1990.
26
17-Aug-90  02:12 PM        UNDO
```

The extracted data is moved into the AUGPL1.WK1 file.

■ *10* Select /File, Save, press ⏎, and select
Replace to save the edited version of
AUGPL1.WK1.

■ *Linking Your Worksheets*

1-2-3's file linking feature enables you to create a new worksheet (called a *target* worksheet) that contains formulas that refer to cells in already existing worksheets (called *source* worksheets). When files are connected with these *linking formulas*, any change that affects the linked cells in the source worksheets is automatically recalculated by the linking formula when the target worksheet is retrieved. File linking saves you the work of updating every worksheet affected by a change made in another worksheet.

Creating the Target Worksheet

In this exercise you'll create a target worksheet that summarizes the income totals from the AUGPL1 and JULYPL1 worksheets, which are the source worksheet.

■ *1* The AUGPL1 worksheet should be on your screen. If not, press / and retrieve it, then press HOME .

```
A1: 'BRIARCLIFF AVIATION                                          READY

          A         B         C         D         E         F
1   BRIARCLIFF AVIATION
2   Santa Clarita, CA.
3   August 1990 Profit-and-Loss Statement
4
5                             Week 1    Week 2    Week 3    Week 4
6                        ×××××××××××××××××××××××××××××××××××××××××××
7   INCOME
8   Flight Instruction      1,600.00  1,200.00  1,600.00  1,200.00
9   Charter                 6,200.00  4,800.00  6,200.00  4,800.00
10  Aircraft Rental         5,600.00  7,000.00  5,600.00  7,000.00
11  Maintenance             8,600.00  9,200.00  8,600.00  9,200.00
12  TOTAL INCOME           22,000.00 22,200.00 22,000.00 22,200.00
13
14  EXPENSES
15  Wages                   6,800.00  6,600.00  6,800.00  6,600.00
16  Fuel/Oil/Parts         10,300.00  8,400.00 10,300.00  8,400.00
17  Rent                    2,000.00  2,000.00  2,000.00  2,000.00
18  Insurance               1,200.00  1,200.00  1,200.00  1,200.00
19  TOTAL EXPENSES         20,300.00 18,200.00 20,300.00 18,200.00
20
17-Aug-90  02:13 PM        UNDO
```

■*2*   Move the pointer to cell G5, type **^TOTAL**,
and press ⬇.

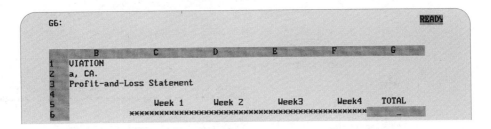

```
G6:                                                          READY

          B          C          D          E          F          G
1  UIATION
2  a, CA.
3  Profit-and-Loss Statement
4
5                      Week 1      Week 2      Week3       Week4    TOTAL
6  ××××××××××××××××××××××××××××××××××××××××××××××××××    —
```

■*3*   Type * and press ⬇.

■*4*   Move the pointer to cell G12, type
@SUM(C12..F12), and press ↵.

```
4
5                      Week 1      Week 2      Week3       Week4     TOTAL
6  ×××××××××××××××××××××××××××××××××××××××××××××××××××××××××××××
7
8   uction          1,600.00    1,200.00    1,600.00    1,200.00
9                   6,200.00    4,800.00    6,200.00    4,800.00
10  tal             5,600.00    7,000.00    5,600.00    7,000.00
11                  8,600.00    9,200.00    8,600.00    9,200.00
12                 22,000.00   22,200.00   22,000.00   22,200.00    88,400.00
13
14
```

The total income for the four weeks in August 1990 appears here. Make a note of cell G12; you will use it later in a linking formula in the target worksheet.

■*5*   Save this file using the /File, Save command.

You've already created a formula for the total income in the JULYPL1 worksheet.
Now retrieve JULYPL1 in order to locate the cell containing the formula.

6

■6   Select /File, Retrieve.

```
E9: 1600                                                        READY

         A         B          C          D          E          F
1  BRIARCLIFF AVIATION
2  Santa Clarita, CA.
3  July 1990 Profit-and-Loss Statement
4
5                            Week 1     Week 2     Week 3     Week 4
6                         xxxxxxxxxxxxxxxxxxxxxxxxxxxxxxxxxxxxxxxxxxxxxxx
7
8  INCOME
9  Flight Instruction       1600       1300       1600       1200
10 Charter                  6200       5000       6200       4800
11 Aircraft Rental          5600       6000       5600       7000
12 Maintenance              6600       9000       8600       9200
13 TOTAL INCOME            20000      21300      22000      22200
14
15 EXPENSES
16 Wages                    6800       6600       6800       6600
17 Fuel/Oil/Parts          10300       8400      10300       8400
18 Rent                     2000       2000       2000       2000
19 Insurance                1200       1200       1200       1200
20 TOTAL EXPENSES          20300      18200      20300      18200
17-Aug-90  02:17 PM       UNDO
```

■7   Move the pointer to cell G13 and make a note
      of this cell. You will refer to this cell in a link-
      ing formula in the target worksheet.

```
7
8
9   uction        1600       1300       1600       1200
10                6200       5000       6200       4800
11  tal           5600       6000       5600       7000
12                6600       9000       8600       9200
13               20000      21300      22000      22200      85500
```

■*8*   Save this file using the /File, Save command.

Now you're ready to create the target worksheet.

■*1*   Select /Worksheet, Erase, Yes to clear
JULYPL1 from the screen.

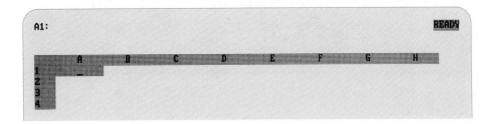

■*2*   Type the labels shown in the following screen
illustration in cells A1 and A2 (remember to
place an ' in front of the 1990 Year-to-Date
Summary label).

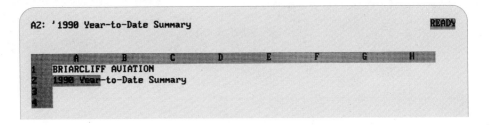

6

■*3*   Move the pointer to cell B4. Type the labels
      ^July, **^August**, and **^TOTAL** in cells B4,
      C4, and D4 respectively. (The ^ symbol
      centers the labels in the cells.)

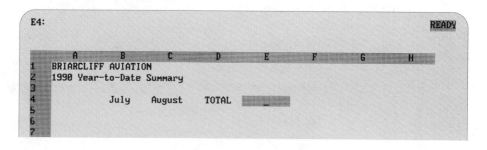

■*4*   Move the pointer to cell B5 and type * into
      cells B5 through D5.

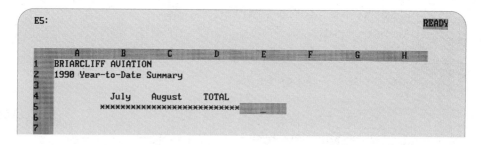

■5 Move the pointer to cell A7, type **^IN-COME**, and press →.

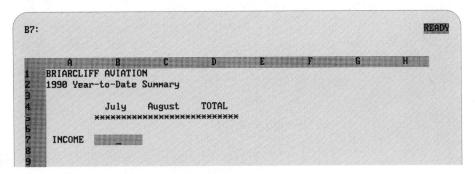

Adding the Linking Formulas

Now you're ready to create the linking formulas that will pull the income figures from the JULYPL1 and AUGPL1 files automatically. Cell G13 from JULYPL1 and cell G12 from AUGPL1 will be used in the linking formulas you will create.

6

■1 With the pointer in cell B7, type **+<<JULYPL1>>G13**. If the source file resides in a different directory, type the complete path, as in: **+<<C:\123\JULYPL.WK1>>**.

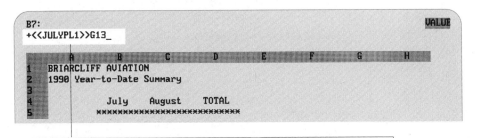

The + sign tells 1-2-3 that you are entering a formula. The << and >> brackets enclose the name of the source file. G13 is the cell in the source file that you want to link the target file

> **Note** *Assigning a Range Name to Source Cells* You can use the /Range, Name, Create command to assign a range name to your source cells. This is helpful if the source cell's contents get moved to different cells in the source worksheet. The linking formula will adjust to the new location. If you use a specific cell address, such as G13 in our example, the linking formula would refer to that specific cell and would provide inaccurate computations if G13's content were to be moved to another cell.

■2 ⇥ to place the linking formula in cell B7.

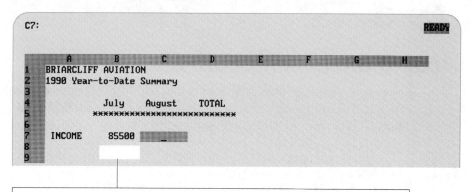

The total income from JULYPL1 is automatically placed in cell B7.

> **Note** *The ERR Message* If you receive an ERR prompt when entering a linking formula, check for one of the following:
>
> - Is the range name accurate?
> - Does the source file exist?
> - Did you enter the correct path to the source file location?
> - Is the source file password-protected?
> - Is the drive latch on the floppy drive closed?
> - Is another network user saving or retrieving the source file?
> - If you used a source worksheet created in 1-2-3 releases 1A, 2.0, or 2.01, or in Symphony versions 1.1, 1.2, or 2.0, be sure to include correct file extensions when you type the file name in the linking formula.

■ *3*   Type **+<<AUGPL1>>G12** and press →.

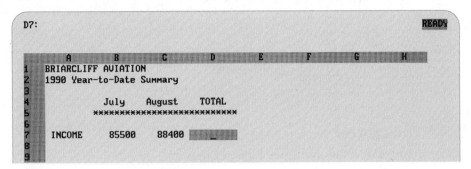

■ *4*   Type **+B7+C7** and press →.

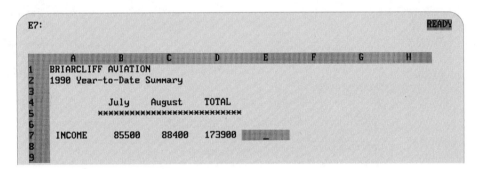

■ *5*   Select /File, Save, type **SUMMARY**, and press ↵ to save the target worksheet and make the links permanent.

Now let's see how file-linking works.

■ *6*   Retrieve JULYPL1 or AUGPL1, edit an
         INCOME value, and save the worksheet.

■ *7*   Retrieve SUMMARY. The appropriate
         INCOME value will be automatically updated
         and a new value will appear on the worksheet.

■ *8*   Please return the source values to their
         original values for use in future exercises.

Note *Tips for Linking Files* The following information may prove helpful when working with linked files.

■ On a network, if other users have worked on the source files while you worked in the target file, use the /File, Admin, Link-Refresh command to update the target file.

■ The /File, List, Linked command displays a list of linked worksheets.

■ Refer to your 1-2-3 documentation for more advanced tips on using file linking.

■ *Summary*

In this chapter you've learned how to use some time-saving 1-2-3 features for exchanging and moving worksheet data. You've seen how to link worksheets together using target and source files. You've also learned how to share information between 1-2-3 and other programs by using either ASCII files or 1-2-3's Translate utility. Finally, you saw two methods for moving information from one worksheet to another.

S E V E N

After you create your worksheets, you'll probably want to use the information in one type of presentation or another. You can simply print a copy of the worksheet if only numerical detail is needed, or you can transform the worksheet data into a graph. Graphs are great for visually representing relationships between numerical values while at the same time greatly enhancing a presentation. 1-2-3 lets you view a graph on your monitor prior to printing it, as long as your computer has a graphics card. However, you can still print graphs without a graphics card—you just can't see them beforehand.

Creating and Enhancing Bar Graphs

■

Playing the "What If " Game with Graphs

■

Saving and Naming Graphs

■

Creating Line Graphs

■

Creating a Pie Chart

■

Printing Graphs

■

Using /Graph, Group (Quick Graph)

■ *Creating and Viewing Bar Graphs*

In this section you'll create and view on the screen a common type of graph—the bar graph. Bar graphs display data as a series of vertical bars that represent each numerical value.

Creating a Bar Graph

Let's create a bar graph for the INCOME items on your AUGPL1.WK1 worksheet.

■ *1*   Select /File, Retrieve and retrieve the
AUGPL1.WK1 file. Press HOME to move
the pointer to cell A1.

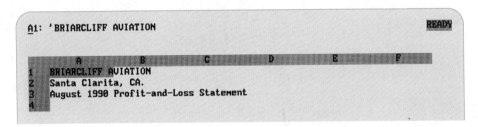

7

■*2* Select /Graph. The Graph main menu and
Graph Settings sheet are displayed.

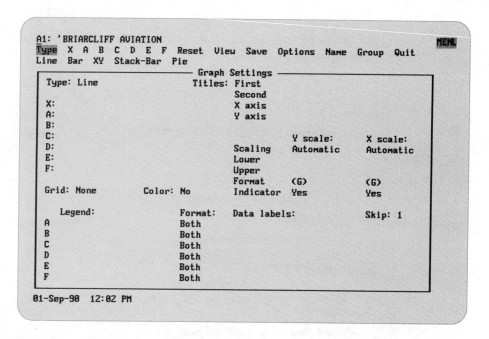

Note *Using the Graph Main Menu* These options let you access 1-2-3's graph capabilities:

- Use *Type* to select one of five types of graphs: Line, Bar, XY, Stack-Bar, and Pie Chart.
- Use *X* to create labels along the x-axis (horizontal) of a graph.
- Use options *A* through *F* to specify up to six ranges of data to be graphed.
- *Reset* clears some or all of the current graph settings.
- *View* displays the graph on the screen.
- Use *Save* to save the graph as a graphics file with a .PIC extension for use in a graphics program.
- Use *Options* to place titles, legends, and labels on graphs.
- Use *Name* to create, modify, and delete named graphs.
- Use *Group* to specify several data ranges at one time as long as they are in consecutive rows or columns.

■*3* Select Type.

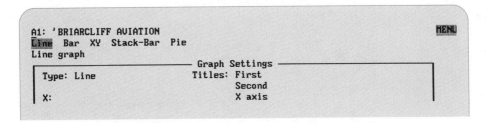

```
A1: 'BRIARCLIFF AVIATION                                    MENU
Line  Bar  XY  Stack-Bar  Pie
Line graph
                        ┌──── Graph Settings ──────────────────────┐
   Type: Line            Titles: First
                                 Second
   X:                            X axis
```

■*4* Select Bar.

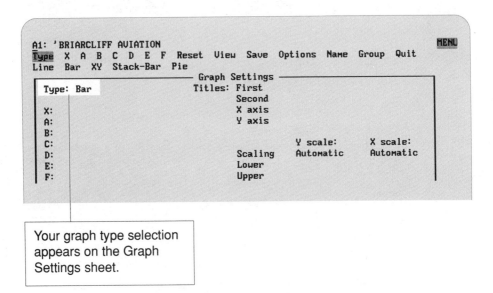

```
A1: 'BRIARCLIFF AVIATION                                    MENU
Type  X  A  B  C  D  E  F  Reset  View  Save  Options  Name  Group  Quit
Line  Bar  XY  Stack-Bar  Pie
                        ┌──── Graph Settings ──────────────────────┐
   Type: Bar             Titles: First
                                 Second
   X:                            X axis
   A:                            Y axis
   B:
   C:                                     Y scale:      X scale:
   D:                            Scaling  Automatic     Automatic
   E:                            Lower
   F:                            Upper
```

Your graph type selection appears on the Graph Settings sheet.

The next step is to designate the range of data you want to graph. You can choose up to six ranges, indicated by choosing a letter A through F. You'll choose four ranges.

■5   Select A to designate the first range of values.

```
A1: 'BRIARCLIFF AVIATION                                        POINT
Enter first data range: A1

      A        B         C         D         E         F
1   BRIARCLIFF AVIATION
2   Santa Clarita, CA.
3   August 1990 Profit-and-Loss Statement
4
5                       Week 1    Week 2    Week 3    Week 4
6   ×××××××××××××××××××××××××××××××××××××××××××××××××××××××
7   INCOME
8   Flight Instruction  1,600.00  1,200.00  1,600.00  1,200.00
9   Charter             6,200.00  4,800.00  6,200.00  4,800.00
10  Aircraft Rental     5,600.00  7,000.00  5,600.00  7,000.00
11  Maintenance         8,600.00  9,200.00  8,600.00  9,200.00
12  TOTAL INCOME       22,000.00 22,200.00 22,000.00 22,200.00
13
14  EXPENSES
```

■6   Type **C8..F8**, the range of cells that contain
the INCOME data for Flight Instruction;
press ⏎.

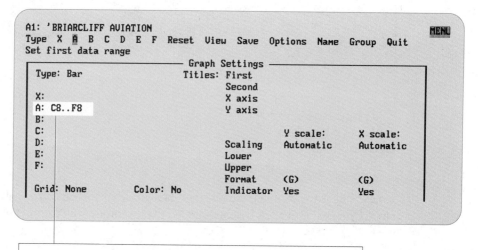

```
A1: 'BRIARCLIFF AVIATION                                        MENU
Type X A B C D E F  Reset  View  Save  Options  Name  Group  Quit
Set first data range
                        ── Graph Settings ──
  Type: Bar              Titles: First
                                 Second
  X:                             X axis
  A: C8..F8                      Y axis
  B:
  C:                                        Y scale:     X scale:
  D:                             Scaling    Automatic    Automatic
  E:                             Lower
  F:                             Upper
                                 Format     (G)          (G)
  Grid: None     Color: No       Indicator  Yes          Yes
```

The data range is recorded on the Graph Settings sheet.

■7   Select B, type **C9 . . F9**, and press ⏎.

```
A1: 'BRIARCLIFF AVIATION                                        MENU
Type  X  A  B  C  D  E  F  Reset  View  Save  Options  Name  Group  Quit
Set second data range
                                  ┌─ Graph Settings ─
     Type: Bar                    Titles: First
                                          Second
     X:                                   X axis
     A: C8..F8                            Y axis
     B: C9..F9
     C:                                               Y scale:     X scale:
```

■8   Select C, type **C10 . . F10**, and press ⏎.

```
A1: 'BRIARCLIFF AVIATION                                        MENU
Type  X  A  B  C  D  E  F  Reset  View  Save  Options  Name  Group  Quit
Set third data range
                                  ┌─ Graph Settings ─
     Type: Bar                    Titles: First
                                          Second
     X:                                   X axis
     A: C8..F8                            Y axis
     B: C9..F9
     C: C10..F10                                      Y scale:     X scale:
     D:                           Scaling  Automatic  Automatic
```

■9   Select D, type **C11 . . F11**, and press ⏎.

```
A1: 'BRIARCLIFF AVIATION                                        MENU
Type  X  A  B  C  D  E  F  Reset  View  Save  Options  Name  Group  Quit
Set fourth data range
                                  ┌─ Graph Settings ─
     Type: Bar                    Titles: First
                                          Second
     X:                                   X axis
     A: C8..F8                            Y axis
     B: C9..F9
     C: C10..F10                                      Y scale:     X scale:
     D: C11..F11                  Scaling  Automatic  Automatic
     E:                           Lower
```

Viewing Your Graph

Remember, you must have a graphics card in your computer to view graphs. If you don't, you'll have to print the graph to see the results.

■ *1*   Select View to display the graph on your
screen.

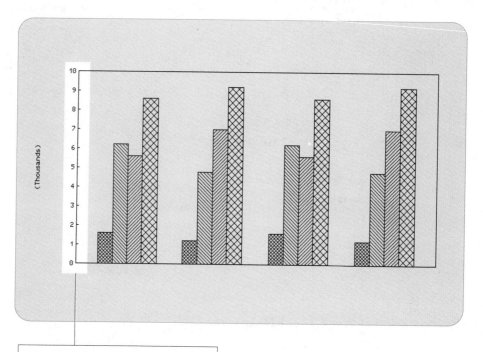

The vertical y-axis values and
tick marks are automatically
created by 1-2-3, based upon
the greatest value plotted.

This is a "bare bones" version of the graph without any titles, labels, or a legend.
You'll add these items in a moment. Notice that 1-2-3 automatically selects a different hatching for each bar.

> **Note** *If You Get a Blank Screen* The problem is probably one of these things: you may not have the correct monitor display card, you installed the wrong screen display driver, or the data ranges are not specified. Press ESC to return to the Graph menu and continue with the next exercise. You can create the graphs in these exercises, but you will not be able to view them until the problem is corrected or until you print them.

■*2*   ⏎ (or any other key) to return to the
Graph menu.

```
A1: 'BRIARCLIFF AVIATION                                          MENU
Type  X  A  B  C  D  E  F   Reset  View  Save  Options  Name  Group  Quit
View the current graph
                          ─────── Graph Settings ───────
   Type: Bar                    Titles: First
                                        Second
   X:                                   X axis
```

Keep this menu on the screen for the next exercise. If you want to take a break before you continue, be sure to save the worksheet as you normally do with the /File, Save command. This will save the work you've done on the graph so far.

■*Enhancing Graphs*

Now that you've created a graph from your worksheet data, you'll want to add some enhancements to it to increase its effectiveness as a presentation aid. 1-2-3 enables you to add titles and labels, place horizontal and vertical grids, or change the scale used to present the data. In this section you'll make all these enhancements to your AUGPL1 graph.

Adding Legends, Titles, and Labels

Legends, titles, and labels enable others to interpret the graphed data. Titles provide an overall description of the graphed material. A legend differentiates between each data range by using different shadings and symbols. Labels are used to name each data entry. Let's first place a legend on the AUGPL1 graph.

■ *1*   Select Options.

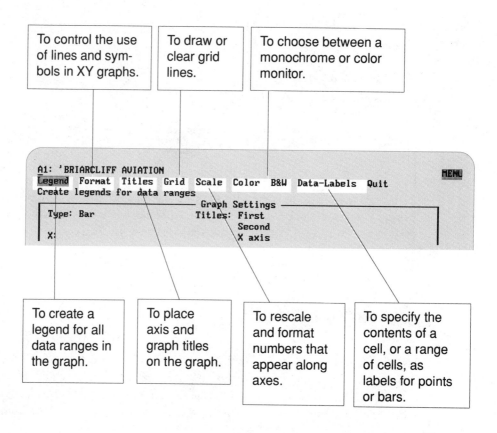

To control the use of lines and symbols in XY graphs.

To draw or clear grid lines.

To choose between a monochrome or color monitor.

```
A1: 'BRIARCLIFF AVIATION                                         MENU
Legend  Format  Titles  Grid  Scale  Color  B&W  Data-Labels  Quit
Create legends for data ranges
                            ───── Graph Settings ─────
    Type: Bar                    Titles: First
                                         Second
    X:                                   X axis
```

To create a legend for all data ranges in the graph.

To place axis and graph titles on the graph.

To rescale and format numbers that appear along axes.

To specify the contents of a cell, or a range of cells, as labels for points or bars.

■*2* Select Legend.

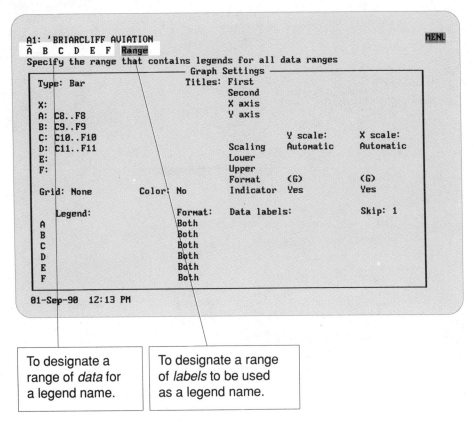

A1: 'BRIARCLIFF AVIATION   MENU
Ā B C D E F **Range**
Specify the range that contains legends for all data ranges
────────────────────────── Graph Settings ──────────────────────────
  Type: Bar   Titles: First
                                       Second
  X: X axis
  A: C8..F8   Y axis
  B: C9..F9
  C: C10..F10   Y scale: X scale:
  D: C11..F11   Scaling   Automatic   Automatic
  E: Lower
  F: Upper
                           Format   (G)   (G)
  Grid: None   Color: No Indicator   Yes   Yes

     Legend: Format: Data labels: Skip: 1
  A   Both
  B   Both
  C   Both
  D   Both
  E   Both
  F   Both

  01-Sep-90 12:13 PM

To designate a
range of *data* for
a legend name.

To designate a range
of *labels* to be used
as a legend name.

7

■*3* Select A.

A1: 'BRIARCLIFF AVIATION   EDIT
Enter legend for first data range:_

────────────────────────── Graph Settings ──────────────────────────
  Type: Bar   Titles: First
                                       Second
  X: X axis

■4   Type **Flight Instruction**, to describe the
first data range on the graph, and press ⏎.
(The legend name can be no longer than 19
characters.)

```
      Legend:                    Format:   Data labels:              Skip: 1
   A  Flight Instruction         Both
   B                             Both
   C                             Both
   D                             Both
   E                             Both
   F                             Both

01-Sep-90  12:15 PM
```

The legend name is placed
on the Graph Settings sheet.

At this point, you could continue to designate legend names by selecting B, C,
and D, and typing in the names of the remaining legends. But there's another
way to create legends. Let's use the Range option to select a range of labels to
used as legends.

■5   Select Legend, Range.

■ *6*   Move the pointer to cell A8 and press
⬚ (period) to anchor the range.

```
A8: 'Flight Instruction                                          POINT
Enter legend range: A8..A8

       A        B          C           D           E           F
1  BRIARCLIFF AVIATION
2  Santa Clarita, CA.
3  August 1990 Profit-and-Loss Statement
4
5                          Week 1      Week 2      Week 3      Week 4
6                      ×××××××××××××××××××××××××××××××××××××××××××
7  INCOME
8  Flight Instruction   1,600.00    1,200.00    1,600.00    1,200.00
9  Charter              6,200.00    4,800.00    6,200.00    4,800.00
10 Aircraft Rental      5,600.00    7,000.00    5,600.00    7,000.00
11 Maintenance          8,600.00    9,200.00    8,600.00    9,200.00
12 TOTAL INCOME        22,000.00   22,200.00   22,000.00   22,200.00
13
14 EXPENSES
15 Wages                6,800.00    6,600.00    6,800.00    6,600.00
16 Fuel/Oil/Parts      10,300.00    8,400.00   10,300.00    8,400.00
17 Rent                 2,000.00    2,000.00    2,000.00    2,000.00
18 Insurance            1,200.00    1,200.00    1,200.00    1,200.00
19 TOTAL EXPENSES      20,300.00   18,200.00   20,300.00   18,200.00
20
01-Sep-90  12:17 PM
```

> If you have typed in a legend, and then wish to use the
> Range option to designate other legends, you must in-
> clude in the range any legend you have already typed in.

■ *7*   Move the pointer to cell A11 to highlight the
cells containing the INCOME labels.

```
5                          Week 1      Week 2      Week 3      Week 4
6                      ×××××××××××××××××××××××××××××××××××××××××××
7  INCOME
8  Flight Instruction   1,600.00    1,200.00    1,600.00    1,200.00
9  Charter              6,200.00    4,800.00    6,200.00    4,800.00
10 Aircraft Rental      5,600.00    7,000.00    5,600.00    7,000.00
11 Maintenance          8,600.00    9,200.00    8,600.00    9,200.00
12 TOTAL INCOME        22,000.00   22,200.00   22,000.00   22,200.00
```

7

■*8* ⏎

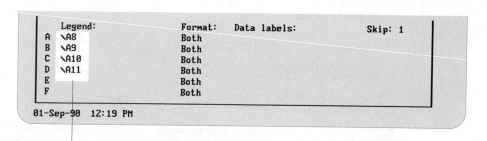

	Legend:	Format:	Data labels:	Skip: 1
A	\A8	Both		
B	\A9	Both		
C	\A10	Both		
D	\A11	Both		
E		Both		
F		Both		

01-Sep-90 12:19 PM

The cell addresses that contain the labels to be used as legends are displayed instead of the legend names.

■*9* Select Quit and View to see the legends.

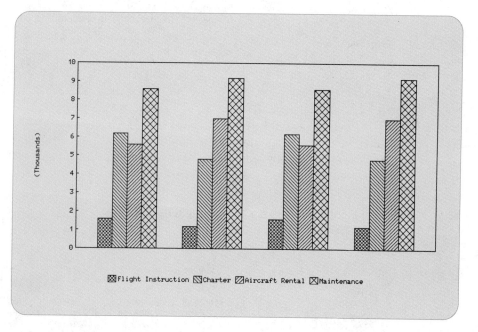

⊠Flight Instruction ⊠Charter ⊠Aircraft Rental ⊠Maintenance

Next you'll place two titles on the graph.

■ *1* ⏎ to return to the Graph menu. Select Options, Titles.

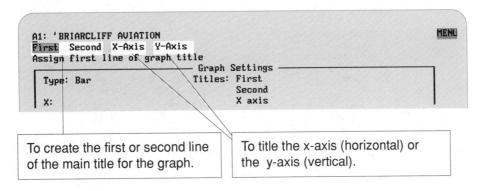

To create the first or second line of the main title for the graph.

To title the x-axis (horizontal) or the y-axis (vertical).

■ *2* Select First and type **INCOME ITEMS**.

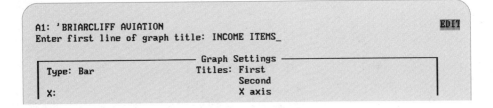

■ *3* ⏎

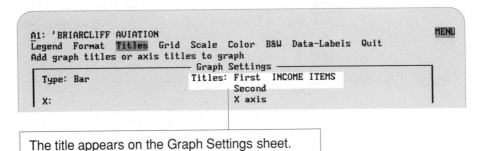

The title appears on the Graph Settings sheet.

7

■4 Select Titles, Second. Type **August 1990**, and
press ⏎.

```
A1: 'BRIARCLIFF AVIATION                                              MENU
Legend  Format  Titles  Grid  Scale  Color  B&W  Data-Labels  Quit
Add graph titles or axis titles to graph
                            ─── Graph Settings ───
  Type: Bar                    Titles: First   INCOME ITEMS
                                       Second  August 1990
  X:                                   X axis
```

■5 Select Quit to return to the Graph menu and
select View to see the titles displayed.

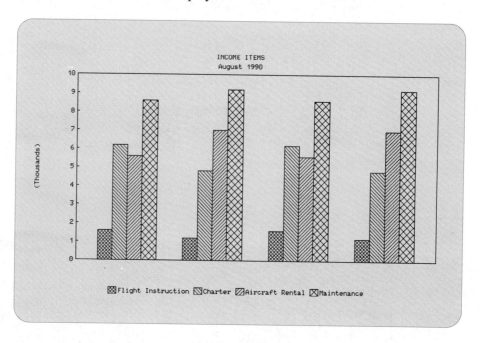

Now let's label the x-axis of the graph with the Week 1 through Week 4 column
labels.

■ *1* ⏎ to return to the Graph menu, and then select X to place labels along the x-axis of the graph.

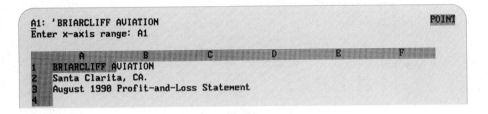

■ *2* Move the pointer to cell C5, which contains the Week 1 label.

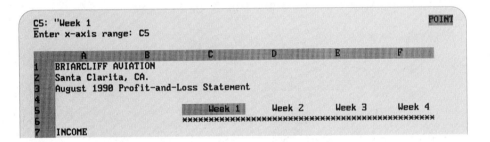

■ *3* . (period) to anchor the range and move the pointer to cell F5.

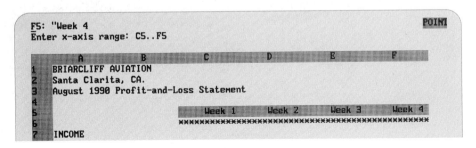

■4 ⏎

```
A1: 'BRIARCLIFF AVIATION                                            MENU
Type X A B C D E F  Reset  VIEW  Save  Options  Name  Group  Quit
View the current graph
                           ─── Graph Settings ───
   Type: Bar              Titles: First   INCOME ITEMS
                                  Second  August 1990
   X: C5..F5                      X axis
   A: C8..F8                      Y axis
   B: C9..F9
   C: C10..F10                                Y scale:     X scale:
   D: C11..F11              Scaling        Automatic     Automatic
```

The X range is displayed on the Graph Settings sheet.

■5 Select View to see the x-axis labels.

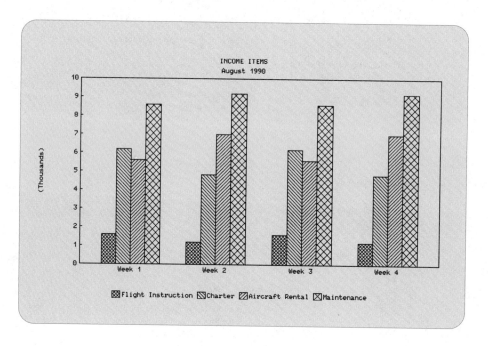

Creating a Grid

Placing a background grid on your graph makes it easier to interpret the graph's data. You can create three types of grids—horizontal, vertical, and a combination of both. Let's place a horizontal grid on the graph you've just created.

■1   ⏎ to return to the Graph menu. Select

Options, Grid.

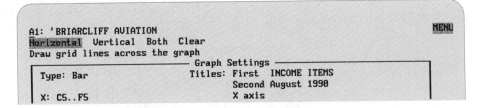

```
A1: 'BRIARCLIFF AVIATION                                    MENU
Horizontal  Vertical  Both  Clear
Draw grid lines across the graph
                            ─── Graph Settings ───
   Type: Bar                    Titles: First   INCOME ITEMS
                                        Second  August 1990
   X: C5..F5                            X axis
```

■2   Select Horizontal.

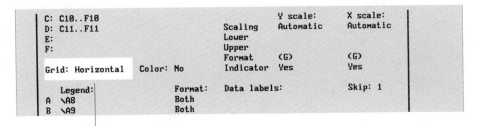

```
   C: C10..F10                             Y scale:     X scale:
   D: C11..F11                    Scaling  Automatic    Automatic
   E:                             Lower
   F:                             Upper
                                  Format   (G)          (G)
   Grid: Horizontal   Color: No   Indicator Yes         Yes

      Legend:          Format:    Data labels:           Skip: 1
   A  \A8              Both
   B  \A9              Both
```

The type of grid is displayed on the Graph Settings sheet.

7

■3 Select Quit and View to see the graph with
the horizontal grid lines.

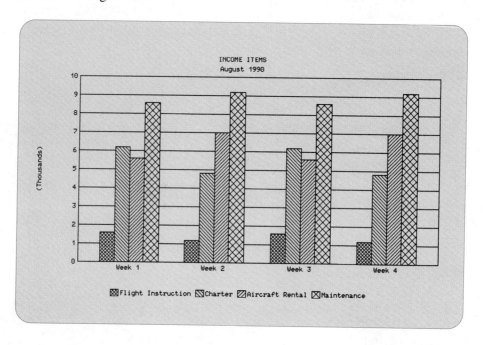

Changing Scale Lines

As you create a graph, 1-2-3 automatically establishes the scale for the x- and
y-axes according to the data selected for graphing. However, if you want to scale
the graph yourself, you can do so. In addition, you can change the look of the
scale indicators.

Let's modify the y-axis scale on the AUGPL graph. First you'll change the scale,
then you'll add dollar signs to the scale indicators.

■ *1*   ⏎ to return to the Graph menu. Select Options, Scale.

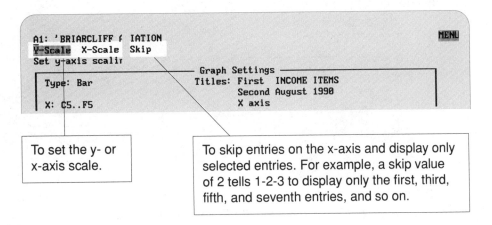

To set the y- or x-axis scale.

To skip entries on the x-axis and display only selected entries. For example, a skip value of 2 tells 1-2-3 to display only the first, third, fifth, and seventh entries, and so on.

■ *2*   Select Y-Scale.

7

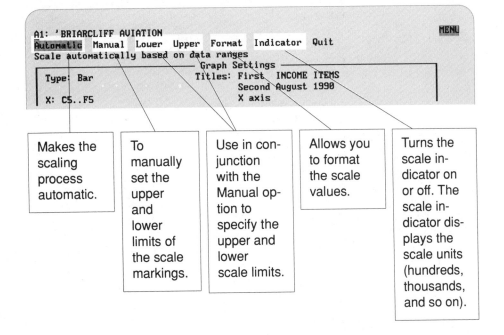

Makes the scaling process automatic.

To manually set the upper and lower limits of the scale markings.

Use in conjunction with the Manual option to specify the upper and lower scale limits.

Allows you to format the scale values.

Turns the scale indicator on or off. The scale indicator displays the scale units (hundreds, thousands, and so on).

■*3*   Select Manual, Upper.

```
A1: 'BRIARCLIFF AVIATION                                              EDIT
Enter upper limit: 0

                          ──── Graph Settings ────
   Type: Bar              Titles: First  INCOME ITEMS
                                  Second August 1990
   X: C5..F5              X axis
   A: C8..F8              Y axis
   B: C9..F9
   C: C10..F10                            Y scale:      X scale:
   D: C11..F11            Scaling         Manual        Automatic
   E:                     Lower           0
   F:                     Upper           0
```

■*4*   Type **15000** to set a new upper limit, and then
       press 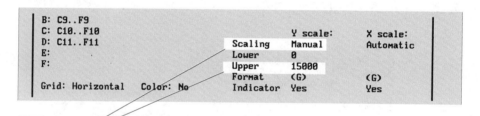 .

```
   B: C9..F9
   C: C10..F10                            Y scale:      X scale:
   D: C11..F11            Scaling         Manual        Automatic
   E:                     Lower           0
   F:                     Upper           15000
                          Format          (G)           (G)
   Grid: Horizontal   Color: No           Indicator     Yes           Yes
```

The Y-scale scaling display changes
from Automatic to Manual, and the
upper limit is now shown as 15000.

Now let's change the format of the scale indicator for the y-axis by adding
dollar signs.

■*5* Select Format, Currency.

```
A1: 'BRIARCLIFF AVIATION                                    EDIT
Enter number of decimal places (0..15): 2

                        ┌──────── Graph Settings ────────
   Type: Bar            Titles: First  INCOME ITEMS
                                Second August 1990
   X: C5..F5            X axis
```

■*6* Type **0** (zero) and press 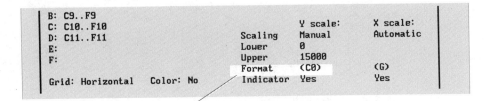 to negate
any decimal points appearing in the
scale indicators.

```
   B: C9..F9
   C: C10..F10                          Y scale:      X scale:
   D: C11..F11            Scaling       Manual        Automatic
   E:                     Lower         0
   F:                     Upper         15000
                          Format        (C0)          (G)
   Grid: Horizontal   Color: No   Indicator   Yes     Yes
```

The Format indicator now
shows that currency (C)
and no decimal points (0)
have been selected.

7

■ 7   Select Quit twice and then select View to see
the dollar signs on the Y-axis scale indicators.

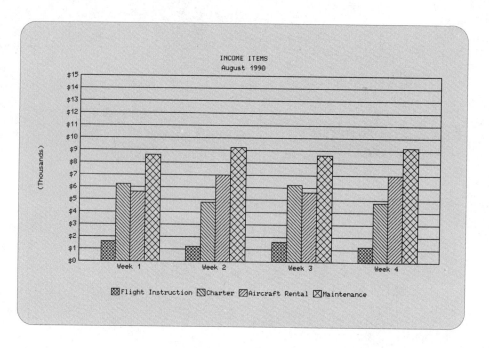

Compare this screen with the one in step 3 of the previous exercise in "Creating
a Grid." Keep this graph on the screen for use in the next exercise.

In the next
exercises
you'll see how
to create other
types of
graphs.

> **Note** *Resetting or Clearing Graph Settings* If you want to clear data ranges, legends, formatting choices, or titles from a graph, use the /Graph, Reset command. In addition to clearing selected settings, you can clear the settings for the entire graph.

Changing a Bar
■ Graph to a Stack-Bar Graph

A stack-bar graph displays the same information as a bar graph, but stacks each bar one on top of the other, rather than lining up the bars next to each other. This is a handy way to see the total amount of all the items added together.

You can take an existing bar graph and turn it into a stack-bar graph very easily. You can also create a stack-bar graph first, and then change it into a bar graph. Let's convert the AUGPL1 bar graph into a stack-bar graph.

7

■ *1*   ⏎ to return to the Graph menu. Select Type, Stack-Bar.

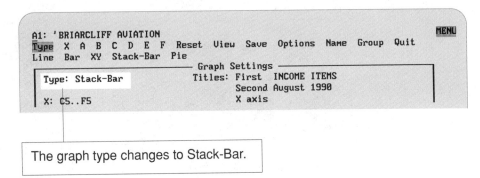

The graph type changes to Stack-Bar.

■2 Select Options, Scale, Y-Axis, Automatic to
change the method of scaling from manual to
automatic. Select Quit twice to return to the
Graph menu.

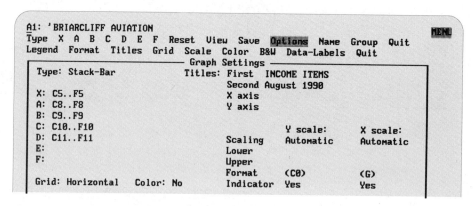

■3 Select View to see the newly created stack-
bar graph.

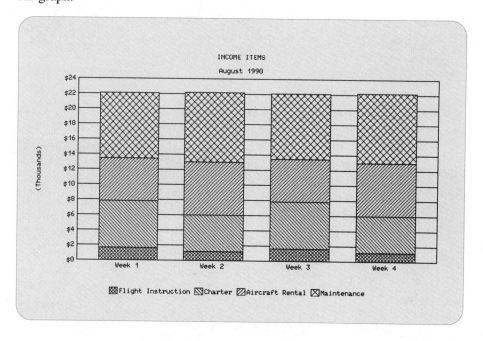

■4   ⏎ and select Type, Bar to change it back to
a bar graph.

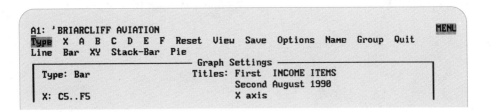

■5   Select Quit to return to the worksheet.

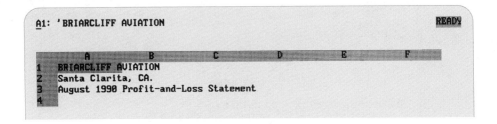

■*Playing "What If" with Graphs*

As you know, when you modify your worksheet data, 1-2-3 automatically recalculates the affected formulas. Well, the graphs associated with the same
worksheet are also automatically updated. This time-saving feature is terrific
when preparing financial projections for presentations that involve graphs. Let's
modify some values on the AUGPL1 worksheet and see how it affects the graph
you've created.

■*1* Move the pointer to the following cells and use **F2** (Edit) to enter the new values for these cells:

E8	1100
E11	7000
F9	3500
F10	8000

```
5
6                              Week 1      Week 2      Week 3      Week 4
7    INCOME            xxxxxxxxxxxxxxxxxxxxxxxxxxxxxxxxxxxxxxxxxxxxxxxxxx
8    Flight Instruction   1,600.00    1,200.00    1,100.00    1,200.00
9    Charter              6,200.00    4,800.00    6,200.00    3,500.00
10   Aircraft Rental      5,600.00    7,000.00    5,600.00    8,000.00
11   Maintenance          8,600.00    9,200.00    7,000.00    9,200.00
12   TOTAL INCOME        22,000.00   22,200.00   19,900.00   21,900.00
13
```

■*2* **F10** (Graph) to display the updated graph without going through the Graph menu.

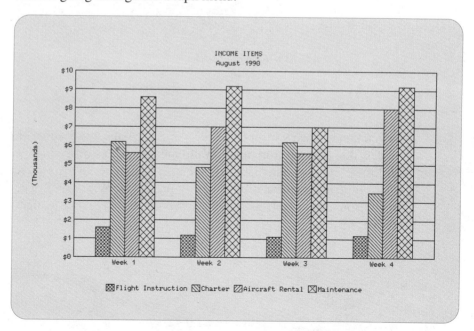

■*3* ⏎ to return to the worksheet.

■*Saving and Naming Graphs*

How you intend to use the graphs you create will determine the method you use to save them. There are two methods for saving graphs—you use one for graphs that will be viewed on-screen, and the other for those you'll be printing.

If you will only be viewing the graph with 1-2-3, you need only save the worksheet as you always do with the /File, Save command. The graph settings will be saved with the worksheet.

If you want to print a graph, you must save the graph with the /Graph, Save command. This creates a graphic file with a .PIC extension for use outside of the 1-2-3 program. You can use PrintGraph or Allways (both programs are included with Release 2.2) to print the graph. Then, you must use the /File, Save command after you use /Graph, Save in order to save the graph settings.

If you create more than one graph for a worksheet, you must name each graph before you save it so 1-2-3 can differentiate between them. You would then save all the named graph settings with the /File, Save command.

Let's name and save the bar and stack-bar graphs of the AUGPL1 worksheet data you've been working with.

Naming Your Graph

You should still have the AUGPL1 worksheet on the screen with the pointer in cell F10.

■ *1* Select /Graph, Name to display the Graph Settings sheet for the bar graph.

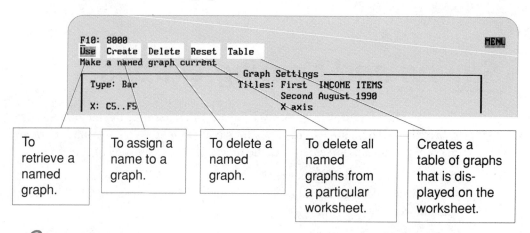

To retrieve a named graph.

To assign a name to a graph.

To delete a named graph.

To delete all named graphs from a particular worksheet.

Creates a table of graphs that is displayed on the worksheet.

■*2* Select Create.

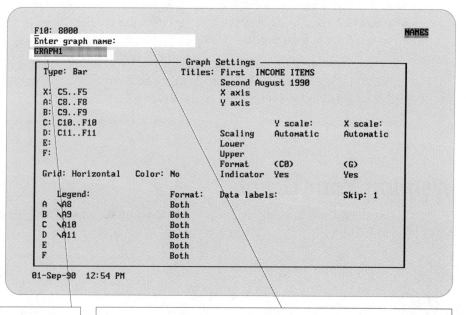

Named graphs appear here.

Do not use spaces, commas, semicolons, or any character that 1-2-3 might interpret as a value: + * – / & { @ and #.

■*3*   Type **AUGUST1** as the bar graph name and
press ⏎.

```
F10: 8000                                                          MENU
Type  X  A  B  C  D  E  F  Reset  View  Save  Options  Name  Group  Quit
Use  Create  Delete  Reset  Table
                       ───────── Graph Settings ─────────
     Type: Bar                    Titles: First   INCOME ITEMS
                                          Second  August 1990
     X: C5..F5                             X axis
```

■*4*   Select Type, Stack-Bar to name the
stack-bar graph.

```
F10: 8000                                                          MENU
Type  X  A  B  C  D  E  F  Reset  View  Save  Options  Name  Group  Quit
Line  Bar  XY  Stack-Bar  Pie
                       ───────── Graph Settings ─────────
     Type: Stack-Bar              Titles: First   INCOME ITEMS
                                          Second  August 1990
     X: C5..F5                             X axis
```

■*5*   Select Name, Create, type **AUGUST2**, and
press ⏎. You have now created a copy of
each type of bar graph.

```
F10: 8000                                                          MENU
Type  X  A  B  C  D  E  F  Reset  View  Save  Options  Name  Group  Quit
Use  Create  Delete  Reset  Table
                       ───────── Graph Settings ─────────
     Type: Stack-Bar              Titles: First   INCOME ITEMS
                                          Second  August 1990
     X: C5..F5                             X axis
```

Keep the Graph main menu on the screen for the next exercise

7

Saving Your Graph for Printing

Let's save a copy of the bar graph (AUGUST1) for printing with the PrintGraph program. The stack-bar graph (AUGUST2) settings are currently displayed on the screen, so we'll have to first select AUGUST1 before we save it.

■ 1 Select Name, Use.

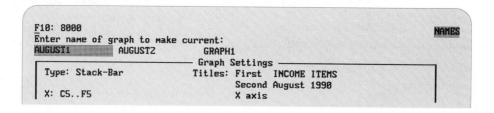

■ 2 Select AUGUST1 to view the bar graph.

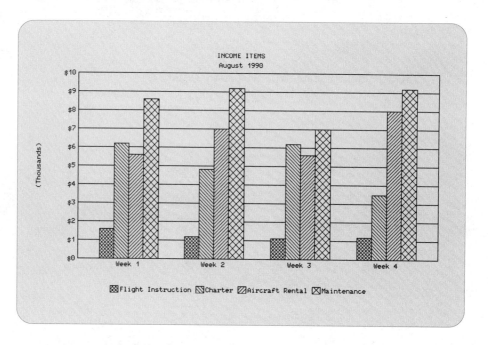

■*3* ⏎ and select Save.

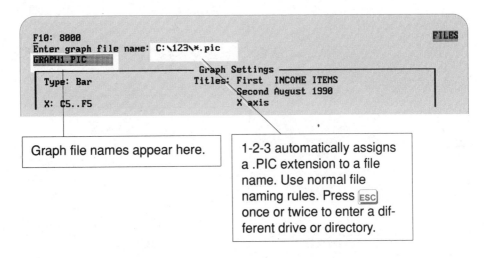

```
F10: 8000                                                      FILES
Enter graph file name: C:\123\*.pic
GRAPH1.PIC
                          Graph Settings
   Type: Bar                   Titles: First  INCOME ITEMS
                                       Second August 1990
   X: C5..F5                           X axis
```

Graph file names appear here.

1-2-3 automatically assigns a .PIC extension to a file name. Use normal file naming rules. Press ESC once or twice to enter a different drive or directory.

■*4* Type **AUGUST1** and press ⏎ to name and save the graphic file.

7

```
F10: 8000                                                      MENU
Type  X  A  B  C  D  E  F  Reset  View  Save  Options  Name  Group  Quit
Save the current graph in 0 file for printing
                          Graph Settings
   Type: Bar                   Titles: First  INCOME ITEMS
                                       Second August 1990
   X: C5..F5                           X axis
```

Saving Graphs for Future Viewing

Use the /File, Save command to save all your graph settings with your worksheet.

■ *1* Select Quit to return to the worksheet.

```
F10: 8000                                                          READY

          A          B          C          D          E          F
1    BRIARCLIFF AVIATION
2    Santa Clarita, CA.
3    August 1990 Profit-and-Loss Statement
4
```

■ *2* Select /File, Save.

```
F10: 8000                                                          EDIT
Enter name of file to save: C:\123\AUGPL1.WK1

          A          B          C          D          E          F
1    BRIARCLIFF AVIATION
2    Santa Clarita, CA.
3    August 1990 Profit-and-Loss Statement
4
```

■ *3* ⏎ and select Replace to accept the
AUGPL1.WK1 file name.

Creating and
■*Formatting Line Graphs*

Line graphs are effective when you want to show worksheet values relative to
elapsed time. This is similar to the way bar graphs display data, except a line
graph uses lines instead of bars to represent the data categories. Each category of
information is represented by a distinctive symbol located along each line at the
appropriate time intervals.

Constructing a line graph is very much the same process that you used to construct a bar graph in the previous exercises. Let's use the settings from the

AUGUST1 bar graph you saved in the last exercise and create a line graph. You'll then reformat the graph by adding labels and removing the grid.

■ *1*   With the AUGPL1.WK1 worksheet on the screen, select /Graph. The bar graph settings from the last exercise are displayed.

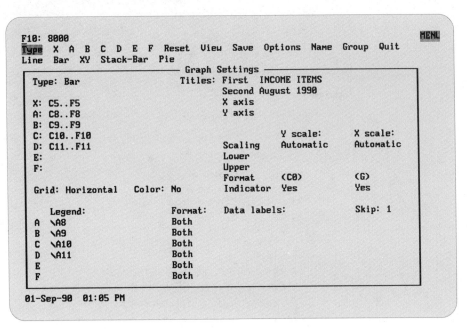

■ *2*   Select Type, Line.

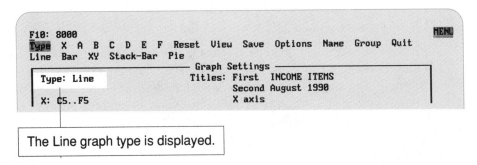

The Line graph type is displayed.

■3   Select View to display the graph.

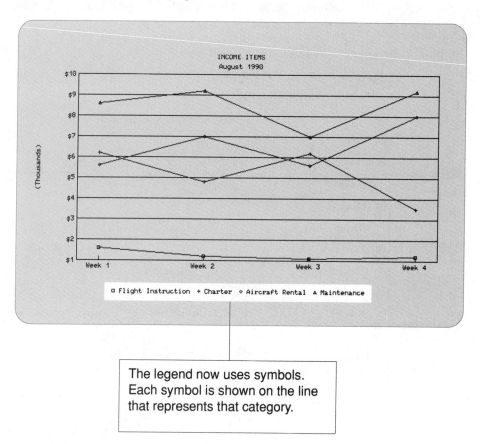

The legend now uses symbols.
Each symbol is shown on the line
that represents that category.

Adding Data-Labels

The Data-Label option in the Graph Options menu takes the contents of a range of cell addresses and uses this data to label the corresponding points on a line graph. The ranges of cell addresses are the same ranges of data designated in the A-F data ranges, which you chose when you created the graph. Let's place data labels on the line graph you just created.

■ *1*   ⏎ to return to the Graph menu. Select
Options, Data-Labels.

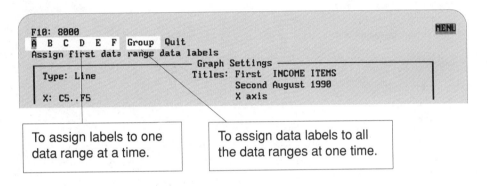

To assign labels to one
data range at a time.

To assign data labels to all
the data ranges at one time.

■ *2*   Select Group to place data labels on all the
graph points.

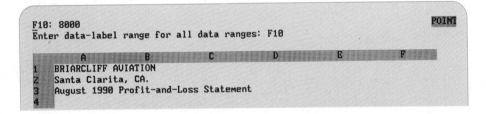

7

■ *3*   Move the pointer to cell C8, press ⎡.⎤
(period) to anchor the range, and move the
pointer to cell F11.

	Week 1	Week 2	Week 3	Week 4
5				
6	xxxxxxxxxxxxxxxxxxxxxxxxxxxxxxxxxxxxxxxxxxxxxxx			
7 INCOME				
8 Flight Instruction	1,600.00	1,200.00	1,100.00	1,200.00
9 Charter	6,200.00	4,800.00	6,200.00	3,500.00
10 Aircraft Rental	5,600.00	7,000.00	5,600.00	8,000.00
11 Maintenance	8,600.00	9,200.00	7,000.00	9,200.00
12 TOTAL INCOME	22,000.00	22,200.00	19,900.00	21,900.00
13				

■*4* ⏎

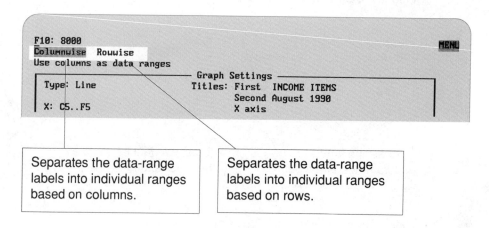

Separates the data-range labels into individual ranges based on columns.

Separates the data-range labels into individual ranges based on rows.

■*5* Select Rowwise, because the range data is displayed in rows.

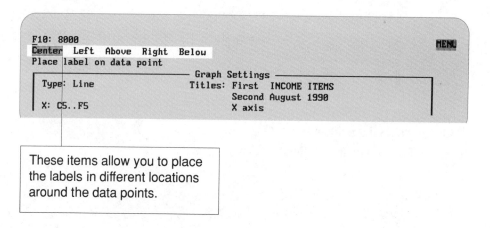

These items allow you to place the labels in different locations around the data points.

■ *6*   Select Above.

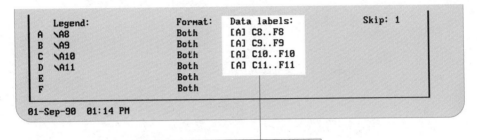

```
    Legend:         Format:   Data labels:              Skip: 1
A   \A8             Both      [A] C8..F8
B   \A9             Both      [A] C9..F9
C   \A10            Both      [A] C10..F10
D   \A11            Both      [A] C11..F11
E                   Both
F                   Both

01-Sep-90  01:14 PM
```

The [A] code indicates the
labels are placed above the
data points. The data label
ranges are also displayed.

The horizontal grid conflicts with the lines in this graph, which also run horizontally, so let's remove it.

7

■ *7*   Select Quit, Grid, Clear. The Grid indication
changes to None.

```
D: C11..F11                        Scaling    Automatic    Automatic
E:                                 Lower
F:                                 Upper
                                   Format     (C0)         (G)
Grid: None        Color: No        Indicator  Yes          Yes

    Legend:         Format:   Data labels:              Skip: 1
A   \A8             Both      [A] C8..F8
```

■ *8* Select Quit, View to display the graph.

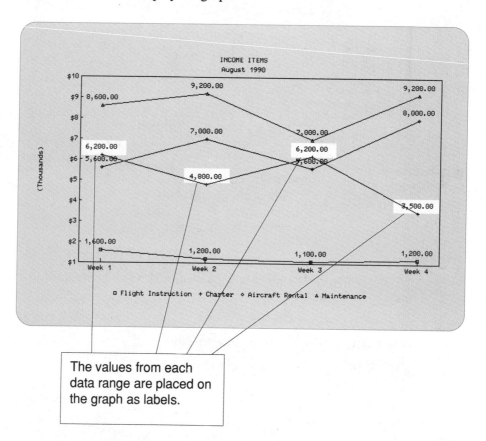

The values from each data range are placed on the graph as labels.

Hiding Line Graph Components

There may be times when you want to create a second graph that emphasizes only a portion of the graph. Let's hide the Flight Instruction and Aircraft Rental symbols and lines from the line graph created in the last exercise.

■ *1* ⏎ to return to the Graph menu. Select
Options, Format.

```
F10: 8000                                                    MENU
Graph  A  B  C  D  E  F  Quit
Set format for all ranges
                          ┌──────── Graph Settings ────────────────┐
   Type: Line                  Titles: First  INCOME ITEMS
                                       Second August 1990
   X: C5..F5                    X axis
   A: C8..F8                    Y axis
   B: C9..F9
   C: C10..F10                                  Y scale:    X scale:
   D: C11..F11                  Scaling         Automatic   Automatic
   E:                          Lower
   F:                          Upper
```

■ *2* Select A, the Flight Instruction range of data.

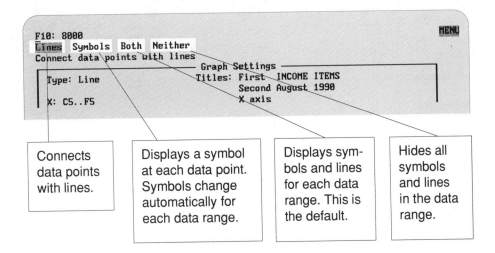

```
F10: 8000                                                    MENU
Lines  Symbols  Both  Neither
Connect data points with lines
                          ┌──────── Graph Settings ──────
   Type: Line                  Titles: First  INCOME ITEMS
                                       Second August 1990
   X: C5..F5                    X axis
```

| Connects data points with lines. | Displays a symbol at each data point. Symbols change automatically for each data range. | Displays symbols and lines for each data range. This is the default. | Hides all symbols and lines in the data range. |

7

■*3*   Select Neither to hide lines and symbols in
the Flight Instruction data range.

```
F10: 8000                                                      MENU
Graph  A  B  C  D  E  F  Quit
Set format for first data range
                    ───────── Graph Settings ─────────
   Type: Line              Titles: First  INCOME ITEMS
                                   Second August 1990
   X: C5..F5                       X axis
   A: C8..F8                       Y axis
```

■*4*   Select C, Neither to hide the lines and symbols in the Aircraft Rental data range.

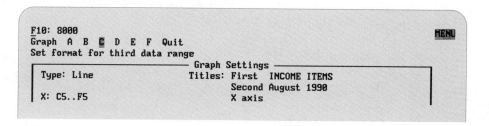

```
F10: 8000                                                      MENU
Graph  A  B  C  D  E  F  Quit
Set format for third data range
                    ───────── Graph Settings ─────────
   Type: Line              Titles: First  INCOME ITEMS
                                   Second August 1990
   X: C5..F5                       X axis
```

■*5* Select Quit twice, and then select View.

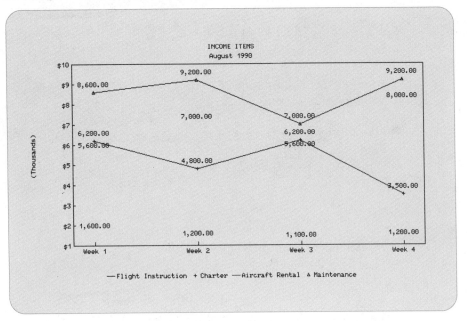

■*6* ⏎ and select Quit to return to the worksheet.

Creating and
■Enhancing a Pie Chart

Pie charts are useful when you want to compare individual values with each other and as parts of a whole. Each "slice" of the pie represents a value. In 1-2-3 you can even add emphasis to one or more slices of the pie by adding hatch patterns and by "exploding" (separating) them from the rest of the pie.

Let's create and format a pie chart using data from the AUGPL1.WK1 worksheet.

Creating a Pie Chart

■ *1*   Retrieve the AUGPL1.WK1 file. Press `HOME`
to place the pointer in cell A1.

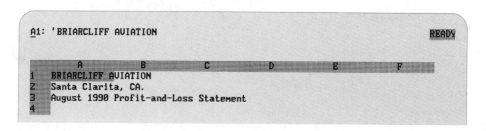

■ *2*   Select /Graph, Reset, Graph to clear all the
settings from the previously created graph.

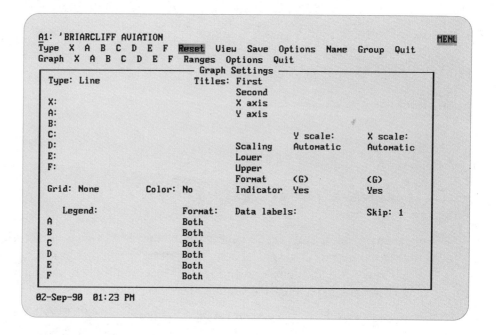

■*3* Select Type, Pie.

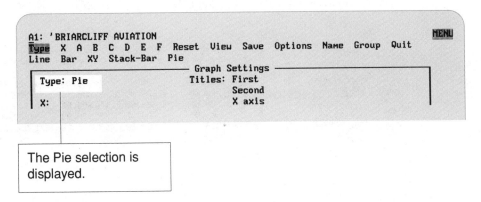

The Pie selection is
displayed.

Labeling a Pie Chart

You only need to designate the X-range and the A-range to create a pie chart.
The X-range is always used for labels and the A-range for values.

■*1* Select X to determine the labels for each slice
of the pie.

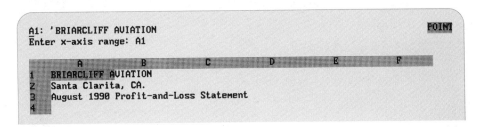

■*2*   Move the pointer to cell A8, press [.]
(period) and highlight cells A8 through A11.

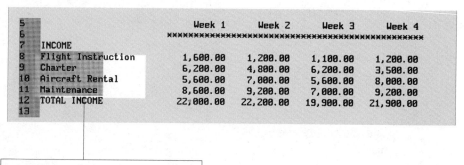

5		Week 1	Week 2	Week 3	Week 4
6		×××			
7	INCOME				
8	Flight Instruction	1,600.00	1,200.00	1,100.00	1,200.00
9	Charter	6,200.00	4,800.00	6,200.00	3,500.00
10	Aircraft Rental	5,600.00	7,000.00	5,600.00	8,000.00
11	Maintenance	8,600.00	9,200.00	7,000.00	9,200.00
12	TOTAL INCOME	22,000.00	22,200.00	19,900.00	21,900.00
13					

These labels will be assigned to slices of the pie.

■*3*   Press [↵].

```
A1: 'BRIARCLIFF AVIATION                                          MENU
Type X A B C D E F Reset View Save Options Name Group Quit
Set X data range
                        ┌──── Graph Settings ────────────
 Type: Pie              Titles: First
                               Second
 X: A8..A11                    X axis
 A:                            Y axis
```

The label range is displayed.

■*4* Select A to determine the values for each slice
of the pie.

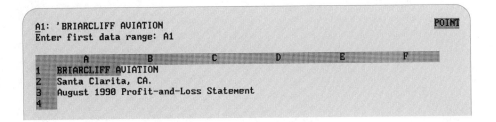

```
A1: 'BRIARCLIFF AVIATION                                    POINT
Enter first data range: A1

        A           B           C           D           E           F
1   BRIARCLIFF AVIATION
2   Santa Clarita, CA.
3   August 1990 Profit-and-Loss Statement
4
```

■*5* Type **C8..C11**, the range that contains the
values for the labels determined in step 2.

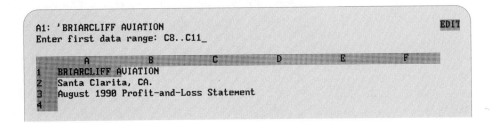

```
A1: 'BRIARCLIFF AVIATION                                    EDIT
Enter first data range: C8..C11_

        A           B           C           D           E           F
1   BRIARCLIFF AVIATION
2   Santa Clarita, CA.
3   August 1990 Profit-and-Loss Statement
4
```

■*6* ⏎ The A data range is displayed.

```
A1: 'BRIARCLIFF AVIATION                                    MENU
Type X A B C D E F  Reset  View  Save  Options  Name  Group  Quit
Set first data range
                            ┌──────── Graph Settings ────────┐
  Type: Pie                 │    Titles: First               │
                            │            Second              │
  X: A8..A11                │            X axis              │
  A: C8..C11                │            Y axis              │
  B:                        │                                │
```

7

■ 7   Select View.

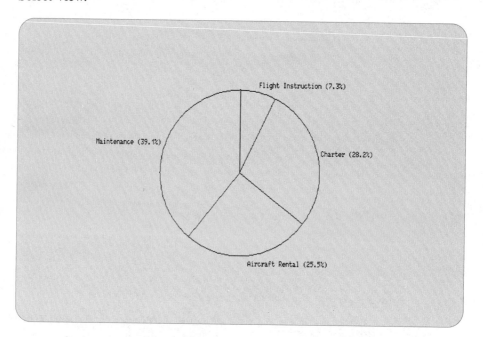

Shading and Exploding a Pie Chart

So you may clearly differentiate between the different slices of a pie chart, 1-2-3 provides eight shade patterns (also called *hatch* patterns) or colors. You choose these patterns by typing shade numbers (each representing a different pattern) into empty cells on the worksheet. You must have the same number of these shade-number cells as you have cells in the A-range of data cells, which determine the number of slices. Then, you add the shade-number cells to the graph settings by using the B-range option on the Graph menu.

For emphasis, you can "explode" one or more slices of the pie away from the rest of the pie. To do this, you type the number *100* in the cell that corresponds to the data you want to explode. You can even shade an exploded slice by adding a shade number (1-7) to the number 100.

Let's shade the pie chart you created in the last exercise and explode the Flight Instruction slice.

■ *1*   ⏎ and select Quit to return to the worksheet
Ready mode.

```
A1: 'BRIARCLIFF AVIATION                                    READY

        A         B          C          D          E        F
1   BRIARCLIFF AVIATION
2   Santa Clarita, CA.
3   August 1990 Profit-and-Loss Statement
4
```

First, specify the slice of the pie you want to explode. You'll also shade this exploded slice by adding the shade number to the number 100 (which designates
this as an exploded slice).

■ *2*   → and ↓ to move the pointer to cell H8,
type **101**, and press ↓.

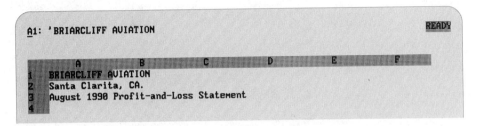

```
            Week 1     Week 2     Week 3     Week 4    TOTAL
     xxxxxxxxxxxxxxxxxxxxxxxxxxxxxxxxxxxxxxxxxxxxxxxxxxxxxxxxxxxxx

       1,600.00   1,200.00   1,100.00   1,200.00                101.00
       6,200.00   4,800.00   6,200.00   3,500.00
       5,600.00   7,000.00   5,600.00   8,000.00
       8,600.00   9,200.00   7,000.00   9,200.00
      22,000.00  22,200.00  19,900.00  21,900.00   86,000.00
```

7

Note *1-2-3's Hatch Patterns* There are nine shade numbers, 0 through 8. The numbers 0 and 8 leave the pie slice blank, while 1 through 7 assign different hatch patterns on a monochrome monitor and different colors on a color monitor (if colors are selected). Here's what each of the patterns looks like.

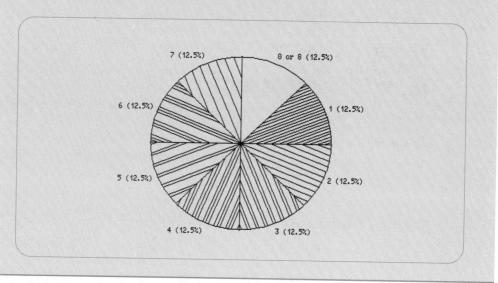

■3   Type the shade numbers **2**, **3**, and **4** into cells H9, H10, and H11 respectively.

7					
8	1,600.00	1,200.00	1,100.00	1,200.00		101.00
9	6,200.00	4,800.00	6,200.00	3,500.00		2.00
10	5,600.00	7,000.00	5,600.00	8,000.00		3.00
11	8,600.00	9,200.00	7,000.00	9,200.00		4.00
12	22,000.00	22,200.00	19,900.00	21,900.00	86,000.00	
13						

This range of cells is the same size as the A-range that defined the four slices of the pie chart. The decimal places appear because the value format is set for two decimal places.

■*4*   Select /Graph. Select B. Then, with the
pointer in cell H11, press ⌷ (period) and
move the pointer to cell H8.

	Week 1	Week 2	Week 3	Week 4	TOTAL	
5						
6	××
7						
8	1,600.00	1,200.00	1,100.00	1,200.00		101.00
9	6,200.00	4,800.00	6,200.00	3,500.00		2.00
10	5,600.00	7,000.00	5,600.00	8,000.00		3.00
11	8,600.00	9,200.00	7,000.00	9,200.00		4.00
12	22,000.00	22,200.00	19,900.00	21,900.00	86,000.00	
13						

■*5*   ⏎ and select View.

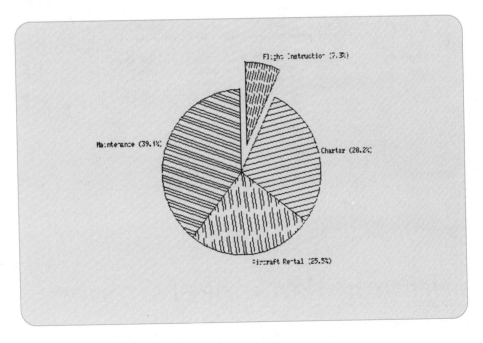

7

■6 ⏎ to return to the Graph menu. Select
Name, Create. Type **AUGUST3** to name the
pie chart.

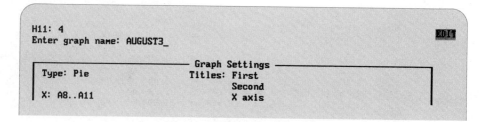

```
H11: 4                                                          EDIT
Enter graph name: AUGUST3_

                           ─ Graph Settings ─
  Type: Pie                  Titles: First
                                     Second
  X: A8..A11                         X axis
```

■7 ⏎ Select Quit to return to the worksheet.

	Week 1	Week 2	Week 3	Week 4	TOTAL	
5						
6	××					
7						
8	1,600.00	1,200.00	1,100.00	1,200.00		101.00
9	6,200.00	4,800.00	6,200.00	3,500.00		2.00
10	5,600.00	7,000.00	5,600.00	8,000.00		3.00
11	8,600.00	9,200.00	7,000.00	9,200.00		4.00
12	22,000.00	22,200.00	19,900.00	21,900.00	86,000.00	
13						

■8 Select /File, Save, press ⏎, and select
Replace to save the named graphs along with
the worksheet.

■*Printing Worksheet Graphs*

In order to print 1-2-3 graphs, you must use a separate program called Print-
Graph. PrintGraph comes with your 1-2-3 program disks. If you have a hard-
disk computer and have followed the instructions for installation in Appendix A,

you will have installed PrintGraph in the 1-2-3 directory. If you have a dual floppy-disk computer, you'll have to use the disk labeled PrintGraph Disk. Remember, you can only print graphs saved with the /Graph, Save command, which stores the graph with the .PIC graphic file extension (see the exercise on saving graphs earlier in this chapter).

Starting PrintGraph and Selecting PrintGraph Settings

Let's start PrintGraph and print a copy of AUGUST1.PIC, the bar graph you created and saved earlier. Be sure your printer is turned on and ready to print.

■ *1*   If you are currently running 1-2-3, save your work and exit to DOS or the Access System, depending on how you started 1-2-3. If you exit to a DOS prompt, type **LOTUS** to start the Access System.

```
1-2-3  PrintGraph  Translate  Install  Exit
Use 1-2-3

                        1-2-3 Access System
                      Copyright  1986, 1989
                   Lotus Development Corporation
                        All Rights Reserved
                           Release 2.2

The Access system lets you choose 1-2-3, PrintGraph, the Translate utility,
and the Install program, from the menu at the top of this screen.  If
you're using a two-diskette system, the Access system may prompt you to
change disks.  Follow the instructions below to start a program.

o  Use → or ← to move the menu pointer (the highlighted rectangle
   at the top of the screen) to the program you want to use.

o  Press ENTER to start the program.

You can also start a program by typing the first character of its name.

Press HELP (F1) for more information.
```

Note You may also start PrintGraph directly from a DOS prompt by typing **PGRAPH**.

■*2* Select Print Graph. (Floppy-disk users will be prompted to place the PrintGraph Disk into drive A; do so.)

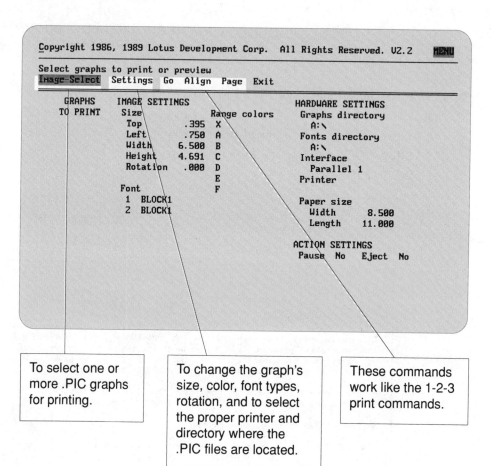

Copyright 1986, 1989 Lotus Development Corp. All Rights Reserved. V2.2   MENU

Select graphs to print or preview
Image Select Settings Go Align Page Exit

GRAPHS TO PRINT	IMAGE SETTINGS			HARDWARE SETTINGS
	Size		Range colors	Graphs directory
	Top	.395	X	A:\
	Left	.750	A	Fonts directory
	Width	6.500	B	A:\
	Height	4.691	C	Interface
	Rotation	.000	D	Parallel 1
			E	Printer
	Font		F	
	1 BLOCK1			Paper size
	2 BLOCK1			Width 8.500
				Length 11.000
				ACTION SETTINGS
				Pause No Eject No

To select one or more .PIC graphs for printing.

To change the graph's size, color, font types, rotation, and to select the proper printer and directory where the .PIC files are located.

These commands work like the 1-2-3 print commands.

■ *3* Select Settings to set up the PrintGraph program. (You only need to do this once, unless
you want to modify the settings later.)

```
Copyright 1986, 1989 Lotus Development Corp.  All Rights Reserved. V2.2    MENU

Select graph size, fonts, and colors
Image  Hardware  Action  Save  Reset  Quit

    GRAPHS      IMAGE SETTINGS                    HARDWARE SETTINGS
   TO PRINT     Size              Range colors    Graphs directory
                  Top      .395  X                  A:\
                  Left     .750  A                Fonts directory
```

■ *4* Select Hardware.

To specify the drive and directory
where the PrintGraph fonts are stored.

To select the printer you will be
using during the printing session.

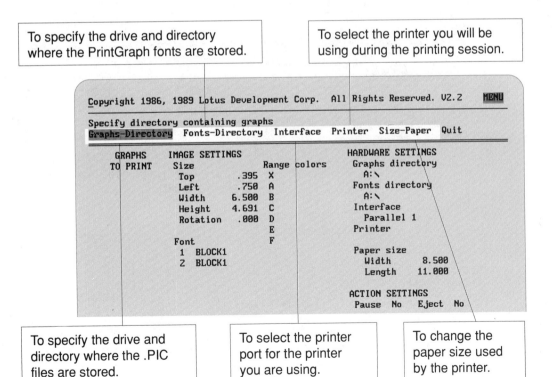

```
Copyright 1986, 1989 Lotus Development Corp.  All Rights Reserved. V2.2    MENU

Specify directory containing graphs
Graphs-Directory  Fonts-Directory  Interface  Printer  Size-Paper  Quit

    GRAPHS      IMAGE SETTINGS                    HARDWARE SETTINGS
   TO PRINT     Size              Range colors    Graphs directory
                  Top      .395  X                  A:\
                  Left     .750  A                Fonts directory
                  Width   6.500  B                  A:\
                  Height  4.691  C                Interface
                  Rotation .000  D                  Parallel 1
                                 E                Printer
                Font             F
                  1  BLOCK1                       Paper size
                  2  BLOCK1                         Width     8.500
                                                   Length   11.000

                                                 ACTION SETTINGS
                                                   Pause  No   Eject  No
```

To specify the drive and
directory where the .PIC
files are stored.

To select the printer
port for the printer
you are using.

To change the
paper size used
by the printer.

7

■*5*   Select Graphs-Directory.

```
Copyright 1986, 1989 Lotus Development Corp.  All Rights Reserved. U2.2   MENU

Enter directory containing graph (.PIC) files
A:\

      GRAPHS    IMAGE SETTINGS                        HARDWARE SETTINGS
      TO PRINT    Size              Range colors      Graphs directory
                  Top       .395  X                     A:\
                  Left      .750  A                    Fonts directory
```

■*6*   Hard-disk users type **C:\123** and press ⏎.
      (If .PIC files are stored in a different direc-
      tory, replace *123* with the correct name.)
      Floppy-disk users type **B:** and press ⏎.

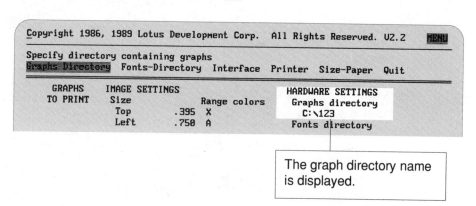

```
Copyright 1986, 1989 Lotus Development Corp.  All Rights Reserved. U2.2   MENU

Specify directory containing graphs
Graphs Directory  Fonts-Directory  Interface  Printer  Size-Paper  Quit

      GRAPHS    IMAGE SETTINGS                        HARDWARE SETTINGS
      TO PRINT    Size              Range colors      Graphs directory
                  Top       .395  X                     C:\123
                  Left      .750  A                    Fonts directory
```

The graph directory name
is displayed.

■7   Select Fonts-Directory.

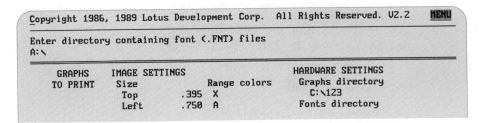

■8   Hard-disk users type **C:\123** and press ⏎.
(If the .FNT files are stored in a different
directory, replace *123* with the correct
name.) Floppy-disk users type **A:** and
press ⏎.

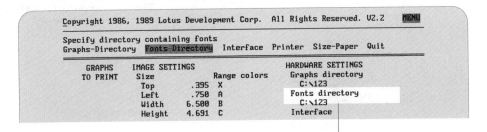

The fonts directory name
is displayed.

■ *9* Select Printer. The printers listed here depend on the printers you selected during the installation of your 1-2-3 program. If the printers you see here cannot print graphs, you will not be able to select them. You will have to install a suitable graphics printer, if you have one available (see Appendix A).

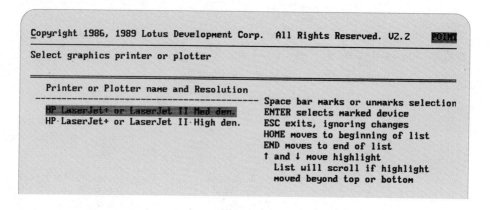

■ *10* Place the highlight on the printer of choice and press ⏎.

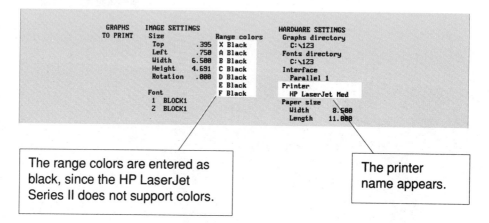

The range colors are entered as black, since the HP LaserJet Series II does not support colors.

The printer name appears.

■ *11*   Select Quit, Save to save the printer settings.

```
Copyright 1986, 1989 Lotus Development Corp.  All Rights Reserved. V2.2   MENU

Set, save or reset image, hardware, and action settings
Image-Select  Settings  Go  Align  Page  Exit

    GRAPHS     IMAGE SETTINGS                      HARDWARE SETTINGS
   TO PRINT    Size                               Graphs directory
               Top      .395   X Black            C:\123
               Left     .750   A Black            Fonts directory
```

Selecting a Graph for Printing

Now that you have established your print settings, you're ready to print a copy of the AUGUST1.PIC file. Be sure your printer is turned on and the paper is adjusted properly.

7

Remember, you must install PrintGraph before you can print the graph. See Appendix A.

■ *1*   Select Image-Select.

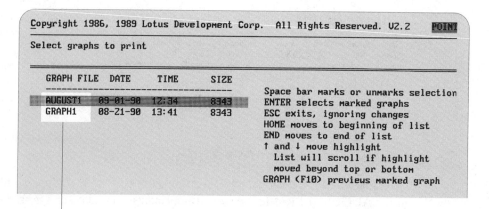

```
Copyright 1986, 1989 Lotus Development Corp.  All Rights Reserved. V2.2    POINT

Select graphs to print


    GRAPH FILE   DATE      TIME      SIZE
    ---------------------------------------      Space bar marks or unmarks selection
    AUGUST1      09-01-90  12:34     8343         ENTER selects marked graphs
    GRAPH1       08-21-90  13:41     8343         ESC exits, ignoring changes
                                                  HOME moves to beginning of list
                                                  END moves to end of list
                                                  ↑ and ↓ move highlight
                                                    List will scroll if highlight
                                                    moved beyond top or bottom
                                                  GRAPH (F10) previews marked graph
```

A list of all .PIC files are displayed. If the graph you
want is not listed, you may
be looking in the wrong
directory.

If you want to view the graph prior to printing, highlight the file name and press [F10]
(Graph).

■*2* Move the highlight to AUGUST1 and press
the space bar to place a # symbol next to the
file name.

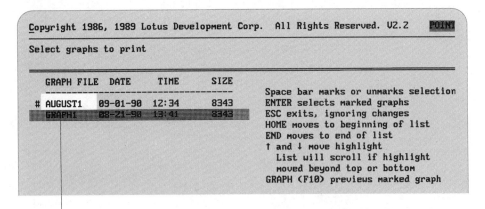

```
Copyright 1986, 1989 Lotus Development Corp.  All Rights Reserved. V2.2    POINT

Select graphs to print


    GRAPH FILE  DATE      TIME     SIZE
    --------------------------------------    Space bar marks or unmarks selection
  # AUGUST1    09-01-90  12:34    8343        ENTER selects marked graphs
    GRAPH1      08-21-90  13:41    8343        ESC exits, ignoring changes
                                              HOME moves to beginning of list
                                              END moves to end of list
                                              ↑ and ↓ move highlight
                                                List will scroll if highlight
                                                moved beyond top or bottom
                                              GRAPH (F10) previews marked graph
```

When you want to print more than one file at a time, you must
place the # symbol next to each file name. To remove the #
symbol, highlight the file name and press the space bar again.

7

■*3* ⏎ to accept the file(s) for printing.

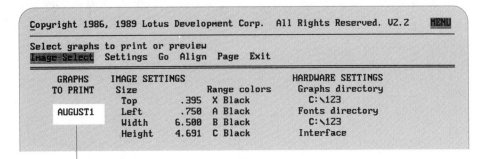

```
Copyright 1986, 1989 Lotus Development Corp.  All Rights Reserved. V2.2    MENU

Select graphs to print or preview
Image-Select  Settings  Go  Align  Page  Exit

    GRAPHS     IMAGE SETTINGS                 HARDWARE SETTINGS
   TO PRINT    Size            Range colors   Graphs directory
              Top       .395   X Black          C:\123
    AUGUST1   Left      .750   A Black        Fonts directory
              Width    6.500   B Black          C:\123
              Height   4.691   C Black        Interface
```

A list of the graphs you select for printing
is displayed here.

■*4* Select Align, Go to print the graph. (Laser
printer users must also select Page to move the
paper through the printer. Dot-matrix printer
users have to select Page *after* the graph prints
to move the paper through the printer.)

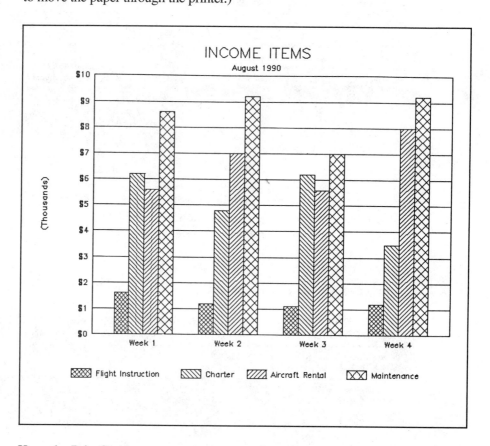

Keep the PrintGraph menu on your screen for the next exercise.

Customizing Your Graph's Printout

PrintGraph allows you to select different fonts and colors and to change the size of a graph.

■ *1*   Select Settings, Image.

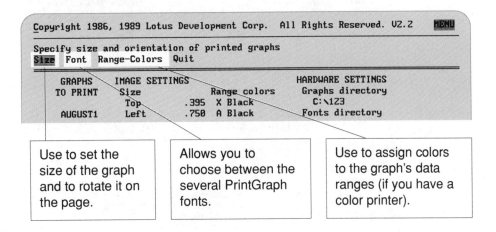

Use to set the size of the graph and to rotate it on the page.

Allows you to choose between the several PrintGraph fonts.

Use to assign colors to the graph's data ranges (if you have a color printer).

■ *2*   Select Size.

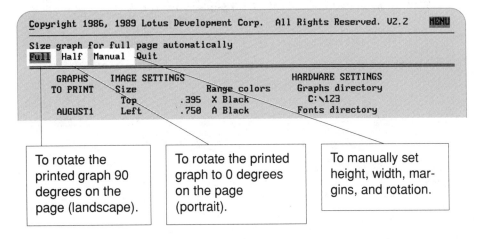

To rotate the printed graph 90 degrees on the page (landscape).

To rotate the printed graph to 0 degrees on the page (portrait).

To manually set height, width, margins, and rotation.

■*3*   Select Full, Quit to rotate the printed graph 90 degrees and return to the Image menu.

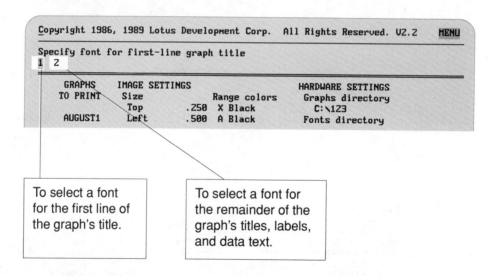

■*4*   Select Font.

To select a font for the first line of the graph's title.

To select a font for the remainder of the graph's titles, labels, and data text.

Note *PrintGraph Fonts* Some PrintGraph fonts, such as Italic and Script, do not work well with dot-matrix printers. You may want to experiment with fonts to determine which ones work best on your printer.

■*5*   Select 1 to display a list of fonts.

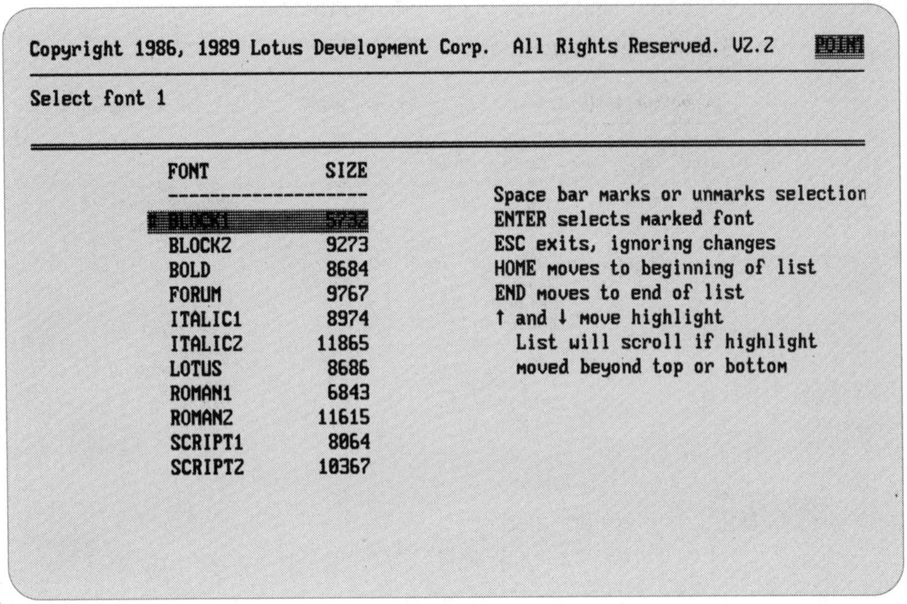

```
Copyright 1986, 1989 Lotus Development Corp.  All Rights Reserved. V2.2   POINT

Select font 1
_____

           FONT        SIZE
           --------------------
         ▓ BLOCK1       5752      Space bar marks or unmarks selection
           BLOCK2       9273      ENTER selects marked font
           BOLD         8684      ESC exits, ignoring changes
           FORUM        9767      HOME moves to beginning of list
           ITALIC1      8974      END moves to end of list
           ITALIC2      11865     ↑ and ↓ move highlight
           LOTUS        8686        List will scroll if highlight
           ROMAN1       6843        moved beyond top or bottom
           ROMAN2       11615
           SCRIPT1      8064
           SCRIPT2      10367
```

7

Use the space
bar to unmark
and mark your
font selection.

■ 6　Highlight Roman 2, press the space bar to
mark the font, and press ⏎ to change the
first line font to Roman.

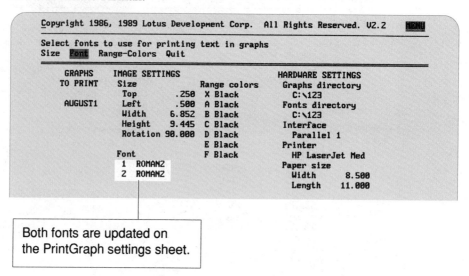

Both fonts are updated on
the PrintGraph settings sheet.

1-2-3 assumes you will want Font 1 and 2 to be the same, so Font 2 automatically changes to match Font 1. To select a different font for Font 2, repeat the
procedure above, but select a new font for Font 2. Font 1 remains as is when you
change Font 2.

■ 7　Select Quit twice to return to the
PrintGraph menu.

■*8*   Select Align, Go, Page to print the graph.

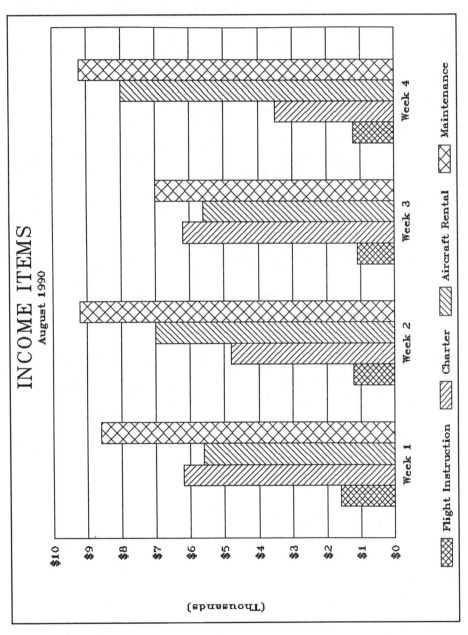

7

■ 9   Select Exit, Yes to return to the Access System.

Using the /Graph, Group
■ *Command (Quick Graph)*

1-2-3 has a unique feature called Quick Graph, which uses the /Graph, Group command to select the X-range and all the data ranges of a worksheet at once. The data to be graphed must be located in consecutive columns and rows. Let's create a small worksheet and use Quick Graph to speed up the graphing process.

■ 1   Start 1-2-3. At a blank worksheet, enter the information shown in the screen below in the appropriate cells (Use the caret symbol (^) to center the QTR heading.).

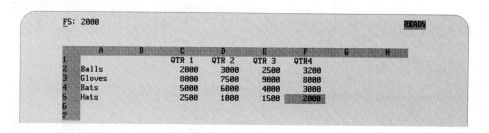

```
F5: 2000                                                                    READY

          A        B        C        D        E        F        G        H
   1                       QTR 1    QTR 2    QTR 3    QTR4
   2   Balls               2000     3000     2500     3200
   3   Gloves              8000     7500     9000     8000
   4   Bats                5000     6000     4000     3000
   5   Hats                2500     1000     1500     2000
   6
   7
```

■*2*   Select /Graph, Group.

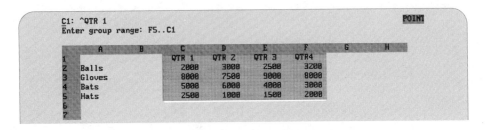

■*3*   `⌐.` (period) to anchor the range and move
the pointer to cell C1.

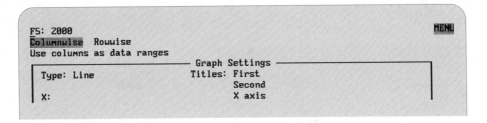

■*4*   `⏎` to accept the range.

```
F5: 2000                                                    MENU
Columnwise  Rowwise
Use columns as data ranges
                              ── Graph Settings ──
   Type: Line              Titles: First
                                   Second
   X:                              X axis
```

7

■ 5   Select Rowwise, because the QTR labels are
across the screen in row 1.

```
F5: 2000                                                             MENU
Type X A B C D E F  Reset  View  Save  Options  Name  Group  Quit
Set all data ranges at once
┌──────────────────────── Graph Settings ──────────────────────
│  Type: Line                     Titles: First
│                                         Second
│  X: C1..F1                      X axis
│  A: C2..F2                      Y axis
│  B: C3..F3
│  C: C4..F4                                 Y scale:      X scale:
│  D: C5..F5                      Scaling    Automatic     Automatic
│  E:                             Lower
```

The X-range and the A–D range data are created automatically.

■ 6   Select Type, Bar to change from the default
line graph to a bar graph, then select View.

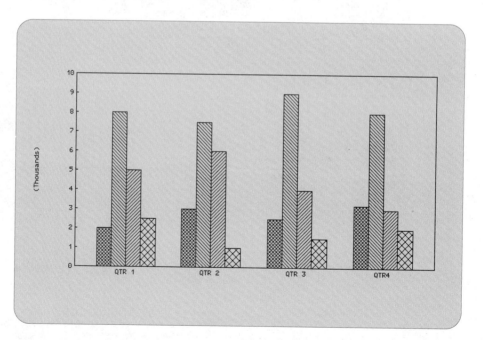

■7　　⏎ to return to the Graph menu. You can now place legends, labels, currency signs, grid lines, and so on to enhance the graph.

■8　　Select Quit to exit the graph.

■*Summary*

In this chapter you learned how to turn your worksheets into graphs. Bar, stack-bar, line, and pie charts are at your finger tips, waiting to perk up any presentation. Remember, when you create a graph, be sure to use the /File, Save command to save the graph settings. If you want to print the graph, save it as a .PIC file with the /Graph, Save command and then use the /File, Save command to save the graph settings. You can format your graphs with shading and patterns, or use different fonts to add interest to the text. The /Graph, Group feature lets you create a graph quickly, though there are some limitations to this method.

Graphs are very useful and a lot of fun to create and edit. With a little experimentation, you'll become an expert in a short period of time.

7

■ ■ ■ ■ ■
E I G H T

Using 1-2-3 as a Database ■ Manager

A database is a comprehensive grouping of related data that is organized for ease of access. Your telephone book is an excellent example of a database. You can create your own databases with 1-2-3 and use the Data menu commands to manipulate the information stored in them. This chapter will guide you through the basics of creating and working with a small database. 1-2-3 databases are constructed on the same worksheet screen that you create spreadsheets on. As a matter of fact, you'll use the same commands for placing and editing data in a database that you use when working with spreadsheets.

▪*Creating a Database*

The information in a database is organized into records and fields. A *record* consists of all the information that pertains to one database item. In our phone book example, a record would be one person's name, address, and phone number. A *field* consists of similar data shared by all the records. Again, in our example, a field would be all the addresses in the phone book.

In this section you'll build this small database. It consists of five fields and eight records:

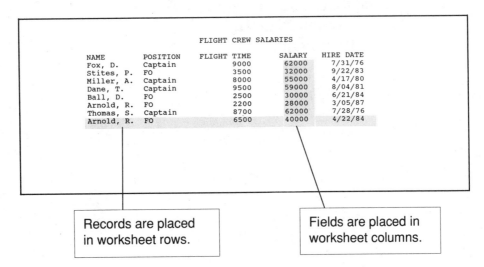

```
                         FLIGHT CREW SALARIES

        NAME         POSITION   FLIGHT TIME     SALARY    HIRE DATE
        Fox, D.      Captain          9000      62000     7/31/76
        Stites, P.   FO               3500      32000     9/22/83
        Miller, A.   Captain          8000      55000     4/17/80
        Dane, T.     Captain          9500      59000     8/04/81
        Ball, D.     FO               2500      30000     6/21/84
        Arnold, R.   FO               2200      28000     3/05/87
        Thomas, S.   Captain          8700      62000     7/28/76
        Arnold, R.   FO               6500      40000     4/22/84
```

Records are placed in worksheet rows.	Fields are placed in worksheet columns.

8

Entering Fields and Records

The *input range* is the complete range of data stored in the database. Except for the database title, the first row of a database input range must consist of the field names. Subsequent rows will contain the database records. Do not place a separating blank row or a row of symbols (such as asterisks) between the field names and the first record. Also, field names must be unique. Do not duplicate a field name in a database. You can have one field name per column, up to 256 columns, and you can have up to 8,191 records.

■ *1*   Start 1-2-3 with a blank worksheet.

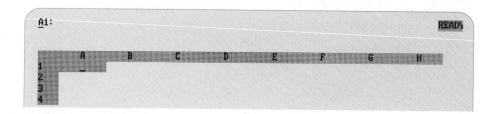

■ *2*   Move the pointer to cell C1 and type the
database title: **'FLIGHT CREW
SALARIES**. Press ⏎.

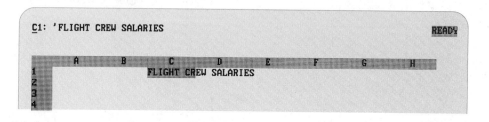

■ *3*   Select /Worksheet, Global, Column-Width.
Type **12** and press ⏎ to widen the columns to
12 characters.

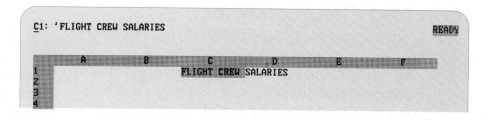

■*4* Move the pointer to cell A3 and place the
field names shown in the screen below in the
displayed cells. Left-align (use the ' prefix)
the labels in columns A and B. Right-align
(use the " prefix) the labels in columns C, D,
and E.

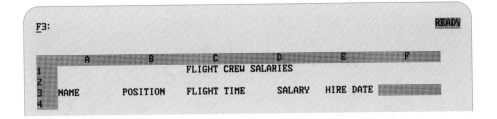

The "Labeling
Your Worksheet"
section of Chapter
2 provides details
on label alignment
and entry.

8

■*5* Move the pointer to cell A4 and enter the database records shown in the screen below in rows 4 through 11. Left-align (use the ' prefix) the labels in columns A and B. Right-align (use the " prefix) the labels in column E. The values in columns C and D will automatically be right-aligned.

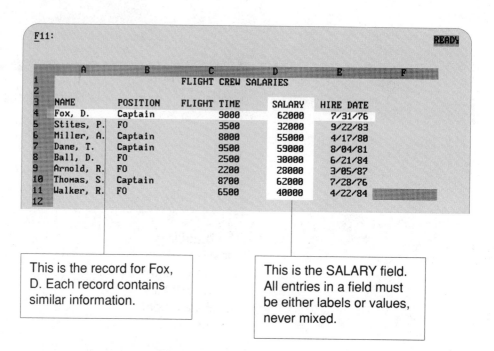

F11:   READY

	A	B	C	D	E	F
1			FLIGHT CREW SALARIES			
2						
3	NAME	POSITION	FLIGHT TIME	SALARY	HIRE DATE	
4	Fox, D.	Captain	9000	62000	7/31/76	
5	Stites, P.	FO	3500	32000	9/22/83	
6	Miller, A.	Captain	8000	55000	4/17/80	
7	Dane, T.	Captain	9500	59000	8/04/81	
8	Ball, D.	FO	2500	30000	6/21/84	
9	Arnold, R.	FO	2200	28000	3/05/87	
10	Thomas, S.	Captain	8700	62000	7/28/76	
11	Walker, R.	FO	6500	40000	4/22/84	
12						

This is the record for Fox, D. Each record contains similar information.

This is the SALARY field. All entries in a field must be either labels or values, never mixed.

■*6* Select /File, Save. Save the file under the name SALARIES. Press ⏎.

■*Sorting the Database*

The /Data, Sort command lets you arrange, or sort, the database records in any order you wish. For example, in the sample database created in the last exercise, you can arrange the data according to salary amounts, flight time, position, or by the date (if you convert the date displays to the Julian date numbers). 1-2-3 can arrange the records in ascending or descending order. *Ascending* order arranges data alphabetically from A to Z or numerically from the lowest number to the highest. *Descending* order arranges data in the reverse direction, from Z to A and from the highest number to the lowest.

There are two keys for sorting database records—the primary key and the secondary key. The *primary key* is used to sort records according to a selected field. The *secondary key* is used to further sort the records that were sorted by the primary key. The following two examples show you how to use these two keys.

Using the Primary Key

Let's sort the database alphabetically, by name. The SALARIES.WK1 file should be on the screen.

8

> Sorting database records makes it easier to locate, organize, and work with related database entries.

■ *1* Select /Data. This is the Data menu.

Creates a table of values.

Locates records that conform to a specified criteria.

Determines the relationship between variables and is used to predict possible future data based on current data.

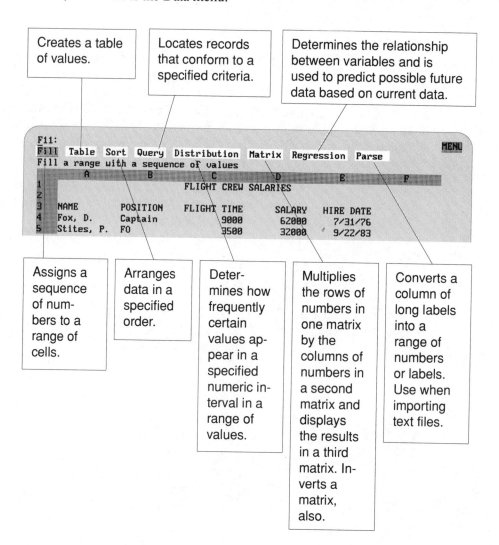

```
F11:
Fill  Table  Sort  Query  Distribution  Matrix  Regression  Parse        MENU
Fill a range with a sequence of values
        A            B           C            D        E           F
1                              FLIGHT CREW SALARIES
2
3   NAME         POSITION    FLIGHT TIME    SALARY   HIRE DATE
4   Fox, D.      Captain          9000      62000    7/31/76
5   Stites, P.   FO               3500      32000    9/22/83
```

Assigns a sequence of numbers to a range of cells.

Arranges data in a specified order.

Determines how frequently certain values appear in a specified numeric interval in a range of values.

Multiplies the rows of numbers in one matrix by the columns of numbers in a second matrix and displays the results in a third matrix. Inverts a matrix, also.

Converts a column of long labels into a range of numbers or labels. Use when importing text files.

■2   Select Sort, Data-Range.

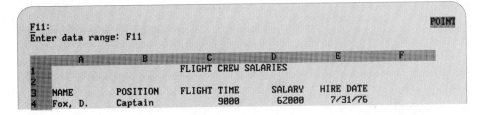

```
F11:                                                              POINT
Enter data range: F11

        A           B           C           D           E        F
1                      FLIGHT CREW SALARIES
2
3   NAME        POSITION    FLIGHT TIME    SALARY   HIRE DATE
4   Fox, D.     Captain          9000      62000     7/31/76
```

■3   Move the pointer to cell E11, press ⌐.⌐
      (period), and move the pointer to cell A4.

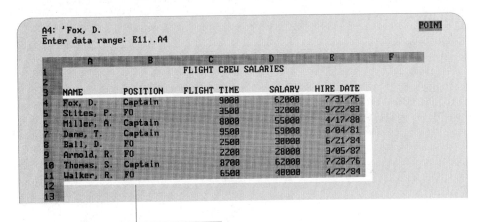

```
A4: 'Fox, D.                                                      POINT
Enter data range: E11..A4

        A           B           C           D           E        F
1                      FLIGHT CREW SALARIES
2
3   NAME        POSITION    FLIGHT TIME    SALARY   HIRE DATE
4   Fox, D.     Captain          9000      62000     7/31/76
5   Stites, P.  FO               3500      32000     9/22/83
6   Miller, A.  Captain          8000      55000     4/17/80
7   Dane, T.    Captain          9500      59000     8/04/81
8   Ball, D.    FO               2500      30000     6/21/84
9   Arnold, R.  FO               2200      28000     3/05/87
10  Thomas, S.  Captain          8700      62000     7/28/76
11  Walker, R.  FO               6500      40000     4/22/84
12
13
```

Do not include the
field names when
designating the data
range.

8

■4 ⮐

```
F11:
Data-Range  Primary-Key  Secondary-Key  Reset  Go  Quit        MENU
Select records to be sorted
                          ─── Sort Settings ───
   Data range:      A4..E11

   Primary key:
     Field (column)
     Sort order

   Secondary key:
     Field (column)
     Sort order
```

The range is displayed on the Sort
Settings sheet.

■5   Select Primary-Key to specify the primary
      field on which you want to sort the database.

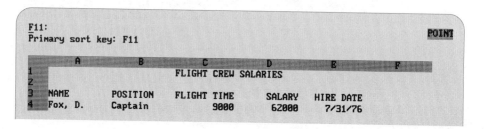

```
F11:
Primary sort key: F11                                          POINT

      A            B           C          D          E         F
1
2                          FLIGHT CREW SALARIES
3  NAME         POSITION   FLIGHT TIME    SALARY    HIRE DATE
4  Fox, D.      Captain          9000     62000     7/31/76
```

■*6* Type **A1** and press ⏎. The database names
are located in column A. Typing the name of
any cell in this column would work. You are
asked for the sort order.

```
F11:                                                                   EDIT
Primary sort key: A1                        Sort order (A or D): D
                              ┌───── Sort Settings ─────
    Data range:        A4..E11

    Primary key:
      Field (column)  A1..A1
      Sort order

    Secondary key:
      Field (column)
      Sort order

 11  Walker, R.  FO              6500       40000       4/22/84
```

■*7* Type **A** (for *ascending*) and press ⏎.

```
F11:                                                                   MENU
Data-Range  Primary-Key  Secondary-Key  Reset  Go  Quit
Specify primary order for records
                              ┌───── Sort Settings ─────
    Data range:        A4..E11

    Primary key:
      Field (column)  A1..A1
      Sort order      Ascending

    Secondary key:
      Field (column)
      Sort order
```

The primary sort field and sort order are
displayed on the Sort Settings sheet.

8

■8   Select Go. The database is now in alphabetical order.

```
F11:                                                          READY

           A          B          C          D          E        F
 1                          FLIGHT CREW SALARIES
 2
 3   NAME          POSITION   FLIGHT TIME   SALARY    HIRE DATE
 4   Arnold, R.    FO             2200      28000      3/05/87
 5   Ball, D.      FO             2500      30000      6/21/84
 6   Dane, T.      Captain        9500      59000      8/04/81
 7   Fox, D.       Captain        9000      62000      7/31/76
 8   Miller, A.    Captain        8000      55000      4/17/80
 9   Stites, P.    FO             3500      32000      9/22/83
10   Thomas, S.    Captain        8700      62000      7/28/76
11   Walker, R.    FO             6500      40000      4/22/84
12
```

Using the Secondary Key

The secondary key allows you to perform a secondary sort within the records sorted according to the primary key. For example, if you sort your database by the POSITION and SALARY fields, the positions (in this case, *Captain* and *FO*) are first grouped alphabetically. These positions are then sorted by the salary amounts. The following exercise illustrates this concept. The SALARY database should still be on the screen.

■1   Select /Data, Sort, Primary-Key.

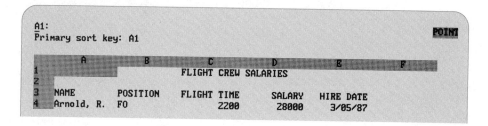

```
A1:                                                          POINT
Primary sort key: A1

           A          B          C          D          E        F
 1                          FLIGHT CREW SALARIES
 2
 3   NAME          POSITION   FLIGHT TIME   SALARY    HIRE DATE
 4   Arnold, R.    FO             2200      28000      3/05/87
```

■*2*　Move the cursor to any cell in column B that
contains the POSITION field and press ⏎.

```
F11:                                                                    EDIT
Primary sort key: B1                        Sort order (A or D): A
                         ─────────── Sort Settings ───────────
     Data range:        A4..E11

     Primary key:
       Field (column)   B1..B1
       Sort order       Ascending

     Secondary key:
       Field (column)
       Sort order
```

■*3*　Type **A** and press ⏎ to select ascending
order.

```
F11:                                                                    MENU
Data-Range  Primary-Key  Secondary-Key  Reset  Go  Quit
Specify primary order for records
                         ─────────── Sort Settings ───────────
     Data range:        A4..E11

     Primary key:
       Field (column)   B1..B1
       Sort order       Ascending

     Secondary key:
       Field (column)
       Sort order
```

8

■*4*   Select Secondary-Key.

■*5*   Move the pointer to any cell in column D,
which contains the SALARY field, and
press ⏎ .

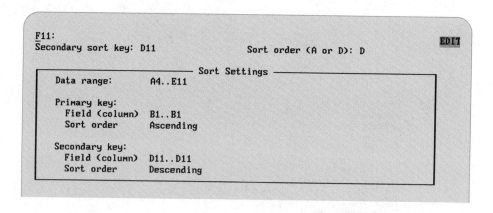

■6   Type **A** and press ⏎ to select ascending
order.

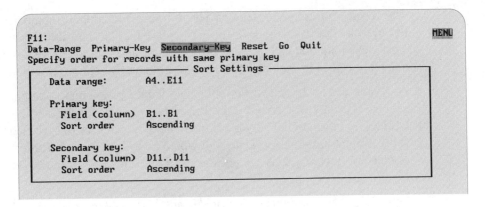

■7   Select Go to sort the database.

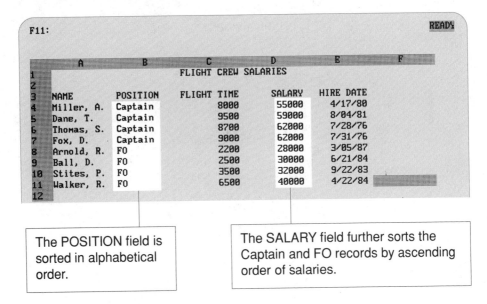

The POSITION field is sorted in alphabetical order.

The SALARY field further sorts the Captain and FO records by ascending order of salaries.

8

■*Numbering Database Entries*

The /Data, Fill command allows you to place sequentially numbered values throughout a specified range of cells. You place the starting value for the numerical series in the first cell of the specified range, and subsequent values are automatically placed in each cell of the range, column by column, from left to right.

An exotic use of the /Data, Fill command would be to create a calendar of sequential dates by first entering the Julian date number for the starting date and telling 1-2-3 to automatically place the remaining dates into a specified range of cells. A more basic use of /Data, Fill would be to assign identification numbers to database records. This would make it easier, in some instances, to locate a specific database entry.

Let's assign identification numbers to the individual pilot records in the SALARIES database.

■*1*   Move the pointer to cell F11 and select
/Data, Fill.

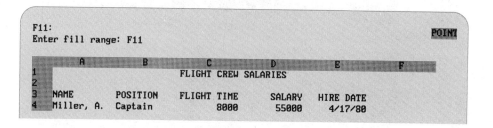

■*2*   [.] (period) to anchor the range and move
the pointer to cell F4. This is the *fill range*
(the range of cells to be "filled" by numbers).

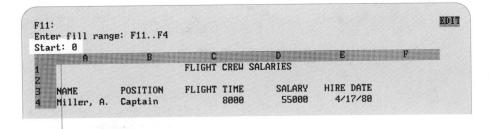

```
F4:                                                                        POINT
Enter fill range: F11..F4

          A            B           C           D           E          F
1                               FLIGHT CREW SALARIES
2
3   NAME          POSITION    FLIGHT TIME    SALARY     HIRE DATE
4   Miller, A.    Captain         8000       55000      4/17/80
5   Dane, T.      Captain         9500       59000      8/04/81
6   Thomas, S.    Captain         8700       62000      7/28/76
7   Fox, D.       Captain         9000       62000      7/31/76
8   Arnold, R.    FO              2200       28000      3/05/87
9   Ball, D.      FO              2500       30000      6/21/84
10  Stites, P.    FO              3500       32000      9/22/83
11  Walker, R.    FO              6500       40000      4/22/84
12
13
```

■*3*   [↵]

```
F11:                                                                        EDIT
Enter fill range: F11..F4
Start: 0
          A            B           C           D           E          F
1                               FLIGHT CREW SALARIES
2
3   NAME          POSITION    FLIGHT TIME    SALARY     HIRE DATE
4   Miller, A.    Captain         8000       55000      4/17/80
```

This is the start value—the
first number in the range.

■*4*   Type **100** and press ⏎.

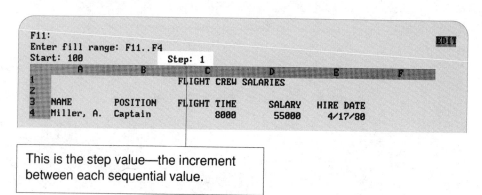

This is the step value—the increment
between each sequential value.

■*5*   ⏎ to sequentially increase the numbers by 1.

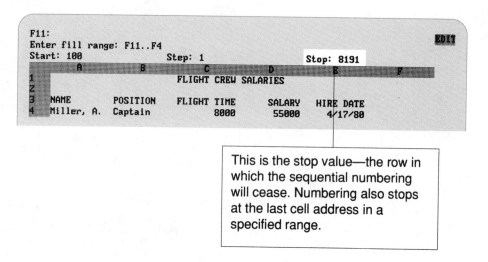

This is the stop value—the row in
which the sequential numbering
will cease. Numbering also stops
at the last cell address in a
specified range.

■6 ⏎ It is not necessary to enter a stop value,
since 1-2-3 will automatically stop numbering
in cell F11, the end of the input range.

```
F11: 107                                                    READY

          A          B          C          D          E          F
 1                        FLIGHT CREW SALARIES
 2
 3   NAME       POSITION   FLIGHT TIME    SALARY   HIRE DATE
 4   Miller, A. Captain         8000      55000     4/17/80       100
 5   Dane, T.   Captain         9500      59000     8/04/81       101
 6   Thomas, S. Captain         8700      62000     7/28/76       102
 7   Fox, D.    Captain         9000      62000     7/31/76       103
 8   Arnold, R. FO              2200      28000     3/05/87       104
 9   Ball, D.   FO              2500      30000     6/21/84       105
10   Stites, P. FO              3500      32000     9/22/83       106
11   Walker, R. FO              6500      40000     4/22/84       107
12
```

■7 Move the pointer to cell F3 and type in this
label: **"IDENT #**. This column of numbers is
the identification number field for this
database.

8

```
F3: "IDENT #                                                 READY

          A          B          C          D          E          F
 1                        FLIGHT CREW SALARIES
 2
 3   NAME       POSITION   FLIGHT TIME    SALARY   HIRE DATE   IDENT #
 4   Miller, A. Captain         8000      55000     4/17/80       100
 5   Dane, T.   Captain         9500      59000     8/04/81       101
```

■8 Save the database with the /File, Save,
Replace command.

Constructing the Input,
▪Criteria, and Output Ranges

To search or *query* the database is to ask 1-2-3 to look for a specific record or a group of records within the database and to place them in a list so they may be reviewed. For example, you can ask 1-2-3 to list all the Captains that make over $60,000. Or, you can ask for a list of all pilots with flight time between 3,000 and 8,000 hours.

Before you can query a database, however, you must construct three ranges: the input range, the criteria range, and the output range. The *input range* consists of the database records that you want 1-2-3 to search through. The SALARY database you just created can be used as an input range. The *criteria* range is where you enter the data that you want 1-2-3 to find in the input range. The *output range* is where 1-2-3 places the data that is found in the search.

In the following exercises, we'll use the SALARY database you just created to establish all three of these ranges. Then, we'll apply some basic query commands to the database.

Creating the Criteria
and Output Range Headings

The first step to querying the database is to create headings for the criteria and output ranges. The criteria range must contain not only the row containing the headings, but also an additional row where the search data is entered. Both the criteria and output ranges must have column headings that exactly match the field names of the input range.

Let's use the /Copy command to place a copy of the input range field names into rows 13 and 16.

■ *1* Move the pointer to cell A3 and select /Copy.

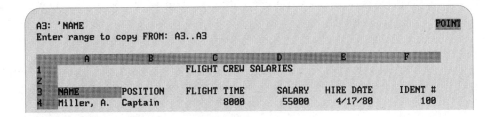

```
A3: 'NAME                                                              POINT
Enter range to copy FROM: A3..A3

         A            B          C          D          E          F
1                              FLIGHT CREW SALARIES
2
3    NAME         POSITION  FLIGHT TIME     SALARY   HIRE DATE   IDENT #
4    Miller, A.   Captain          8000      55000    4/17/80       100
```

■ *2* Move the pointer to cell F3 and press ⏎.

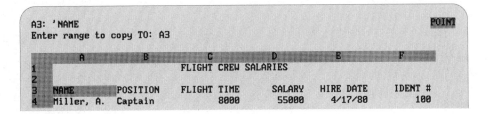

```
A3: 'NAME                                                              POINT
Enter range to copy TO: A3

         A            B          C          D          E          F
1                              FLIGHT CREW SALARIES
2
3    NAME         POSITION  FLIGHT TIME     SALARY   HIRE DATE   IDENT #
4    Miller, A.   Captain          8000      55000    4/17/80       100
```

■ *3* Type **A13** and press ⏎ to place the criteria
range column headings in row 13.

8

```
10   Stites, P.   FO               3500      32000    9/22/83       106
11   Walker, R.   FO               6500      40000    4/22/84       107
12
13   NAME         POSITION  FLIGHT TIME     SALARY   HIRE DATE   IDENT #
14
15
16
17
```

■*4* Repeat steps 1-3 (except in step 3, type **A16**)
to place another copy of the input range field
names in row 16.

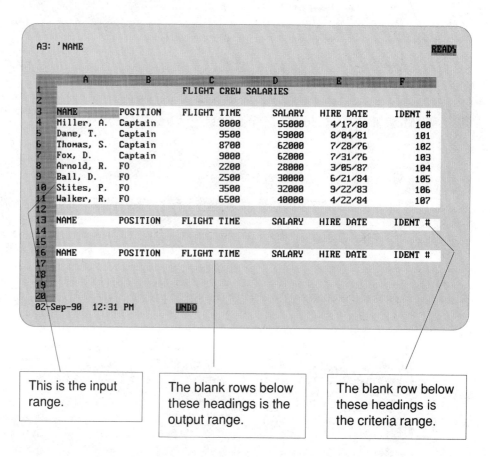

This is the input range.

The blank rows below these headings is the output range.

The blank row below these headings is the criteria range.

■*5* Select /File, Save, press ⏎, and select
Replace to save the worksheet.

∎*Selecting the Query Ranges*

Now that the criteria and output ranges have column headings that exactly match the input range headings, you need to select the input range of data to be searched, the criteria range, and the output range. Let's do that now. If the query results on your screen should differ from what you see in these exercises, use the /File, Retrieve command to retrieve the original version of the database, and then start over.

∎ *1*   Select /Data, Query.

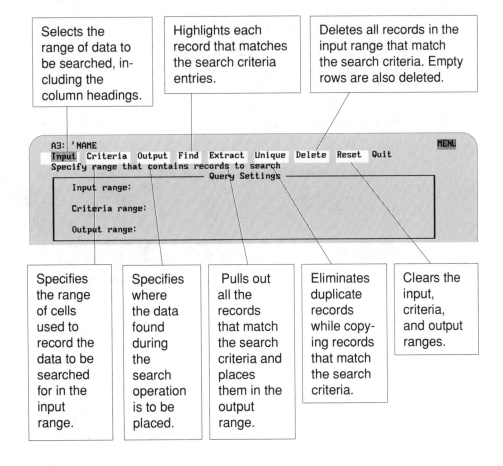

Selects the range of data to be searched, including the column headings.

Highlights each record that matches the search criteria entries.

Deletes all records in the input range that match the search criteria. Empty rows are also deleted.

```
A3: 'NAME                                                    MENU
  Input  Criteria  Output  Find  Extract  Unique  Delete  Reset  Quit
  Specify range that contains records to search
                          Query Settings
     Input range:
     Criteria range:
     Output range:
```

Specifies the range of cells used to record the data to be searched for in the input range.

Specifies where the data found during the search operation is to be placed.

Pulls out all the records that match the search criteria and places them in the output range.

Eliminates duplicate records while copying records that match the search criteria.

Clears the input, criteria, and output ranges.

8

■*2* Select Input.

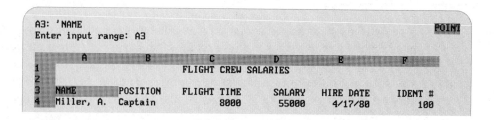

```
A3: 'NAME                                                        POINT
Enter input range: A3

        A           B           C           D           E           F
1                               FLIGHT CREW SALARIES
2
3     NAME          POSITION    FLIGHT TIME     SALARY    HIRE DATE   IDENT #
4     Miller, A.    Captain         8000        55000      4/17/80      100
```

■*3* With the pointer in cell A3, press [.]
      (period) and move the pointer to cell F11.
      This designates the entire database as the
      input range (including the column headings).

```
F11: 107                                                        POINT
Enter input range: A3..F11

        A           B           C           D           E           F
1                               FLIGHT CREW SALARIES
2
3     NAME          POSITION    FLIGHT TIME     SALARY    HIRE DATE   IDENT #
4     Miller, A.    Captain         8000        55000      4/17/80      100
5     Dane, T.      Captain         9500        59000      8/04/81      101
6     Thomas, S.    Captain         8700        62000      7/28/76      102
7     Fox, D.       Captain         9000        62000      7/31/76      103
8     Arnold, R.    FO              2200        28000      3/05/87      104
9     Ball, D.      FO              2500        30000      6/21/84      105
10    Stites, P.    FO              3500        32000      9/22/83      106
11    Walker, R.    FO              6500        48000      4/22/84      107
12
13    NAME          POSITION    FLIGHT TIME     SALARY    HIRE DATE   IDENT #
```

■*4* ⏎

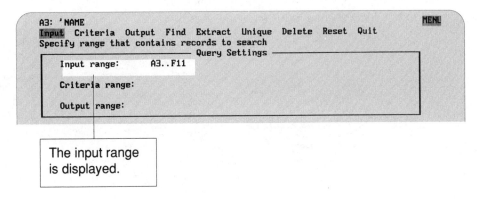

The input range
is displayed.

■*5* Select Criteria.

8

■6   Type **A13..F14** and press ⏎. You must
      specify the column headings, plus at least one
      additional row that will contain the search
      criteria (in this case, row 14).

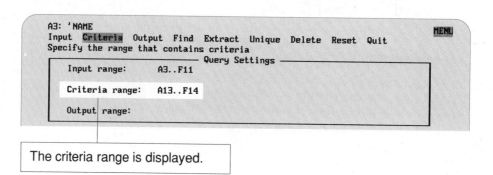

The criteria range is displayed.

■7   Select Output.

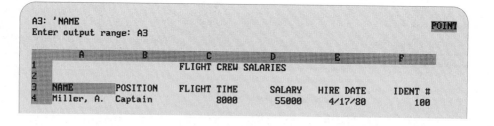

Note *Output Range* When selecting the output range, specify only the row containing the output range headings if there are no cell entries below the output range headings. Should these cell entries exist, specify a specific number of rows that will prevent the output data from overwriting the existing data.

■ *8*   Type **A16..F16** and press ⏎.

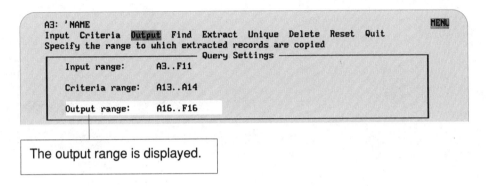

The output range is displayed.

■ *9*   Select Quit to return to the database.

■*Specifying the Search Criteria*

Now that you have selected the input, criteria, and output ranges, it's time to specify the criteria that 1-2-3 will use when searching the database. You can write criterion in order to search for matching labels, values, and formulas. You can write formulas that use logical operators like #AND# and #OR#. And you can use wild cards (*, ?, and ~) to search for items when you aren't exactly sure of the spelling. Let's look at a few examples.

8

Writing a Single Criteria

Let's search for all the pilots that work in the FO (First Officer) position.

■ *1*   Move the pointer to cell B14. Type **FO** and press ⏎. The search criteria must be an *exact* match of the database data, including upper- and lowercase letters.

	NAME	POSITION	FLIGHT TIME	SALARY	HIRE DATE	IDENT #
10	Stites, P.	FO		3500	32000	9/22/83	106
11	Walker, R.	FO		6500	40000	4/22/84	107
12							
13	NAME	POSITION	FLIGHT TIME	SALARY	HIRE DATE	IDENT #
14		FO					
15							
16	NAME	POSITION	FLIGHT TIME	SALARY	HIRE DATE	IDENT #
17							

■ *2*   Select /Data, Query, Extract.

	NAME	POSITION	FLIGHT TIME	SALARY	HIRE DATE	IDENT #
13	NAME	POSITION	FLIGHT TIME	SALARY	HIRE DATE	IDENT #
14		FO					
15							
16	NAME	POSITION	FLIGHT TIME	SALARY	HIRE DATE	IDENT #
17	Arnold, R.	FO	2200	28000	3/05/87	104
18	Ball, D.	FO	2500	30000	6/21/84	105
19	Stites, P.	FO	3500	32000	9/22/83	106
20	Walker, R.	FO	6500	40000	4/22/84	107

02-Sep-90 12:41 PM

All four records from the input range that match the FO criteria are copied into the output range.

Note   If there is no criterion entered in the criteria range, and you use the Extract command, *all* the records in the input range will be copied into the output range.

■ *3*   Select Quit to return to the worksheet.

Writing Multiple Criteria

You have the FO criteria already entered in cell B14. Let's add a second criteria to the same row. This means that a record must match both these criterion before it will appear in the output range. Let's enter a formula criteria in cell C14 to see which FOs have more than 3000 flight hours.

■ *1*   Move the pointer to cell C14. Type
+C4>3000 and press ⏎. (+C4>3000
means: search for all FOs with greater
than 3000 flight hours. See the note below.)

	NAME	POSITION	FLIGHT TIME	SALARY	HIRE DATE	IDENT #
10	Stites, P.	FO	3500	32000	9/22/83	106
11	Walker, R.	FO	6500	40000	4/22/84	107
12						
13	NAME	POSITION	FLIGHT TIME	SALARY	HIRE DATE	IDENT #
14		FO	1			
15						
16	NAME	POSITION	FLIGHT TIME	SALARY	HIRE DATE	IDENT #
17	Arnold, R.	FO	2200	28000	3/05/87	104

The number 1 means that the first record in the database matches. A 0 here would indicate that the first record did not match. This is only incidental information and does not affect the query operation.

Note   When searching for values using a formula with logical operators (<, >, #AND#, #OR#, and so on), you must specify the first cell address in the corrosponding field to be searched. In the above example, cell C4 is the first cell in the FLIGHT TIME field.

8

■*2* Select /Data, Query, Extract. The two items
that meet the multiple criterion appear in the
output range.

```
13 NAME       POSITION    FLIGHT TIME      SALARY   HIRE DATE   IDENT #
14            FO                     1
15
16 NAME       POSITION    FLIGHT TIME      SALARY   HIRE DATE   IDENT #
17 Stites, P. FO                  3500      32000    9/22/83      106
18 Walker, R. FO                  6500      40000    4/22/84      107
19
20
   02-Sep-90   12:43 PM
```

■*3* Select Quit to return to the database.

Displaying Criterion Formulas

The number 1 in cell C14 can be replaced with a written formula for greater
clarity. Let's do so, and at the same time, let's include cell D14, since column D
contains values that could be used in formulas in the future.

■*1* Select /Range, Format, Text.

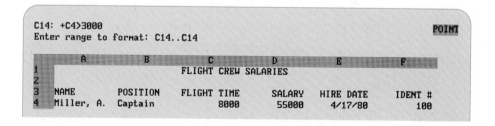

```
C14: +C4>3000                                              POINT
Enter range to format: C14..C14

        A          B          C          D        E          F
1                          FLIGHT CREW SALARIES
2
3  NAME       POSITION    FLIGHT TIME      SALARY   HIRE DATE   IDENT #
4  Miller, A. Captain              8000     55000    4/17/80      100
```

■2 Move the pointer to D14 to expand the range and press ⏎. The formula appears in cell C14. (The (T) in the control panel means text format is on.)

```
10  Stites, P.  FO              3500      32000    9/22/83      106
11  Walker, R.  FO              6500      40000    4/22/84      107
12
13  NAME        POSITION    FLIGHT TIME    SALARY   HIRE DATE   IDENT #
14              FO          +C4>3000
15
16  NAME        POSITION    FLIGHT TIME    SALARY   HIRE DATE   IDENT #
17  Stites, P.  FO              3500      32000    9/22/83      106
```

Erasing Data from the Criteria Range

Use the /Range, Erase command to remove data in the criteria range. Let's erase the FO and +C4>3000 criterion so you can enter new criterion in the following exercises. The pointer should still be in cell C14.

■1 Select /Range, Erase.

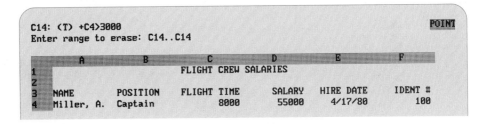

```
C14: (T) +C4>3000                                              POINT
Enter range to erase: C14..C14

         A          B           C          D         E           F
1                           FLIGHT CREW SALARIES
2
3  NAME        POSITION    FLIGHT TIME    SALARY   HIRE DATE   IDENT #
4  Miller, A.  Captain         8000      55000    4/17/80      100
```

8

■ *2*   Type **B14..C14** (the two cells that contain
criteria) and press ⏎. The criteria range
is clear.

10	Stites, P.	FO		3500	32000	9/22/83	106
11	Walker, R.	FO		6500	40000	4/22/84	107
12							
13	NAME	POSITION	FLIGHT TIME		SALARY	HIRE DATE	IDENT #
14							
15							
16	NAME	POSITION	FLIGHT TIME		SALARY	HIRE DATE	IDENT #
17	Stites, P.	FO		3500	32000	9/22/83	106

Writing Multiple Criteria for a Single Field

You can search the database for several different entries in a single field of data.
For example, you can search for records in one field (FLIGHT TIME) that contain 8000 and 9000 hours of flight time. Let's try this. The first step is to increase
the criterion range from the current two rows (13 and 14) to three rows—one
row for the field names, and two rows for the criteria. The pointer should be in
cell C14.

■ *1*   Select /Data, Query, Criteria. The current two
rows in the criteria range are highlighted.

10	Stites, P.	FO		3500	32000	9/22/83	106
11	Walker, R.	FO		6500	40000	4/22/84	107
12							
13	NAME	POSITION	FLIGHT TIME		SALARY	HIRE DATE	IDENT #
14							
15							
16	NAME	POSITION	FLIGHT TIME		SALARY	HIRE DATE	IDENT #
17	Stites, P.	FO		3500	32000	9/22/83	106

■ *2* Move the pointer down one row to include
row 15 and press ⏎.

```
C14: <T>                                                          MENU
   Input  Criteria  Output  Find  Extract  Unique  Delete  Reset  Quit
   Specify the range that contains criteria
   ────────────────────────── Query Settings ──────────────────────────
   │  Input range:       A3..F11                                        │
   │                                                                    │
   │  Criteria range:    A13..F15                                       │
   │                                                                    │
   │  Output range:      A16..F16                                       │
   └────────────────────────────────────────────────────────────────────┘
```

The new criteria range
is displayed.

■ *3* Select Quit. Type **8000** and press ↓. Type
9000 and press ⏎.

10	Stites, P.	FO		3500	32000	9/22/83	106
11	Walker, R.	FO		6500	40000	4/22/84	107
12							
13	NAME	POSITION	FLIGHT TIME		SALARY	HIRE DATE	IDENT #
14				8000			
15				9000			
16	NAME	POSITION	FLIGHT TIME		SALARY	HIRE DATE	IDENT #
17	Stites, P.	FO		3500	32000	9/22/83	106

8

■*4*   Select /Data, Query, Extract. The two pilot
records with 8000 and 9000 hours are placed
in the output range.

13	NAME	POSITION	FLIGHT TIME	SALARY	HIRE DATE	IDENT #
14			8000			
15			9000			
16	NAME	POSITION	FLIGHT TIME	SALARY	HIRE DATE	IDENT #
17	Miller, A.	Captain	8000	55000	4/17/80	100
18	Fox, D.	Captain	9000	62000	7/31/76	103
19						
20						

02-Sep-90   12:51 PM

■*5*   Select Quit, then select /Range, Erase and
erase the criteria in cells C14 and C15.

13	NAME	POSITION	FLIGHT TIME	SALARY	HIRE DATE	IDENT #
14						
15						
16	NAME	POSITION	FLIGHT TIME	SALARY	HIRE DATE	IDENT #
17	Miller, A.	Captain	8000	55000	4/17/80	100
18	Fox, D.	Captain	9000	62000	7/31/76	103
19						
20						

02-Sep-90   12:52 PM   UNDO

■*6*   Select /Data, Query, Criteria and change the
criteria range back to A13..F14.

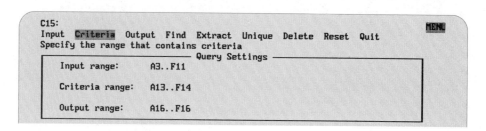

C15:
Input **Criteria** Output Find Extract Unique Delete Reset Quit   MENU
Specify the range that contains criteria
```
────────────────── Query Settings ──────────────────
  Input range:     A3..F11

  Criteria range:  A13..F14

  Output range:    A16..F16
```

> **Note** If you leave blank rows in the criteria range, you will copy the *entire* input range into the output range the next time you use /Data, Query, Extract.

■ 7   Select Quit to return to the database.

Using the Logical Operators #AND# and #OR#

Logical operators are used in search criteria formulas to tell 1-2-3 to match data that meets two or more different conditions. For example, the criterion

    +C4>2500#AND#+C4<8000

tells 1-2-3 to look for pilots that have more than 2500 hours, but less that 8000 hours of flight time. An example of the #OR# operator is

    +C4<3000#OR#+C4>8000

which tells 1-2-3 to look for those pilots with less than 3000 hours or more than 8000 hours of flight time, but none in between.

Let's use both these examples in this exercise. The pointer should be in cell C14 to begin.

8

■ *1*   Type **+C4>2500#AND#+C4<8000** and
press ⏎.

```
C14: (T) +C4>2500#AND#+C4<8000                                    READY

          A           B            C          D          E          F
                                FLIGHT CREW SALARIES
 1
 2
 3    NAME        POSITION    FLIGHT TIME    SALARY   HIRE DATE    IDENT #
 4    Miller, A.  Captain          8000      55000    4/17/80       100
 5    Dane, T.    Captain          9500      59000    8/04/81       101
 6    Thomas, S.  Captain          8700      62000    7/28/76       102
 7    Fox, D.     Captain          9000      62000    7/31/76       103
 8    Arnold, R.  FO               2200      28000    3/05/87       104
 9    Ball, D.    FO               2500      30000    6/21/84       105
10    Stites, P.  FO               3500      32000    9/22/83       106
11    Walker, R.  FO               6500      40000    4/22/84       107
12
13    NAME        POSITION    FLIGHT TIME    SALARY   HIRE DATE    IDENT #
14                            +C4>2500#AN
15
16    NAME        POSITION    FLIGHT TIME    SALARY   HIRE DATE    IDENT #
17    Miller, A.  Captain          8000      55000    4/17/80       100
```

Only part of the long formula appears in the cell.
The full formula appears in the control panel.

■ *2*   Select /Data, Query, Extract. The two pilot
records that have greater than 2500 but less
than 8000 hours appear in the output range.

```
13    NAME        POSITION    FLIGHT TIME    SALARY   HIRE DATE    IDENT #
14                            +C4>2500#AN
15
16    NAME        POSITION    FLIGHT TIME    SALARY   HIRE DATE    IDENT #
17    Stites, P.  FO               3500      32000    9/22/83       106
18    Walker, R.  FO               6500      40000    4/22/84       107
19
20
02-Sep-90  12:55 PM
```

■*3* Select Quit. Type **+C4<2500#OR#+C4>8000**
and press ⏎ .

10	Stites, P.	FO	3500	32000	9/22/83	106
11	Walker, R.	FO	6500	40000	4/22/84	107
12						
13	NAME	POSITION	FLIGHT TIME	SALARY	HIRE DATE	IDENT #
14			+C4<2500#OR			
15						
16	NAME	POSITION	FLIGHT TIME	SALARY	HIRE DATE	IDENT #
17	Dane, T.	Captain	9500	59000	8/04/81	101

The new formula replaces the previous one.

■*4* Select /Data, Query, Extract. The four pilot
records that have less than 2500 or greater
than 8000 hours appear in the output range.

13	NAME	POSITION	FLIGHT TIME	SALARY	HIRE DATE	IDENT #
14			+C4<2500#OR			
15						
16	NAME	POSITION	FLIGHT TIME	SALARY	HIRE DATE	IDENT #
17	Dane, T.	Captain	9500	59000	8/04/81	101
18	Thomas, S.	Captain	8700	62000	7/28/76	102
19	Fox, D.	Captain	9000	62000	7/31/76	103
20	Arnold, R.	FO	2200	28000	3/05/87	104

02-Sep-90 12:57 PM

8

■*5* Select Quit to return to the database.

Using Wild Cards in the Criterion

A *wild card* is a special symbol that you use when you do not know the exact spelling of a label or if you want to type in only a portion of the label to save time. 1-2-3 uses three wild cards: the asterisk (*), the question mark (?), and the tilde (~). The asterisk matches all the characters from the asterisk position to the end of the label. For example, C* matches any label beginning with the letter C and cap* matches labels such as cap, captain, and capsize. The question mark represents a single letter in a label: b?t matches bat, but, bit, and bet, but not both or bath. The tilde is placed in front of a label and tells 1-2-3 to match every label *except* that label: ~Miller, A. matches every record in the database except Miller, A.

Let's use the SALARIES database and extract some records using wild cards.

■ *1* Select /Range, Erase to erase the criteria formula in cell C14. There should be no criteria written in the criteria range.

■ *2* Move the pointer to cell B14, type **Cap*** and press ⏎.

10	Stites, P.	FO		3500	32000	9/22/83	106
11	Walker, R.	FO		6500	40000	4/22/84	107
12							
13	NAME	POSITION	FLIGHT TIME	SALARY	HIRE DATE	IDENT #
14		Cap*					
15							
16	NAME	POSITION	FLIGHT TIME	SALARY	HIRE DATE	IDENT #
17	Dane, T.	Captain	9500	59000	8/04/81	101

■*3*   Select /Data, Query, Extract. All the pilots
with the position of Captain appear in the
output range.

NAME	POSITION	FLIGHT TIME	SALARY	HIRE DATE	IDENT #
13					
14 Cap*					
15					
16 NAME	POSITION	FLIGHT TIME	SALARY	HIRE DATE	IDENT #
17 Miller, A.	Captain	8000	55000	4/17/80	100
18 Dane, T.	Captain	9500	59000	8/04/81	101
19 Thomas, S.	Captain	8700	62000	7/28/76	102
20 Fox, D.	Captain	9000	62000	7/31/76	103

02-Sep-90 12:59 PM

■*4*   Select Quit to return to the database.

Now let's use the ? and * wild cards together.

■*5*   Select /Range, Erase and erase Cap* from
cell B14.

■*6*   Move the pointer to cell A14. Type **??ll*** and
press ⏎.

8

	NAME	POSITION	FLIGHT TIME	SALARY	HIRE DATE	IDENT #
10 Stites, P.	FO		3500	32000	9/22/83	106
11 Walker, R.	FO		6500	40000	4/22/84	107
12						
13 NAME		POSITION	FLIGHT TIME	SALARY	HIRE DATE	IDENT #
14 ??ll*						
15						
16 NAME		POSITION	FLIGHT TIME	SALARY	HIRE DATE	IDENT #
17 Miller, A.		Captain	8000	55000	4/17/80	100

■ 7   Select /Data, Query, Extract.

NAME	POSITION	FLIGHT TIME	SALARY	HIRE DATE	IDENT #
??ll*					
NAME	POSITION	FLIGHT TIME	SALARY	HIRE DATE	IDENT #
Miller, A.	Captain	8000	55000	4/17/80	100
Ball, D.	FO	2500	30000	6/21/84	105

02-Sep-90 01:01 PM

> The names Miller, A. and Ball, D. have two letters before the double l's and therefore match the two ? wild cards. The * matched the remaining letters in the two names.

■ 8   Select Quit to return to the database.

Now use the ~ wild card.

■ 9   Select /Range, Erase to erase the ??ll* criteria from cell A14.

■ 10   Move the pointer to cell B14, type **~Captain**, and press ⏎.

Stites, P.	FO	3500	32000	9/22/83	106
Walker, R.	FO	6500	40000	4/22/84	107
NAME	POSITION	FLIGHT TIME	SALARY	HIRE DATE	IDENT #
	~Captain				
NAME	POSITION	FLIGHT TIME	SALARY	HIRE DATE	IDENT #
Miller, A.	Captain	8000	55000	4/17/80	100

■ *11* Select /Data, Query, Extract. All the pilot
records other than those containing the Captain label are placed into the output range.

NAME	POSITION	FLIGHT TIME	SALARY	HIRE DATE	IDENT #
13 NAME	POSITION	FLIGHT TIME	SALARY	HIRE DATE	IDENT #
14	Captain				
15					
16 NAME	POSITION	FLIGHT TIME	SALARY	HIRE DATE	IDENT #
17 Arnold, R.	FO	2200	28000	3/05/87	104
18 Ball, D.	FO	2500	30000	6/21/84	105
19 Stites, P.	FO	3500	32000	9/22/83	106
20 Walker, R.	FO	6500	40000	4/22/84	107

02-Sep-90 01:03 PM

■ *12* Select Quit to return to the database.

■*Finding and Editing Records*

The /Data, Query, Find command allows you to find specific records that you
may want to edit. You only use the input and criteria ranges when using the Find
command; you do not need to copy data to the output range. Let's find and edit
a record in the input range.

8

■ *1* Move the pointer to cell B14 and select
/Range, Erase to erase the ~Captain criteria.

10 Stites, P.	FO	3500	32000	9/22/83	106
11 Walker, R.	FO	6500	40000	4/22/84	107
12					
13 NAME	POSITION	FLIGHT TIME	SALARY	HIRE DATE	IDENT #
14					
15					
16 NAME	POSITION	FLIGHT TIME	SALARY	HIRE DATE	IDENT #
17 Arnold, R.	FO	2200	28000	3/05/87	104

■2 Type **Captain** and press ⏎.

10	Stites, P.	FO		3500	32000	9/22/83	106
11	Walker, R.	FO		6500	40000	4/22/84	107
12							
13	NAME	POSITION	FLIGHT TIME	SALARY	HIRE DATE	IDENT #
14		Captain					
15							
16	NAME	POSITION	FLIGHT TIME	SALARY	HIRE DATE	IDENT #
17	Arnold, R.	FO		2200	28000	3/05/87	104

■3 Select /Data, Query, Find.

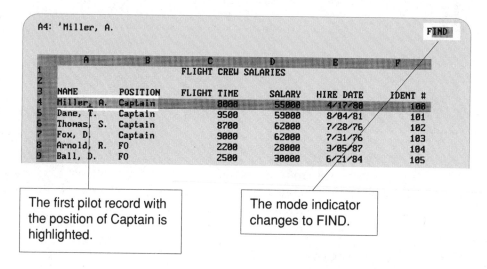

The first pilot record with the position of Captain is highlighted.

The mode indicator changes to FIND.

Note *Cursor Movement for Editing* Use ⬅ and ➡ to move the cursor between cells. Use ⬆ and ⬇ to move the highlight between records.

■*4*   ⬇ and move the highlight to row 6
(Thomas, S.).

```
A6: 'Thomas, S.                                                      FIND

             A          B          C          D          E          F
   1                              FLIGHT CREW SALARIES
   2
   3   NAME       POSITION   FLIGHT TIME      SALARY   HIRE DATE    IDENT #
   4   Miller, A. Captain          8000       55000    4/17/80        100
   5   Dane, T.   Captain          9500       59000    8/04/81        101
   6   Thomas, S. Captain          8700       62000    7/28/76        102
   7   Fox, D.    Captain          9000       62000    7/31/76        103
   8   Arnold, R. FO               2200       28000    3/05/87        104
   9   Ball, D.   FO               2500       30000    6/21/84        105
```

■*5*   F2 (Edit) to place the name in the control
panel for editing.

```
A6: 'Thomas, S.                                                      EDIT
    'Thomas, S._
             A          B          C          D          E          F
   1                              FLIGHT CREW SALARIES
   2
   3   NAME       POSITION   FLIGHT TIME      SALARY   HIRE DATE    IDENT #
   4   Miller, A. Captain          8000       55000    4/17/80        100
```

8

■6 Delete the *h* in *Thomas* so the name reads
Tomas, S. and press ⏎.

```
A6: 'Tomas, S.                                                    FIND

          A           B          C          D         E        F
 1                          FLIGHT CREW SALARIES
 2
 3    NAME        POSITION    FLIGHT TIME   SALARY   HIRE DATE  IDENT #
 4    Miller, A.  Captain         8000      55000    4/17/80    100
 5    Dane, T.    Captain         9500      59000    8/04/81    101
 6    Tomas, S.   Captain         8700      62000    7/28/76    102
 7    Fox, D.     Captain         9000      62000    7/31/76    103
 8    Arnold, R.  FO              2200      28000    3/05/87    104
 9    Ball, D.    FO              2500      30000    6/21/84    105
```

■7 ⎋ESC to exit from the Find mode.

■8 Select Quit and use the /File, Save, Replace
command to save the database.

Performing
■ Calculations with @Functions

There are several @functions you can use to perform calculations on database
values. In this section you'll learn about three of the basic database @functions:
@DCOUNT, @DSUM, and @DAVG. As you know, an @function is a built-in
formula that performs a specific calculation. When writing a database @function,
you must include three location elements: the input range, the field, and the criteria
range. The input range is the database information. The field is a database column

containing field data and is determined by an *offset number*. Each field is numbered from left to right starting with the offset number 0. Field number one is offset 0, field two is offset 1, field three is offset 2, and so on. The criteria range is the same range you created in the previous exercise—the place where you write the criteria data.

Note *The Parts of an @Function* Here is an example of how you would write a database @function:

@DCOUNT(A3..F11,0,A13..F13)

- @DCOUNT is the database @function.
- A3..F11 is the input range.
- 0 is the field offset number, corresponding to the first field (left-most column) in the database.
- A13..F14 is the criteria range.

In this exercise, you'll first label an area of the database according to the functions you want to perform. (These labels could be anything you want; they are not a part of the function, per se.) Then you'll create the database @functions. Finally, you'll execute the @functions using various criteria.

8

■ *1*   If SALARIES.WK1 is not on your screen,
select /File, Retrieve and retrieve it. The
pointer should be in cell B14.

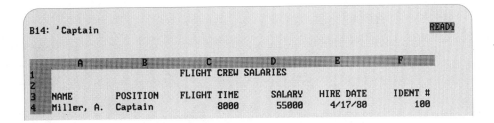

■2   Select /Range, Erase and erase the criteria in
row 14.

10	Stites, P.	FO		3500	32000	9/22/83	106
11	Walker, R.	FO		6500	40000	4/22/84	107
12							
13	NAME	POSITION	FLIGHT TIME		SALARY	HIRE DATE	IDENT #
14							
15							
16	NAME	POSITION	FLIGHT TIME		SALARY	HIRE DATE	IDENT #
17	Arnold, R.	FO		2200	28000	3/05/87	104

■3   Since you will not use the output range in this
exercise, select /Worksheet, Insert, Row, type
A16..A20, and press ⏎ . Five rows are
added between the criteria range and output
range, pushing the output range off the screen.

13	NAME	POSITION	FLIGHT TIME	SALARY	HIRE DATE	IDENT #
14						
15						
16						
17						
18						
19						
20						

02-Sep-90   01:12 PM   UNDO

■4 Move the pointer to cell B16 and type these labels into cells B16, C16, and D16 respectively: **"COUNT**, **"SUM**, and **"AVG**.

■5 Move the pointer to cell B17 and type **@DCOUNT(A3..F11,0,A13..F14)**.

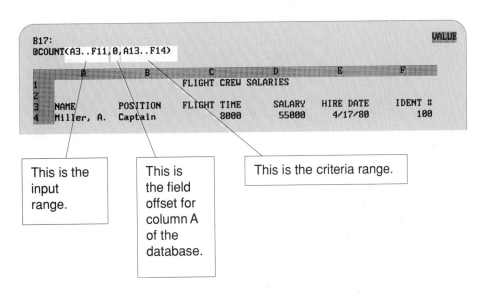

This is the input range.

This is the field offset for column A of the database.

This is the criteria range.

8

■*6* →

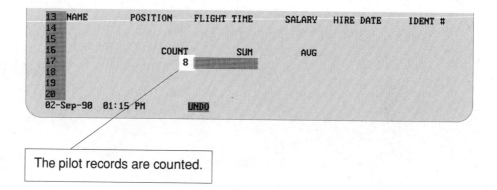

The pilot records are counted.

■*7* Type **@DSUM(A3..F11,2,A13..F14)** and press →.

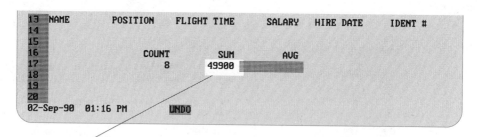

The flight time (for all pilots) in column C (field offset number 2) is totalled.

■ *8*   Type **@DAVG(A3..F11,2,A13..F14)** and
press ⟶.

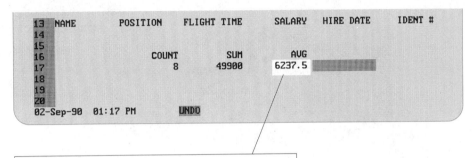

```
13 NAME        POSITION    FLIGHT TIME    SALARY   HIRE DATE    IDENT #
14
15
16              COUNT          SUM         AVG
17               8            49900       6237.5
18
19
20
02-Sep-90  01:17 PM           UNDO
```

The average flight time per pilot is computed.

The @functions used in steps 6, 7, and 8 selected all the records in the database because there is no criteria entered in the criteria range. Now change the criteria.

■ *9*   Move the pointer to cell B14, type **FO**, and
press ⏎. The @function formulas are immediately recalculated according to the new
criteria.

8

```
13 NAME        POSITION    FLIGHT TIME    SALARY   HIRE DATE    IDENT #
14              FO
15
16              COUNT          SUM         AVG
17               4            14700       3675
18
19
20
02-Sep-90  01:18 PM           UNDO
```

There are four FOs with a total of 14,700 hours of flight time, and an average of 3,675 hours per pilot.

■ *10* Type **Captain** and press ⏎. The values are recalculated once again.

13	NAME	POSITION	FLIGHT TIME	SALARY	HIRE DATE	IDENT #
14		Captain				
15						
16		COUNT	SUM	AVG		
17		4	35200	8800		
18						
19						
20						

02-Sep-90 01:19 PM   UNDO

■ *11* Select /File, Save, Replace to save the database.

■*Creating a Database Table*

The /Data, Table command allows you to perform database calculations on several items at the same time. For example, you can create a database table that will simultaneously compute the COUNT, SUM, and AVG values for all the pilots, the Captains, and the FOs from the SALARIES.WK1 database. When creating this table, a database table range must be constructed. This database table range is where the computed information is displayed, and is very similar to the COUNT, SUM, and AVG output range you created in the last exercise in "Performing Calculations with @Functions."

The best way to understand a database table range is to build one.

■ *1* Select /File, Retrieve and retrieve the
SALARIES.WK1 database.

```
B14: 'Captain                                                    READY

          A           B            C            D           E          F
                               FLIGHT CREW SALARIES
 1
 2
 3   NAME        POSITION    FLIGHT TIME     SALARY     HIRE DATE    IDENT #
 4   Miller, A.  Captain           8000      55000      4/17/80        100
```

■ *2* Select /Range, Erase and erase the criteria
from cell B14.

```
 9   Ball, D.    FO                2500      30000      6/21/84        105
10   Stites, P.  FO                3500      32000      9/22/83        106
11   Walker, R.  FO                6500      40000      4/22/84        107
12
13   NAME        POSITION    FLIGHT TIME     SALARY     HIRE DATE    IDENT #
14
15
16               COUNT             SUM          AVG
17                   8            49900       6237.5
18
```

Database table headings are placed in a clear area of the worksheet and the formulas are placed in the cells under the labels. Instead of creating new headings
and formulas, we'll use the headings and formulas from the last exercise. The
currently displayed numerical totals are for all the pilot records in the database.

8

■*3*   Type the following labels in cells A17, A18,
and A19 respectively: **'Pilots**, **'Captain**,
and **'FO**.

	NAME	POSITION	FLIGHT TIME	SALARY	HIRE DATE	IDENT #
13						
14						
15						
16		COUNT	SUM	AVG		
17	Pilots	8	49900	6237.5		
18	Captain					
19	FO					
20						

02-Sep-90   01:22 PM   UNDO

These labels identify the numerical data that will be computed by the formulas
under the COUNT, SUM, and AVG headings. The Captain and FO labels must
exactly match the input range field entries that are being evaluated. If they do not
match, zeros and an ERR message will appear in the table when you try to calculate the data.

The database table structure is now built—headings, formulas, and identifying
labels are in place. Now place the formulas in cells B18 through D19 that will be
used to compute any totals for the Captains and FOs. You will use the /Data,
Table command to compute the new totals in one operation.

■*4*   Select /Data, Table.

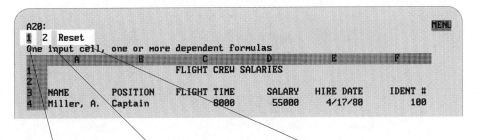

Calculates the results of using one or more formulas that use only one variable (input cell).

Calculates the results of one formula that uses two variables (two input cells).

Clears all the table range and input cell entries. Use when you do not want to save the table range and input cell settings when you save the file.

8

■*5*   Select 1.

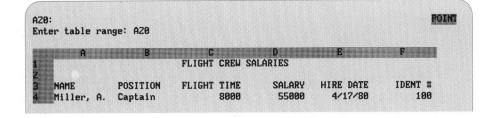

■6 Move the pointer to cell A17, press ⌷
(period), and move the pointer to cell D19.

```
13 NAME          POSITION    FLIGHT TIME      SALARY   HIRE DATE    IDENT #
14
15
16                           COUNT        SUM        AVG
17 Pilots                        8      49900     6237.5
18 Captain
19 FO
20
02-Sep-90  01:25 PM
```

The table range includes the item labels, the formulas,
and the cells in which the calculated results will appear.

■7 ⏎ You are prompted to enter the input cell
location.

```
A20:                                                              POINT
Enter input cell 1: A20

        A         B          C          D         E          F
1                           FLIGHT CREW SALARIES
2
3 NAME          POSITION    FLIGHT TIME      SALARY   HIRE DATE    IDENT #
4 Miller, A.    Captain          8000      55000    4/17/80        100
```

The input cell is always located in a criteria range below the field name for the
variable you want to analyze (in this case the POSITION field, which contains
the Captain and FO labels). You can use an existing criteria range, or create a
separate criteria range for the database table.

■ *8*   Move the pointer to cell B14.

11	Walker, R.	FO		6500	40000	4/22/84	107
12							
13	NAME	POSITION	FLIGHT TIME		SALARY	HIRE DATE	IDENT #
14							
15							
16		COUNT		SUM	AVG		
17	Pilots	8		49900	6237.5		
18	Captains						
19	FOs						

■ *9*   ⏎

13	NAME	POSITION	FLIGHT TIME		SALARY	HIRE DATE	IDENT #
14							
15							
16		COUNT		SUM	AVG		
17	Pilots	8		49900	6237.5		
18	Captain	4		35200	8800		
19	FO	4		14700	3675		
20							

02-Sep-90   02:28 PM   **UNDO**

The formulas are computed and the table is filled with the resultant data for each item.

8

■ *10*   Select /File, Save, Replace to save the database.

Note   *Advanced Table Operations*   This has been an introduction to the /Data, Table command. /Data, Table can be used with spreadsheet worksheets as well as with databases. Refer to your 1-2-3 documentation or to *The Complete Lotus 1-2-3 Release 2.2 Handbook* (SYBEX, 1990) for a more comprehensive discussion of the /Data, Table command.

▪*Determining Data Distribution*

The /Data, Distribution command makes it possible to determine how often certain values occur in a range of values. This is very useful when you want to determine the number of records that fall into certain numerically defined categories.

To use /Data, Distribution you must create a *bin range*, which holds the criteria values used in determining the data distribution. You can use values and formulas in the bin range, each of which must be unique; the values must be in ascending order (lowest value on the top). You must also select a *values range*, which contains the values you want to analyze according to the criteria entered into the bin range.

Let's look at the SALARIES.WK1 file and calculate how many pilots fall into certain salary categories in the SALARY field.

▪ *1*   Select /File, Retrieve and retrieve the
SALARIES.WK1 file.

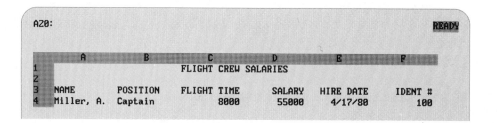

■ *2* Use the arrow keys to move the pointer to
cell G3.

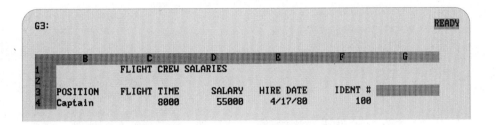

■ *3* Type **"Bin Range** and press ⇥. This titles
the bin range.

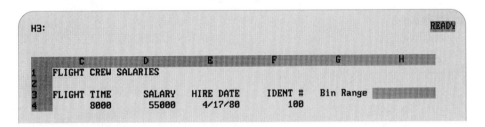

■ *4* Type **"Frequency** and press ⏎. This titles
the frequency range where the distribution
results will appear.

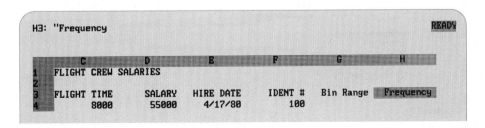

8

■*5*   Move the pointer to cell G4 and type the following values in cells G4, G5, and G6 respectively: **30000**, **45000**, and **60000**.

```
G7:                                                          READY

        C           D          E          F         G          H
1  FLIGHT CREW SALARIES
2
3  FLIGHT TIME      SALARY   HIRE DATE   IDENT #   Bin Range   Frequency
4          8000      55000    4/17/80      100      30000
5          9500      59000    8/04/81      101      45000
6          8700      62000    7/28/76      102      60000
7          9000      62000    7/31/76      103
8          2200      28000    3/05/87      104
9          2500      30000    6/21/84      105
```

These values will be evaluated to see how many salaries in the values range
(which you'll select next) are less than or equal to $30,000 (category 1), greater
than $30,000 and less than or equal to $45,000 (category 2), greater than
$45,000 and less than or equal to $60,000 (category 3), or greater than $60,000
(category 4). You can see why there must be an ascending order of values in the
bin range.

■ *6* Select /Data, Distribution and move the
pointer to cell D4 in order to select the
values range.

```
D4: 55000                                                           POINT
Enter values range: D4

         C              D            E          F          G          H
 1  FLIGHT CREW SALARIES
 2
 3  FLIGHT TIME         SALARY    HIRE DATE    IDENT #   Bin Range  Frequency
 4         8000          55000     4/17/80       100       30000
 5         9500          59000     8/04/81       101       45000
 6         8700          62000     7/28/76       102       60000
 7         9000          62000     7/31/76       103
 8         2200          28000     3/05/87       104
 9         2500          30000     6/21/84       105
10         3500          32000     9/22/83       106
11         6500          40000     4/22/84       107
12
13  FLIGHT TIME         SALARY    HIRE DATE    IDENT #
14
15
16          SUM            AVG
17        49900         6237.5
18        35200           8800
19        14700           3675
20
02-Sep-90   01:34 PM
```

8

■ *7* Press [.] (period) and move the pointer to
cell D11 to highlight the values range.

```
D11: 40000                                                          POINT
Enter values range: D4..D11

         C              D            E          F          G          H
 1  FLIGHT CREW SALARIES
 2
 3  FLIGHT TIME         SALARY    HIRE DATE    IDENT #   Bin Range  Frequency
 4         8000          55000     4/17/80       100       30000
 5         9500          59000     8/04/81       101       45000
 6         8700          62000     7/28/76       102       60000
 7         9000          62000     7/31/76       103
 8         2200          28000     3/05/87       104
 9         2500          30000     6/21/84       105
10         3500          32000     9/22/83       106
11         6500          40000     4/22/84       107
12
13  FLIGHT TIME         SALARY    HIRE DATE    IDENT #
```

■8 ⏎ You are prompted to enter the bin range.

```
G7:                                                                 POINT
Enter values range: D4..D11           Enter bin range: G7

         C            D            E            F            G            H
 1  FLIGHT CREW SALARIES
 2
 3  FLIGHT TIME      SALARY      HIRE DATE    IDENT #     Bin Range   Frequency
 4          8000      55000      4/17/80        100        30000
 5          9500      59000      8/04/81        101        45000
 6          8700      62000      7/28/76        102        60000
 7          9000      62000      7/31/76        103
 8          2200      28000      3/05/87        104
 9          2500      30000      6/21/84        105
10          3500      32000      9/22/83        106
11          6500      40000      4/22/84        107
12
13  FLIGHT TIME      SALARY      HIRE DATE    IDENT #
14
15
16               SUM         AVG
17             49900      6237.5
18             35200        8800
19             14700        3675
20
02-Sep-90   01:35 PM
```

■9 Type **G4..G6** and press ⏎.

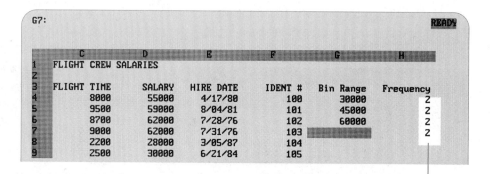

```
G7:                                                                 READY

         C            D            E            F            G            H
 1  FLIGHT CREW SALARIES
 2
 3  FLIGHT TIME      SALARY      HIRE DATE    IDENT #     Bin Range   Frequency
 4          8000      55000      4/17/80        100        30000              2
 5          9500      59000      8/04/81        101        45000              2
 6          8700      62000      7/28/76        102        60000              2
 7          9000      62000      7/31/76        103                          2
 8          2200      28000      3/05/87        104
 9          2500      30000      6/21/84        105
```

The results appear under the Frequency heading.

Two pilots make less than or equal to $30,000; two make more than $30,000 but less than or equal to $45,000; two make more than $45,000 but less than or equal to $60,000; and two make more than $60,000.

■ *10*   Select /File, Save, press ⏎ and select
Replace to save the database.

■*Summary*

In this chapter you learned the basics of creating, sorting, and querying a database. It's important to remember the elements of a database query structure: an input range (you select this from the database itself), a criteria range (include only enough extra rows to accommodate the search criteria), and an output range (where the data found in a search of the database is placed).

You also learned about database @functions—formulas that calculate certain totals of values in the database. You used @functions to create a database table, which also computes the totals for certain values, but does so for more than one database item.

Finally, you learned how to determine the frequency of occurrence of certain database values in a range of values using the /Data, Distribution command. The key elements in determining data distribution are the bin range and values range. Remember, the values range contains the values you want to analyze against the bin range.

8

NINE

Speeding Up Your Work with ◼ Macros

What is a macro? Simply put, a macro is a set of instructions, consisting of 1-2-3 commands and keystrokes, that you create in order to execute specific tasks. Instead of pressing a series of keys or selecting a series of menu items, you can press two macro keys or type a short macro name to automatically do these steps for you. Macros are excellent time savers for performing worksheet procedures that you use regularly. There are many types of macros that can be created—you are limited only by your imagination. For example, you can use macros to place the date in your worksheet, copy a range of cells, type repetitive labels, print worksheets, and save files.

Planning Your Macros

◼

Creating and Running Macros

◼

Creating a Date-Stamp Macro

◼

Debugging a Macro

◼

Remembering Macro Steps with Learn

■*Planning Your Macros*

The first step in creating any macro is planning the actual sequence of key-strokes and commands that you want the macro to execute. You also must plan where to place the macros on your worksheet to insure that inserting or deleting rows and columns won't interfere with the macros. Let's plan the following macros:

Macro Task	Keystrokes
Save an existing file	'/FS~R
Erase a cell	'/RE~
Widen a column to 20	'/WCS20~
Exit 1-2-3 (No edits)	'/QY

Now let's determine the location on the worksheet where you will type in the macros.

■*1*   Select /File, Retrieve and retrieve the
       AUGPL1.WK1 file. Press HOME to return the
       pointer to cell A1.

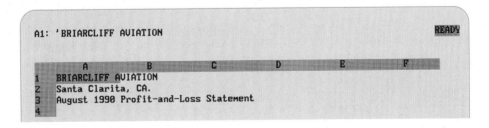

```
A1: 'BRIARCLIFF AVIATION                                    READY

         A          B          C          D          E          F
1  BRIARCLIFF AVIATION
2  Santa Clarita, CA.
3  August 1990 Profit-and-Loss Statement
4
```

9

■2   F5 Type **J23**, and press ↵. This places the
pointer to the right of and below the
worksheet data, therefore avoiding any
problems with the macros if you insert or
delete columns and rows in the worksheet.

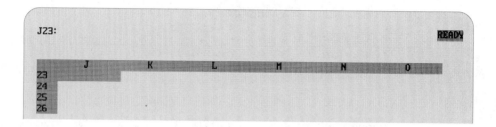

See the section on "Creating a Macro Library" later in this chapter for more information on macro location.

■Creating Macros

There are several steps that must be followed when creating a macro: typing the
macros into the worksheet, documenting the macros, and naming the macros.
The following exercises will take you through each of these steps as you create
a few simple macros.

Typing Macros in the Worksheet

All macro keystrokes are entered into the worksheet cells as labels. Use the '
prefix to insure that 1-2-3 interprets a / or a numerical keystroke as a label, not a
value. Macro commands consist of a series single keystroke characters, each of
which represents a keyboard character or 1-2-3 command. For example, the
macro characters for saving an existing file are '/FS~R. The ' tells 1-2-3 the entry is
a label, the / activates the Main menu, the F and S select the File, Save menu

items, the ~ tells 1-2-3 to press the Enter key, and the R is the Replace menu item. Function keys and pointer-movement keys are enclosed in braces ({ }).

Let's label the column that will contain the different macro steps. Then you'll type in the macros.

■ *1* Move the pointer to cell K23, type **MACRO STEPS**, and press ⬇.

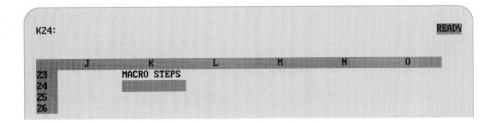

See inside the covers of this book for a list of macro keystroke instructions.

9

■*2*   Type the macro steps shown in the illustration
below in cells K24, K26, K28, and K30.
Be sure to type the apostrophe prefix before
each macro.

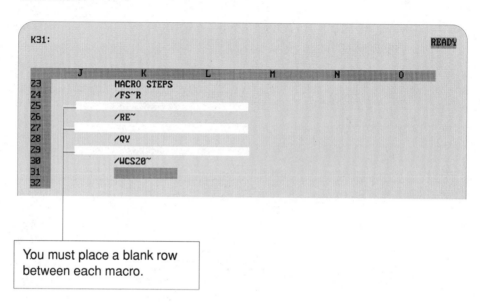

You must place a blank row
between each macro.

1-2-3 executes a macro by starting at the first cell and then moving down that
column until it encounters a blank cell. If you place all the macros on top of each
other, 1-2-3 will execute them all when you select the first one.

Documenting the Macros

Once you've entered the macros on the worksheet, it's helpful to document them
with a short description so you can remember what task the macro was designed
to accomplish. Let's label the column that will contain the descriptions.

■ *1*   Move the pointer to cell L23, type
^DESCRIPTION, and press ⏎.

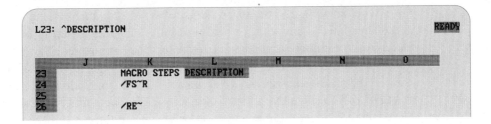

■ *2*   Type the descriptions shown below in the appropriate cells.

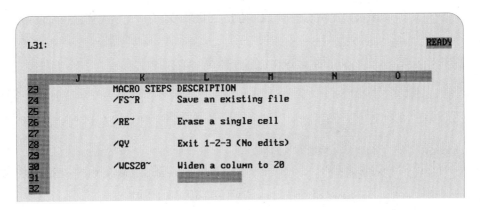

9

■*Naming Macros*

So far you have planned the macro keystrokes, entered them on the worksheet, and documented them with a short description. The next step is to name the macros. You cannot execute the macros unless they are named. Naming macros involves two steps: placing a macro name on the worksheet, then assigning the name to the macro steps so 1-2-3 can run it. You can name individual macros one at a time, or you can name a group of macros at the same time. Let's use both of these methods to name the macros you've created so far.

Naming a Single Macro

Before naming the first macro in column K, let's title the macro name column.

■*1* Move the pointer to cell J23, type **NAME**, and press ⬇.

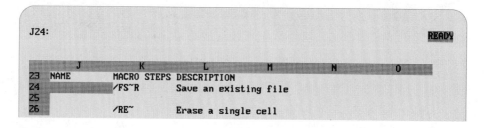

```
J24:                                                            READY

        J           K           L           M         N         O
23  NAME        MACRO STEPS DESCRIPTION
24              /FS~R       Save an existing file
25
26              /RE~        Erase a single cell
```

■*2* In cell J24, type '**\S**, and press ⏎.

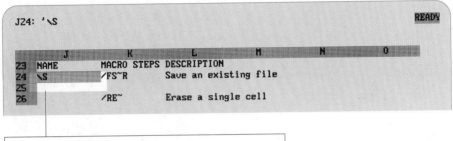

This is the macro name. The \ represents the
Alt key and the S means Save.

When naming macros, try to assign a letter that will remind you of the task being
executed. You may use all the letters of the alphabet plus the 0 (zero) (27 characters in all) when naming a single character macro. (The macro \0 is an
autoexecute macro and is unlike all other macros. The \0 macro automatically
runs when you retrieve a worksheet that contains it.)

■*3* Select /Range, Name, Create to assign the
name to the macro so 1-2-3 can run it.

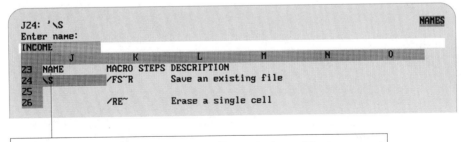

Previously created range names will appear here. These
names include all range names, not just macro range names.

9

■4   Type \S and press ⏎.

```
J24: '\S                                                              POINT
Enter name: \S                        Enter range: J24..J24

        J           K           L           M           N           O
23  NAME        MACRO STEPS  DESCRIPTION
24  \S          /FS~R        Save an existing file
25
26              /RE~         Erase a single cell
```

You are prompted to enter the
name range, which is all the cells
that contain the macro instructions.

■5   Type **K24** (the cell that contains the macro in-
      structions), and press ⏎. The macro is
      named and you return to the worksheet.

Naming a Group of Macros

Now let's place the remaining three macro names on the worksheet. Then you'll assign these names, as a group, to their corresponding macro steps using the /Range, Name, Labels, Right command.

■ *1*

Type the following macro names in cells J26, J28, and J30 respectively: '\E, '\Q, and **COL20**.

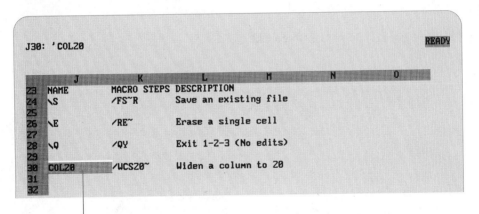

```
J30: 'COL20                                                    READY

          J         K           L            M         N         O
23  NAME        MACRO STEPS DESCRIPTION
24  \S          /FS~R       Save an existing file
25
26  \E          /RE~        Erase a single cell
27
28  \Q          /QY         Exit 1-2-3 (No edits)
29
30  COL20       /WCS20~     Widen a column to 20
31
32
```

You can assign a macro a long name (any name with more than one letter) of up to 15 characters, excluding spaces, commas, semicolons, or periods. You do not need the \ when assigning a long name.

9

■2   Select /Range, Name, Labels, Right to name these three macros at the same time.

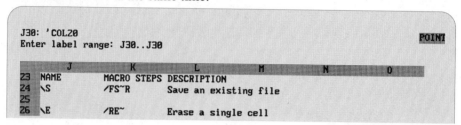

```
J30: 'COL20                                                    POINT
Enter label range: J30..J30

        J         K            L        M       N       O
23  NAME        MACRO STEPS DESCRIPTION
24  \S          /FS~R        Save an existing file
25
26  \E          /RE~         Erase a single cell
```

■3   Move the pointer to cell J26.

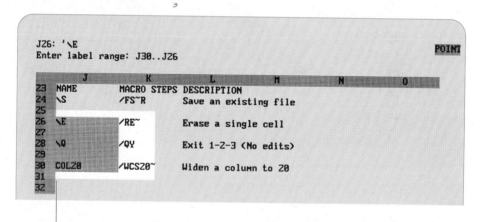

```
J26: '\E                                                       POINT
Enter label range: J30..J26

        J         K            L        M       N       O
23  NAME        MACRO STEPS DESCRIPTION
24  \S          /FS~R        Save an existing file
25
26  \E          /RE~         Erase a single cell
27
28  \Q          /QY          Exit 1-2-3 (No edits)
29
30  COL20       /WCS20~      Widen a column to 20
31
32
```

The /Range, Name, Labels, Right command assigns the macro names in cells J26, J28, and J30 to the macro instructions in cells K26, K28, and K30 because these cells are located to the right of the specified range.

■4 ⏎ The three macros are named and you are
returned to the worksheet.

■*Running Your Macros*

Now that you have planned, created, documented, and named your macros, you
will want to use them. You read earlier that a single keystroke macro is named
with the \ symbol and is executed by holding down the Alt key and pressing the
assigned letter. But what about the macro that has a long name? To execute a
long-name macro, you press ALT F3 (Run) and select the macro name. Let's use
both these methods with the macros you created in the previous exercises.

■1 Move the pointer to cell L30 and press
ALT F3 (Run).

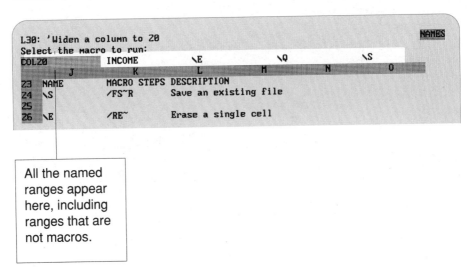

```
L30: 'Widen a column to 20                                          NAMES
Select the macro to run:
COL20          INCOME          \E            \Q           \S
     J       K          L            M         N        O
23 NAME        MACRO STEPS DESCRIPTION
24 \S          /FS~R       Save an existing file
25
26 \E          /RE~        Erase a single cell
```

All the named
ranges appear
here, including
ranges that are
not macros.

9

■2

Select COL20, the macro that widens a
column to 20 characters. Column L is now
expanded.

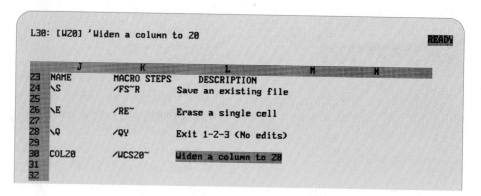

■3 ALT E to erase the contents of cell L30.

■ *4* `ALT` `F4` (Undo) to restore the label.

```
L30: [W20] 'Widen a column to 20                         READY

        J           K              L              M          N
  23  NAME        MACRO STEPS    DESCRIPTION
  24  \S          /FS~R          Save an existing file
  25
  26  \E          /RE~           Erase a single cell
  27
  28  \Q          /QY            Exit 1-2-3 (No edits)
  29
  30  COL20       /WCS20~        Widen a column to 20
  31
  32
```

■ *5* `ALT` `S` to save the worksheet with the new
macros.

■ *6* `ALT` `Q` to exit 1-2-3.

■ *Creating a Date-Stamp Macro*

9

You can create macros that are simple, like the one you've already created, or complex macros involving many steps and functions. Creating a date-stamp macro is an excellent introduction to more complex macros. A date-stamp macro will place the current date into your worksheet. This is handy for dating individual worksheet entries or keeping a record of when a worksheet was last edited.

You use the @NOW function to place the date into a worksheet. 1-2-3 determines the date based on the number of days since January 1, 1900. Time is computed as a fraction of the current day. Twelve noon on September 3, 1990 is represented by the number 33119.5. In order to translate this number into a standard date format, you must use the /Worksheet, Global, Format or /Range, Format, Date command.

Let's add a date-stamp macro to the list of macros in the AUGPL1.WK1 file. Start 1-2-3 if it's not already running.

■ *1*   Select /File, Retrieve and retrieve the AUGPL1.WK1 worksheet.

```
L30: [W20] 'Widen a column to 20                              READY

            J            K            L            M            N
23  NAME         MACRO STEPS     DESCRIPTION
24  \S           /FS~R           Save an existing file
25
26  \E           /RE~            Erase a single cell
27
28  \Q           /QY             Exit 1-2-3 (No edits)
29
30  COL20        /WCS20~         Widen a column to 20
31
32
```

■ *2*   Move the pointer to cell K32 and type the macro keystrokes shown in the illustration below into cells K32, K33, K34, and K35 (be sure to type an apostrophe before each macro):

```
29
30  COL20        /WCS20~         Widen a column to 20
31
32               @NOW
33               {CAL}~
34               /RFD1~
35               /WCS12~
36
37
38
```

The keystrokes you just entered perform the following tasks:

Keystrokes	Task
'@NOW	The date command.
{CAL}~	The F9 function key. (The correct syntax is {CALC}~. You typed it as {CAL}~ in this exercise so you can see how an error is displayed. You'll correct it in the next exercise.)
'/RFD1~	Changes the number into a normal date format.
'/WCS12~	Widens the column to 12 characters.

■3   Move the pointer to cell J32, type **DATE**, and
press ⏎.

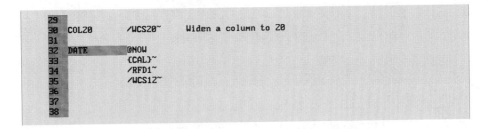

■4   Move the pointer to cell L32 to enter the
description. Type **Enters current date** and
press ⏎.

9

■*5*   Move the pointer to cell K32. Select /Range,
Name, Create.

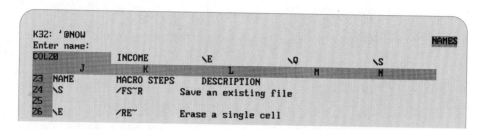

■*6*   Type **DATE** and press ⏎.

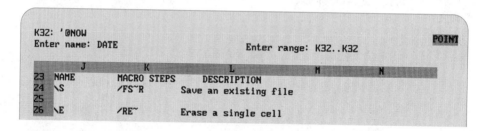

■*7*   Move the pointer to cell K35 (highlighting
cells K32–K35) and press ⏎. The DATE
macro is now named.

■*8*   Move the pointer to cell N32 and press
[ALT][F3] (Name).

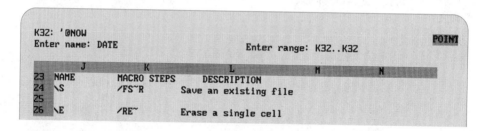

■*9* Select DATE.

```
N32:                                                              ERROR
@NOW

          J             K              L              M        N
 23  NAME          MACRO STEPS      DESCRIPTION
 24  \S            /FS~R            Save an existing file
 25
 26  \E            /RE~             Erase a single cell
 27
 28  \Q            /QY              Exit 1-2-3 (No edits)
 29
 30  COL20         /WCS20~          Widen a column to 20
 31
 32  DATE          @NOW             Enters current date
 33                {CAL}~
 34                /RFD1~
 35                /WCS12~
 36
 37
 38
 39
 40
 41
 42
Unrecognized key/range name {...} (K33)
```

You are alerted to the {CAL}~ mistake with a beep and a descriptive message with the applicable cell name.

The mode indicator displays a flashing error message.

9

■ *10* [ESC] to return to the worksheet. Move on to the next exercise to see how to debug an incorrectly created macro.

Debugging an
■ *Incorrectly Created Macro*

Often, when a macro doesn't execute properly, you will see the error immediately and be able to correct (debug) it right on the worksheet with the [F2] (Edit) key. Sometimes, however, it's not that easy. With 1-2-3 you can use the Step key ([ALT] [F2]) to execute a macro one step at a time so you can check each step for errors.

> **Note** *Some Common Macro Errors* You may find your macro error to be one of the following:
>
> - The Enter key symbol (~) was omitted.
> - Range names or cell addresses were specified that do not exist.
> - A key name was misspelled, for example, {CAL} instead of {CALC}.
> - Formulas or commands contain spaces where they shouldn't.
> - You forgot to assign a name to the macro.
> - A command was omitted from a menu selection sequence.
> - Brackets ([ ]) or parentheses were used around a function or key name instead of braces ({ }).

Let's use the Step mode to debug the DATE macro. The pointer should still be in cell N32.

■ 1   [ALT][F2] (Step). STEP appears on the
status line.

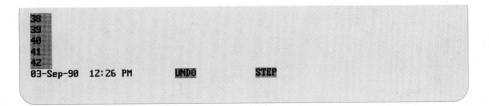

■ 2   [ALT][F3] (Run) and select DATE.

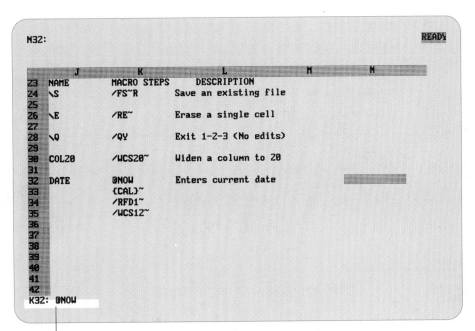

The first instruction in the macro and its location is displayed here. Press the space bar to move through the macro steps one character at a time until you find the error.

9

■*3* @NOW is correct. Press the space bar four
times to move on to the next macro step.

■*4* {CAL} is incorrect. Press CTRL BREAK to stop
running the macro and return to the
worksheet.

■*5* Move the pointer to cell K33. Press F2
(Edit), and edit {CAL}~ to read {CALC}~.

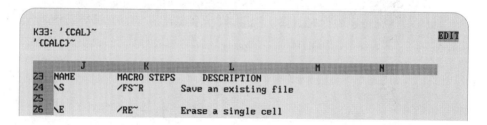

■*6* ⏎ to place {CALC}~ in cell K33.

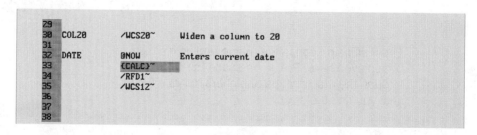

■7 [ALT][F2] to turn the Step mode off.

■8 Move the pointer to cell N32, press [ALT][F3],
and select DATE. The macro now works.

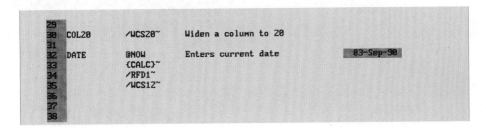

■9 [ALT][E] to erase the date in cell N32.

Using the Learn
■*Feature to Create Macros*

The 1-2-3 Learn feature enables you to create a macro as you type the actual
steps needed to accomplish the 1-2-3 task. An advantage to this method of constructing a macro is that you can spot errors as you are creating the macro steps
because 1-2-3 will alert you immediately to an incorrect entry.

To use Learn, you must specify a *learn range* where the macro steps will be
recorded, activate Learn ([ALT][F5]), go through the sequence of steps for the task
that the macro will execute, turn Learn off, and, finally, name the macro.

Let's redo the DATE macro using the Learn feature. The pointer is in cell N32
on the AUGPL1 worksheet. First you'll specify the learn range.

9

■ *1*   Select /Worksheet, Learn.

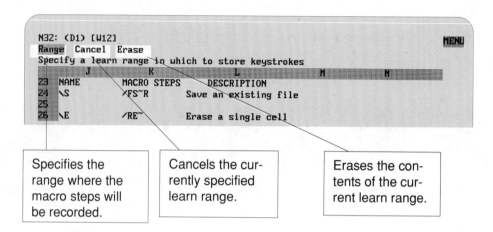

Specifies the range where the macro steps will be recorded.

Cancels the currently specified learn range.

Erases the contents of the current learn range.

■ *2*   Select Range.

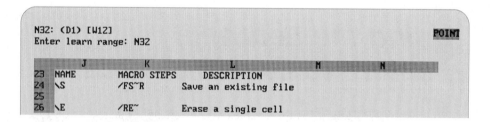

■ *3*   Move the pointer to cell K37, press [.]
(period), and move the pointer to cell K42.

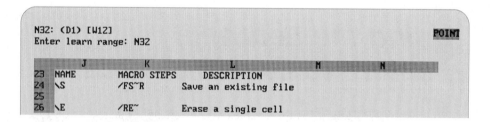

> **Note** *Learn Range Size* Always make the learn range larger than the number of macro steps needed. If it is too small, 1-2-3 will alert you that the range is full and will turn Learn off. If this happens, make the learn range larger, use /Worksheet, Learn, Erase to delete its contents, and then start over from the beginning. If the macro is a very long one, don't delete the contents, just make the range larger and pick up where you left off. Also, a learn range must be contained in one column.

■4   ⏎ to accept the range.

■5   ALT F5 (Learn)

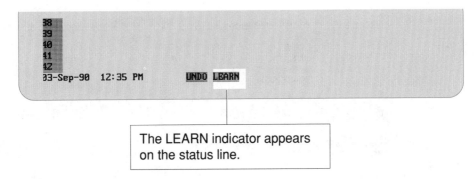

The LEARN indicator appears on the status line.

Now you're ready to go through the steps to create a date-stamp.

■6   Type **@NOW**. (Do *not* press ⏎.)

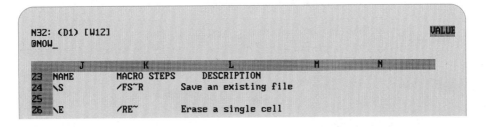

9

■ 7   F9 (Calc)

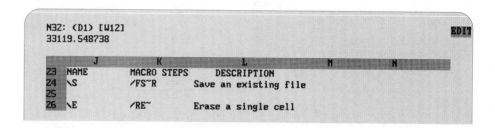

■ 8   ⏎ Select /Range, Format, Date, 1 and
press ⏎.

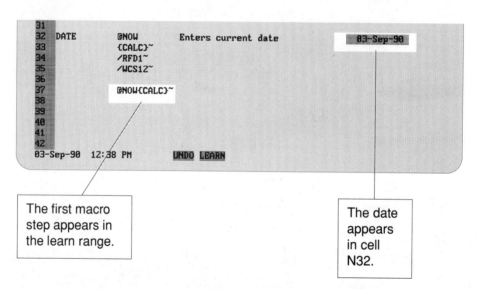

The first macro
step appears in
the learn range.

The date
appears
in cell
N32.

Notice that this is a combined version of steps 1 and 2 from the previously
created date-stamp macro. This version works the same as the earlier one.

■ *9*   Select /Worksheet, Column, Set-Width. Type
12, and press ⏎.

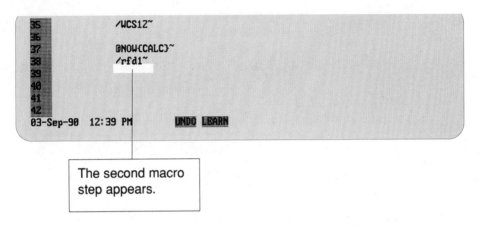

The second macro
step appears.

■ *10*   ALT F5 to turn Learn off, and then move the
pointer to cell M32.

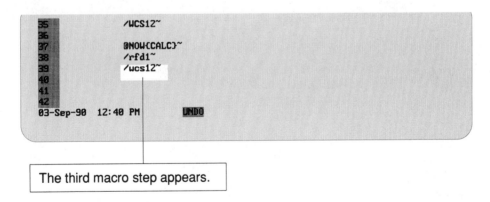

The third macro step appears.

Now you must name the macro.

9

■ *11* Move the pointer to cell K37, select /Range,
Name, Create, and type **NEWDATE**.

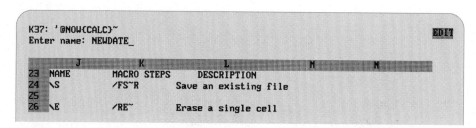

■ *12* ⏎ and move the pointer to cell K39.

■ *13* ⏎ to accept the range. The NEWDATE
macro is created.

■ *14* Move the pointer to cell N32 and press
ALT E to delete the date.

■ *15* `ALT` `F3` (Run), and select NEWDATE.

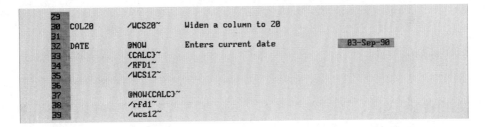

■ *16* `ALT` `S` to save the worksheet.

■ *17* `ALT` `Q` to exit 1-2-3.

■*Creating a Macro Library*

The macros you created in the AUGPL1 worksheet earlier in this chapter only work with that particular worksheet. If you want to use these macros in another worksheet, you have to copy them into the new worksheet with the /File, Combine command you learned about in Chapter 6. This can become confusing and time consuming if you work with many worksheets and use the same macros in all of them.

To facilitate using the same macros with all your worksheets, 1-2-3 has an additional program (such programs are referred to as *add-in* programs) called the Macro Library Manager. The Macro Library Manager lets you create *macro libraries* that consist of one or more macros that are stored in memory (RAM) and in a disk file, called a *library file*.

In this section you'll create a macro libary and edit a macro stored in the library.

9

Note *Steps to Creating a Macro Library* There are three steps in creating and using a macro library:

- Load the Macro Library Manager into memory.
- Invoke the Macro Library Manager.
- Save the macros into the macro library and onto a library file.

Loading the Macro Library Manager into RAM

The file name for the Macro Library Manager add-in is MACROMGR.ADN. It is located on the Install disk. Hard-disk users should have copied this file into the 1-2-3 directory. Floppy-disk users must place the Install disk in one of their floppy-disk drives in order to attach, or load, the Macro Library Manager into memory (RAM).

■ *1* Start 1-2-3 to a blank worksheet. Floppy-disk users place the Install disk in one of your floppy-disk drives.

■ *2* Select /Add-In.

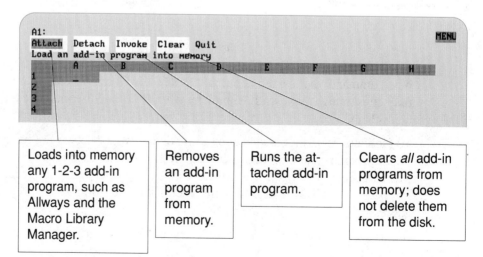

| Loads into memory any 1-2-3 add-in program, such as Allways and the Macro Library Manager. | Removes an add-in program from memory. | Runs the attached add-in program. | Clears *all* add-in programs from memory; does not delete them from the disk. |

■*3*   Select Attach.

```
A1:                                                    FILES
Enter add-in to attach: C:\123\*.ADN
MACROMGR.ADN
        A         B         C         D         E         F         G         H
1
2
3
4
```

All add-ins in the current directory are listed
here. If the add-in you want does not appear
here, press ⌊ESC⌋ once or twice (as necessary)
and type in the new path where the add-in
program (.ADN) is located.

■*4*   Select MACROMGR.ADN.

```
A1:                                                    MENU
No-Key   7  8  9  10
Do not assign add-in to a key
        A         B         C         D         E         F         G         H
1
2
3
4
```

9

Use if you do not
want to assign an
Alt key that will in-
voke the Macro
Library Manager or
another add-in.

Assigns an Alt key combination that will
invoke the Macro Library Manager or
another add-in. You can assign the
⌊ALT⌋⌊F7⌋ , ⌊ALT⌋⌊F8⌋ , ⌊ALT⌋⌊F9⌋ , and ⌊ALT⌋⌊F10⌋ keys
to four different add-ins.

■5 Select 10 to assign the [ALT][F10] key to the
Macro Library Manager.

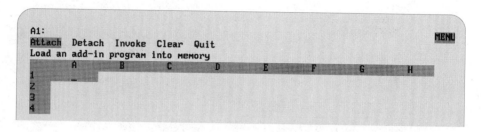

■6 Select Quit to return to the Ready mode. The
Macro Library Manager is now attached into
memory, ready to be called on when needed.

If you want to attach the
Macro Library Manager
automatically whenever
you start 1-2-3, refer to
Chapter 12 in your 1-2-3
documentation where it
discusses the /Worksheet,
Global, Default, Other,
Add-In command.

Invoking the Macro Library Manager and Placing Macros into the Library

You created some basic macros earlier in your AUGPL1 worksheet. Let's activate the Macro Library Manager, and then save and place these macros in a macro library, making them available for use in other worksheets.

■ *1* Select /File, Retrieve and retrieve the AUGPL1.WK1 worksheet. The macros you created earlier are displayed.

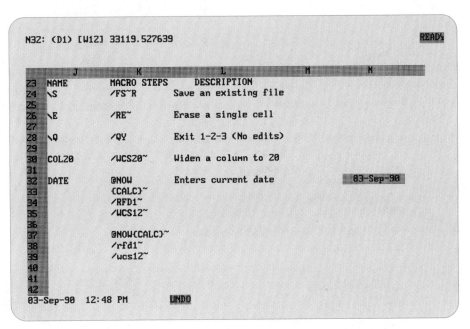

```
N32: (D1) [W12] 33119.527639                                      READY

        J            K              L              M          N
23  NAME         MACRO STEPS     DESCRIPTION
24  \S           /FS~R           Save an existing file
25
26  \E           /RE~            Erase a single cell
27
28  \Q           /QY             Exit 1-2-3 (No edits)
29
30  COL20        /WCS20~         Widen a column to 20
31
32  DATE         @NOW            Enters current date        03-Sep-90
33               {CALC}~
34               /RFD1~
35               /WCS12~
36
37               @NOW{CALC}~
38               /rfd1~
39               /wcs12~
40
41
42
03-Sep-90  12:48 PM        UNDO
```

9

■2   [ALT][F10] to invoke the Macro Library Manager.
(If you did not assign a function key in the previous exercise, select /Add-In, Invoke, and then
select the library file you want.)

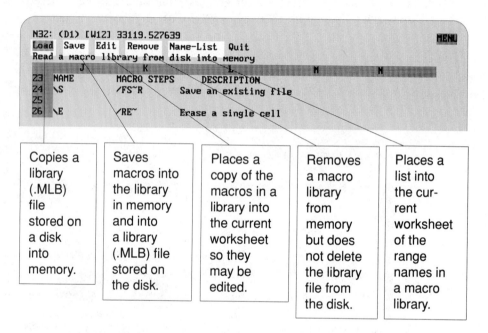

N32: <D1> [W12] 33119.527639   MENU
Load Save Edit Remove Name-List Quit
Read a macro library from disk into memory

	NAME	MACRO STEPS	DESCRIPTION
23			
24	\S	/FS~R	Save an existing file
25			
26	\E	/RE~	Erase a single cell

Copies a library (.MLB) file stored on a disk into memory.	Saves macros into the library in memory and into a library (.MLB) file stored on the disk.	Places a copy of the macros in a library into the current worksheet so they may be edited.	Removes a macro library from memory but does not delete the library file from the disk.	Places a list into the cur- rent worksheet of the range names in a macro library.

■3   Select Save to save the macros into the
macro library.

N32: <D1> [W12] 33119.527639   EDIT
Enter name of macro library to save: C:\123_

	NAME	MACRO STEPS	DESCRIPTION
23			
24	\S	/FS~R	Save an existing file
25			
26	\E	/RE~	Erase a single cell

■4   Type **MACRO1** and press ⏎ .

```
N32: (D1) [W12] 33119.527639                              POINT
Enter macro library range: N32..N32

         J           K            L            M            N
23 NAME        MACRO STEPS    DESCRIPTION
24 \S          /FS~R          Save an existing file
25
26 \E          /RE~           Erase a single cell
```

> **Note**   Name the library file AUTOLOAD.MLB if you want to automatically load the macro library into RAM when you attach the Macro Library Manager. The macros do not execute automatically, but are immediately available for use.

■5   ESC to unanchor the range and move the
      pointer to J23.

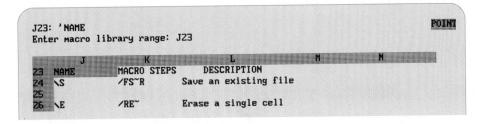

```
J23: 'NAME                                                 POINT
Enter macro library range: J23

         J           K            L            M            N
23 NAME        MACRO STEPS    DESCRIPTION
24 \S          /FS~R          Save an existing file
25
26 \E          /RE~           Erase a single cell
```

9

■ 6   ⌐.⌐ (period) and move the pointer to cell K35.

```
K35: '/WCS12~                                              POINT
Enter macro library range: J23..K35

        J           K              L          M         N
 23  NAME        MACRO STEPS    DESCRIPTION
 24  \S          /FS~R          Save an existing file
 25
 26  \E          /RE~           Erase a single cell
 27
 28  \Q          /QY            Exit 1-2-3 (No edits)
 29
 30  COL20       /WCS20~        Widen a column to 20
 31
 32  DATE        @NOW           Enters current date
 33              {CALC}~
 34              /RFD1~                                03-Sep-90
 35              /WCS12~
 36
```

When specifying the macro library range, remember that the amount of data included in the range will affect the amount of memory (RAM) available for 1-2-3 worksheet data, other macro libraries, or separate memory-resident programs.

■ 7   ⌐↵⌐ You are given the option to enter a password.

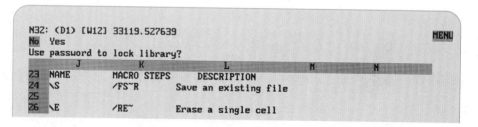

```
N32: (D1) [W12] 33119.527639                              MENU
No  Yes
Use password to lock library?
        J           K              L          M         N
 23  NAME        MACRO STEPS    DESCRIPTION
 24  \S          /FS~R          Save an existing file
 25
 26  \E          /RE~           Erase a single cell
```

Passwords are used to keep others from editing a macro library or viewing macros with the Step mode. They can, however, use the macros in the library. If you use a password, you must remember the exact spelling, including uppercase and lowercase letters, that you typed for the password. Passwords can be up to 80 characters long.

■*8*   Select No. The macro range is completely
removed from the worksheet, loaded into
memory, and saved to the disk as
MACRO1.MLB.

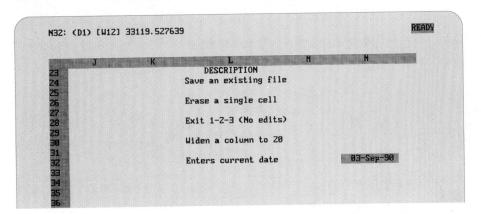

You can have up to 10 macro libraries attached into memory at one time, depending
on the amount of RAM you have available. To minimize the amount of memory
macro libraries occupy, try to keep your macros as compact as possible. I recommend you detach from memory any macro libraries you do not plan to use when
working with a worksheet in order to free up valuable memory.

■*Using the Macro Library*

To use macros saved into a library file, you must first attach and invoke into
memory the Macro Library Manager. You attach the manager with the /Add-In,
Attach command and invoke the manager with the /Add-In, Invoke command,
or by pressing the designated Alt-key combination. You then load the desired
macro library file into memory using the /Add-In, Invoke command (or Alt-key
combination) and then select the Load command. You can then select an existing
macro library from a list displayed in the control panel.

9

When you initially create a macro library file, a copy of it is automatically placed in memory and is available for immediate use. In this exercise, you will load a macro library and then use the macros you just saved in the MACRO1.MLB file to erase the macro description data, the remaining macro steps, and the date that currently appears on your screen.

■ *1* ⌈ALT⌉⌈F10⌉ to display the Macro Manager Library command line menu.

```
N32: (D1) [W12] 33119.527639                              MENU
Load  Save  Edit  Remove  Name-List  Quit
Read a macro library from disk into memory
            J          K              L              M          N
23                                    DESCRIPTION
24                              Save an existing file
25
26                              Erase a single cell
```

■ *2* Select Load.

```
N32: (D1) [W12] 33119.527639                              FILES
Enter name of macro library to load: C:\123\*.MLB
MACRO1.MLB
            J          K              L              M          N
23                                    DESCRIPTION
24                              Save an existing file
25
26                              Erase a single cell
```

■ *3* Select MACRO1.MLB, Yes. The macro library file is loaded into memory, overwriting itself because it was already installed into memory in the last exercise.

■ *4* Select Quit and return to the worksheet.

■5 Move the pointer to cell L23 (the DESCRIP-
TION label), and press [ALT][F3] (Run). The
list of macros in the MACRO1 library file,
plus other range names, appears.

```
L23: [W20] ^DESCRIPTION                                              NAMES
Select the macro to run:
INCOME          NEWDATE          COL20          DATE          \E
         J          K          L          M          N
23                                   DESCRIPTION
24                               Save an existing file
25
26                               Erase a single cell
```

■6 Select the \E macro. The DESCRIPTION
label disappears.

```
L23: [W20]                                                          READY

         J          K          L          M          N
23
24                               Save an existing file
25
26                               Erase a single cell
```

■7 Erase all the data in columns K, L, and N by
using [ALT][F3] or [ALT][E] .

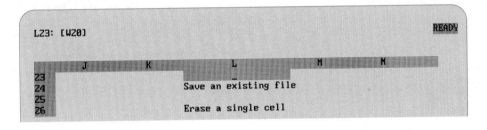

9

■ *8*   [HOME] to move the pointer to cell A1.

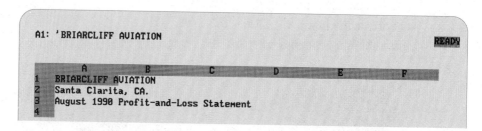

■ *9*   Move the pointer to cell A4 and
press [ALT][F3] .

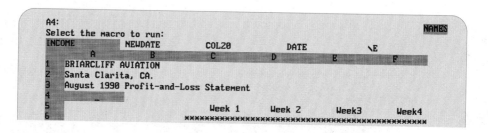

■ *10*   Select DATE to place the current date into
cell A4.

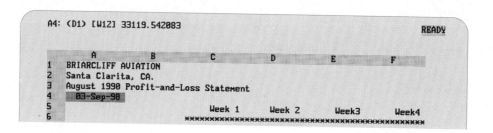

■ *11* [ALT][F3] and select \ S to save the current worksheet.

Now let's remove the macro library from memory. This increases the amount of available RAM for use by worksheet data, other macro libraries, or memory-resident programs.

■ *12* [ALT][F10] and select Remove. A list of macro libraries currently in memory is displayed.

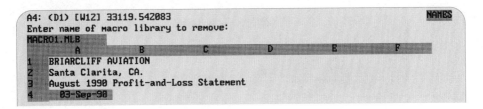

```
A4: (D1) [W12] 33119.542083                                          NAMES
Enter name of macro library to remove:
MACRO1.MLB
     A              B            C           D          E          F
1    BRIARCLIFF AVIATION
2    Santa Clarita, CA.
3    August 1990 Profit-and-Loss Statement
4        03-Sep-90
```

■ *13* Select MACRO1.MLB. The library is removed from memory.

■ *14* Select /File, Save, press [←] , and select Replace to save the current version of the worksheet.

9

Editing Macros
■*in a Macro Library*

The Edit command, which is one of the Macro Library Manager commands, places a copy of the macros located in a macro library into the worksheet you are currently working on. You can then add new macros or make changes to existing macros. Let's place the macros in the MACRO1.MLB file into the AUGPL1 worksheet, which should still be displayed on your screen.

■ *1*   [F5] (Goto). Type **J23** and press [↵]. This moves you to an area of the worksheet where the incoming macro list will not overwrite existing data.

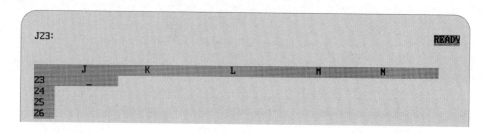

■ *2*   [ALT][F10] and select Load, MACRO1.MLB to load the macro library file into memory.

■*3* Select Edit.

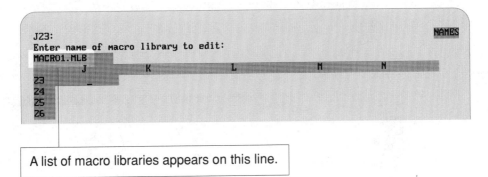

A list of macro libraries appears on this line.

■*4* Select MACRO1.MLB.

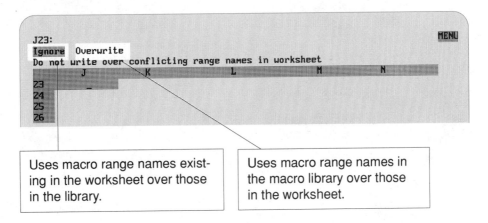

Uses macro range names existing in the worksheet over those in the library.

Uses macro range names in the macro library over those in the worksheet.

9

■*5* Select Ignore.

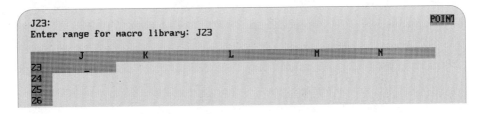

■ 6   ⏎ to accept cell J23 as the range. You only need to specify the upper-left corner of the range.

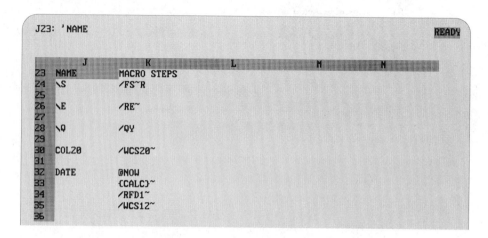

You can add new macros, edit existing macros, or erase unnecessary macros in the macro library.

■ 7   Move the pointer to cell K30.

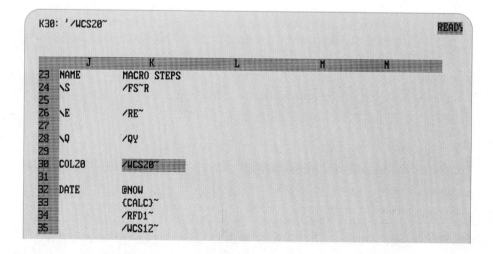

■ *8*   F2 to place the /WCS20~ macro instruction
in the control panel.

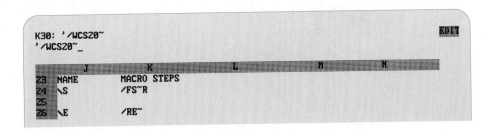

■ *9*   BKSP three times to delete 20 ~. Type **15~** and
press ⏎. The macro has been edited.

■ *10*   ALT F10 Select Save, highlight the
MACRO1.MLB file, and press ⏎.

9

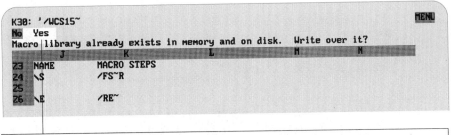

You are asked if you really want to save the data because it will overwrite
the old version of the macros currently stored on the disk. This is to
safeguard inadvertently destroying valuable macros.

■ *11* Select Yes.

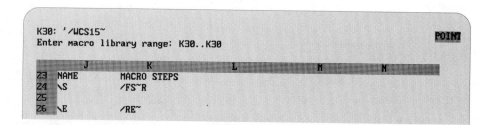

```
K30: '/WCS15~                                                    POINT
Enter macro library range: K30..K30

      J           K              L         M          N
23 NAME        MACRO STEPS
24 \S          /FS~R
25
26 \E          /RE~
```

■ *12* Type **J23..K35**, press ⏎, and select No. The
macros are saved into memory (RAM) and
into the MACRO1.MLB file on the disk.

■ *13* Select /File, Save, press ⏎ and select
Replace to save the current version of the
worksheet.

■*Summary*

In this chapter you learned how to create some basic macros that will speed up
your everyday tasks. Macros can be as simple or as complex as your needs dic-
tate. When you become experienced with basic macros, try creating some of the
advanced macros offered by 1-2-3 that allow you to accomplish some very exotic tasks. Refer to Chapter 14 in your 1-2-3 documentation for a detailed discussion of advanced macros.

You also learned how to use the Macro Library Manager to store macros into
macro libraries for use with more than one worksheet. This add-in program is
helpful in streamlining similar tasks that must be accomplished in several
worksheets.

APPENDIX A

Installing Lotus
■ *1-2-3*

There are three steps in setting up Lotus 1-2-3 Release 2.2. First, you initialize the 1-2-3 System Disk. Second, if you have a hard disk, you copy all the 1-2-3 program disks into a directory on your hard disk. If you have a dual floppy-disk computer, you make backup copies of the program disks. The third procedure is the installation of your computer system equipment. If you are not familiar with DOS or how to work with a directory structure, please read the Introduction to this book before attempting to install 1-2-3. You will need all the program disks provided with your 1-2-3 package except the Allways disks. You should have seven disks if your computer has a 5¼-inch disk drive, or three disks if you have a 3½-inch disk drive.

∎*Initializing 1-2-3 Release 2.2*

When you initialize your 1-2-3 program, you record your name and your company's name on the 1-2-3 System Disk. This permanently identifies you as the licensee of record for your particular 1-2-3 program. Until this initialization process is completed, you will not be able to run the program. This procedure is required only once.

An important note: If you initialize the System Disk on a high-density drive, you will not be able to use it in a double-density drive. In fact, you may not be able to initialize it at all with a high-density drive, in which case you will have to initialize the System Disk in a double-density drive.

∎*1* Start your computer and respond to the date and time prompts by entering the correct date and time or by pressing ⏎ . (If necessary, refer to Chapter 1 for a more detailed discussion on starting your computer.) You will see one of several prompts, such as C, C:, or C:\ for hard drives, or A, A:, or A:\ for floppy drives, depending on which drive you started DOS from.

```
C:>_
```

A

■*2* Place the 1-2-3 System Disk in drive A and
close the latch. Hard-disk users type **A:** and
press ⏎ to change to drive A.

```
C:>A:
A:>_
```

■*3* Type **INIT** and press ⏎.

```
        Thank you for selecting Lotus 1-2-3 Release 2.2 (R).

        Copyright 1985, 1989  Lotus Development Corporation
        All Rights Reserved.

        Lotus Development Corporation retains the ownership of this
        copy of software which is licensed to you according to the
        terms of the Lotus License Agreement.  Use, duplication, or
        sale of this product, except as described in the Lotus
        License Agreement, is strictly prohibited.


                 Press ENTER to continue or press
                 CTRL-BREAK to end this program.
```

■*4* ⏎

```
During initialization, you will be asked to enter your name and
your company's name.  If you are licensing this software as an
individual and not as an employee of a company, then enter your
full name at both the 'Your name:' and 'Your company's name:'
prompt.

If you make a typing error, use the BACKSPACE key to erase
characters to the left of the cursor.  To insert new characters,
use ← and → to move the cursor to the place where you want to
insert the characters.


Press ENTER to continue or press CTRL-BREAK to end this program.
```

■*5* ⏎ to begin initializing 1-2-3.

```
Please enter
Your name:        ██████████████████████
```

A

■6   Type in your first and last name and press
⏎. You may use up to 30 characters. Use
⌫ BKSP to erase typing mistakes.

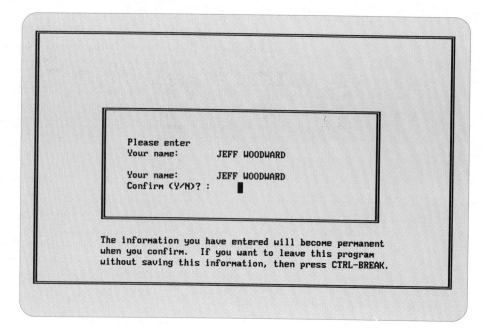

```
            Please enter
            Your name:       JEFF WOODWARD

            Your name:       JEFF WOODWARD
            Confirm (Y/N)? :        █
```

```
       The information you have entered will become permanent
       when you confirm.  If you want to leave this program
       without saving this information, then press CTRL-BREAK.
```

■7   Y ⏎ to confirm your name. (Press N if
you want to delete the name and type another
one. Then press Y ⏎.)

```
       Please enter
       Your company's name: ████████████████████
```

■*8*   Type in your company's name and press ⏎ .
If you do not work for a company, type in
your name again and press ⏎ . You may use
up to 30 characters.

```
Please enter
Your company's name: JEFF WOODWARD

Your company's name: JEFF WOODWARD
     Confirm (Y/N)? :        █


The information you have entered will become permanent
when you confirm.  If you want to leave this program
without saving this information, then press CTRL-BREAK.
```

■9 [Y] [↵] to confirm your company name.
(Press [N] if you want to delete the
company name and type in another one.
Then press [Y] [↵].)

```
FINAL CONFIRMATION SCREEN
The following information will be recorded on your System Disk:

Product: 1-2-3

Release: 2.2

Serial Number:
        0000000-0000000
Your name:
        JEFF WOODWARD
Your company's name:
        JEFF WOODWARD



    Press ENTER to continue or press CTRL-BREAK to end this program.
```

Review the information displayed on this
screen. If it is not accurate, press [CTRL] [BREAK]
to end the initialization process and then start
over with step 3. If the information is correct,
press [↵]. The information is recorded on
your System Disk and will be displayed whenever you start the 1-2-3 program.

■ *10* When you are prompted that the initialization
process is completed, press ⏎ . You are
returned to the DOS prompt.

```
A: >_
```

If you have a hard disk, proceed with the next section, "Copying 1-2-3 onto Your
Hard Disk." If you use dual floppy-disk drives, go first to Appendix B, "Making
Backup Copies of Floppy Disks." When you complete the procedure in Appendix B, return to this appendix and go to the section "Installing 1-2-3" to continue
the 1-2-3 installation.

Copying 1-2-3
■onto Your Hard Disk

In this section you will put into practice some of the information about directories
and DOS that you learned about in the Introduction. You'll create a directory into
which you will copy your 1-2-3 program files.

You should still have an A prompt on your screen. Let's create a directory on
drive C and call it *123*.

A

■ 1   Type **C:** and press ⏎ to change to drive C. If
you wish to create a 1-2-3 directory on a drive
other than C, type that drive letter instead.

```
A:\>C:
C:\>_
```

■ 2   Type **MD 123** and press ⏎.

```
A:>C:
C:>MD 123
C:>_
```

■ 3   Type **CD 123** and press ⏎ to change to the
newly created 1-2-3 directory.

```
A:>C:
C:>MD 123
C:>CD 123
C:>_
```

■4 Place your 1-2-3 System Disk in drive A and close the latch. At the DOS prompt, type **COPY A:*.*** and press ⏎ . The program files are copied into the 1-2-3 directory.

```
A:>C:

C:>MD 123

C:>CD 123

C:>COPY A:*.*
A:123.CMP
A:123.CNF
A:123.DLD
A:123.DYN
A:123.EXE
A:123.RI
A:LICENSE.000
A:LOTUS.COM
A:123.SET
        11 File(s) copied

C:>_
```

■5 Repeat step 4 for all six remaining 1-2-3 program disks. *Do not copy the Allways disks at this time.* When you have completed copying the 1-2-3 disks, proceed with the next section.

A

▪*Installing 1-2-3*

The instructions in this section are for first-time installation of 1-2-3, Release 2.2. If you are upgrading from a previous release, refer to the "Upgraders Handbook" that comes with your 1-2-3 documentation. When you install 1-2-3, you use the Install program to tell 1-2-3 what type of computer equipment you are using. Your 1-2-3 program includes many small program files called drivers. A *driver* is a program that runs a specific type or model of computer equipment. For example, if you have an HP LaserJet Series II printer and an EGA color monitor, you must select drivers for each of them before 1-2-3 can print or display data. You will need to know what kind of computer, monitor, screen display card, and printer(s) make up your system. I suggest you make a list of these items and refer to it when installing 1-2-3.

The Install screens will ask you what type of equipment you have, offer you a list of models to choose from, and provide information to help you select the proper item.

Dual floppy-disk users should use backup copies of their 1-2-3 program (see Appendix B, "Making Backup Copies of Floppy Disks") to install 1-2-3, not the original disks.

Before you start, your computer should be turned on and a C or an A prompt should be displayed on your monitor. If you have a hard disk, change to the 1-2-3 directory (type **CD\123** and press ⏎). If you have a floppy-disk computer, place the System Disk in drive A.

■ *1*   At the DOS prompt, type **LOTUS** and press
⏎ . Read the Access System screen.

```
┌─────┐
│1-2-3│ PrintGraph  Translate  Install  Exit
└─────┘
Use 1-2-3

        ┌──────────────────────────────────────────────────────────────┐
        │                      1-2-3 Access System                      │
        │                     Copyright 1986, 1989                      │
        │                 Lotus Development Corporation                 │
        │                      All Rights Reserved                      │
        │                         Release 2.2                           │
        │                                                               │
        │ The Access system lets you choose 1-2-3, PrintGraph, the Translate utility, │
        │ and the Install program, from the menu at the top of this screen.  If │
        │ you're using a two-diskette system, the Access system may prompt you to │
        │ change disks.  Follow the instructions below to start a program. │
        │                                                               │
        │ o  Use → or ← to move the menu pointer (the highlighted rectangle │
        │    at the top of the screen) to the program you want to use.  │
        │                                                               │
        │ o  Press ENTER to start the program.                          │
        │                                                               │
        │ You can also start a program by typing the first character of its name. │
        │                                                               │
        │ Press HELP (F1) for more information.                         │
        └──────────────────────────────────────────────────────────────┘
```

■ *2*   → three times to move the highlight to Install.

```
1-2-3  PrintGraph  Translate  ┌───────┐  Exit
                              │Install│
Install 1-2-3                 └───────┘

        ┌──────────────────────────────────────────────────────────────┐
        │                      1-2-3 Access System                      │
```

A

■3   Hard-disk users press ⏎ to display the 1-2-3
Install Program instruction screen. Dual floppy-disk users press ⏎ ; you will be
prompted to remove the System Disk and
replace it with the Install Disk. Do so, then
press ⏎ again to display the 1-2-3 Install
Program screen.

```
                    1-2-3 Install Program

                      Copyright 1986, 1989
                  Lotus Development Corporation
                      All Rights Reserved
                         Release 2.2

Note: Before you use Install, follow the "Setting Up 1-2-3" instructions.

The Install program lets you tell 1-2-3 what equipment you have.  You
choose your equipment from a list of options by moving a highlighted
rectangle (the menu pointer) to your choice and pressing ENTER.  You
can start 1-2-3 without using the Install program first, but you will
not be able to display graphs or use a printer.

If you need more information to make a particular choice, press HELP (F1)
to see a Help screen.  You will also find it helpful to complete the
Hardware Chart that came with your 1-2-3 package and have it available
for reference while you are using Install.

            ─── Press ENTER to begin the Install program. ───
```

■4 Hard-disk users press ⌐⌐ to display the Main
menu. Floppy-disk users press ⌐⌐; you will
receive screen prompts to insert the Library
Install Disk in drive A. Do so, then press ⌐⌐.
Next, you'll be prompted to insert the System
Disk in drive A and to press ⌐⌐. The Main
menu appears.

```
                    M A I N   M E N U

                                    ┌──────────────────────────┐
                                    │ First-Time Installation  │
   Use ↓ or ↑ to move menu pointer. │ provides step-by-step    │
                                    │ instructions for completing │
   ┌──────────────────────────┐     │ the installation procedure. │
   │ First-Time Installation  │     │ You will select drivers  │
   ├──────────────────────────┘     │ that allow 1-2-3 to display │
     Change Selected Equipment      │ graphs and print your 1-2-3 │
     Advanced Options               │ worksheets and graphs.   │
     Exit Install Program           │                          │
                                    │ Press ENTER to select    │
                                    │ First-Time Installation. │
                                    └──────────────────────────┘


   ↓ and ↑ move menu pointer        F1  displays a Help screen
   ENTER selects highlighted choice F9  displays the main menu
   ESC   returns to previous screen F10 displays current selections
```

A

■5 ⌐⌐ to move the highlight to each of the three
options below First-Time Installation. Read
the brief description of each option and then
return the highlight to First-Time Installation.

■*6*   ⏎ to display information about the First-
Time Installation option.

Lotus supplies programs, called drivers, that let 1-2-3 work with
different equipment. 1-2-3 comes with generic drivers that let you try
out the program and create a worksheet immediately. When you are ready
to do more with 1-2-3, use the Install program to add drivers that allow
1-2-3 to display graphs and to print your work.

When you select First-Time Installation, the Install program asks you
questions to help you decide which drivers you need to add. Then, it
saves the drivers you select in a file, or driver set, called 123.SET.

If NUM appears in the lower right corner of your screen, press NUM LOCK
to make it disappear. (You should never see the NUM indicator when you
use the Install program.)

──── Press ENTER to continue────

Consult the
"Upgraders
Handbook" if you
are upgrading
from another
Lotus release.

■7 ⏎

```
Can your computer display graphs?          If your computer's monitor
                                           can display graphs, press
   Yes                                     ENTER to select Yes.
   No
                                           If your computer's monitor
                                           cannot display graphs, press
                                           ↓ to move the menu pointer
                                           to No.
```

■8 Place the highlight on Yes or No and press
⏎. If you select No, refer to the screen in
step 10 and proceed with step 11. If you
select Yes, you see the following screen.

```
How many monitors do you have?            If you have a computer with
                                          a single monitor or a portable
   One Monitor                            computer with a built-in
   Two Monitors                           monitor, press ENTER to
                                          select One Monitor.

                                          If you have two monitors,
                                          press ↓ to move the menu
                                          pointer to Two Monitors.
```

A

■*9*   Highlight the appropriate item and press ⏎.
Selecting One Monitor displays the following
screen.

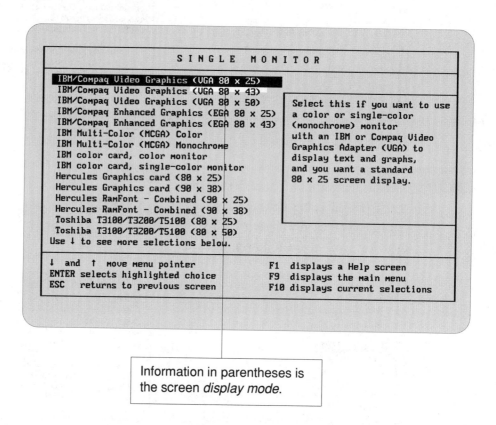

Information in parentheses is
the screen *display mode*.

For a description of the differences between display modes, move the highlight
to different monitors and read the information displayed in the box on the right
side of the screen. An 80 × 25 screen display means 80 characters will be displayed across the screen and 25 rows will be displayed down the screen; 80 × 43
means 80 characters by 43 rows, and so on.

■ *10* Move the highlight to your monitor type and press ⏎. I selected IBM/Compaq Enhanced Graphics (EGA 80 × 25).

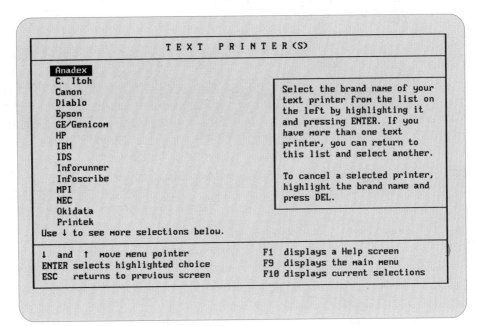

■ *11* Highlight Yes or No and press ⏎. If you select No, refer to the screen in step 14 and proceed to step 15. Selecting Yes gives you the following screen.

A

■ *12* Highlight the brand name of the printer that
you will be using and press ⏎. You are
presented with a list of models and series.
(This list is for Hewlett Packard printers.)

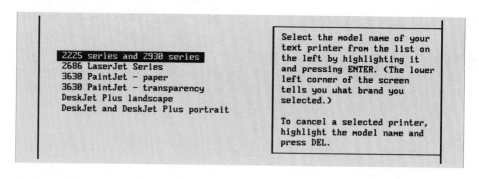

```
2225 series and 2930 series
2686 LaserJet Series
3630 PaintJet - paper
3630 PaintJet - transparency
DeskJet Plus landscape
DeskJet and DeskJet Plus portrait
```

Select the model name of your
text printer from the list on
the left by highlighting it
and pressing ENTER. (The lower
left corner of the screen
tells you what brand you
selected.)

To cancel a selected printer,
highlight the model name and
press DEL.

■ *13* Select the appropriate model or series and
press ⏎.

Do you have another text printer?

```
No
Yes
```

If you do not have another
text printer, press ENTER
to select No.

If you have another text
printer, press ↓ to move the
menu pointer to Yes.

■ *14* With the highlight on No, press ⏎.

Do you want to print graphs?

Yes
No

If you want to print the
graphs you create with 1-2-3
and your printer is able to
print graphs, press ENTER
to select Yes.

If you do not want to print
graphs or your printer is not
capable of printing graphs,
press ↓ to move the menu
pointer to No.

■ *15* If you highlight No and press ⏎, refer to the
screen in step 18 and proceed with step 19. If
you select Yes and press ⏎, you will see the
following screen.

G R A P H I C S P R I N T E R (S)

Amdek
Anadex
C. Itoh
CalComp
Canon
Epson
GE/Genicom
HP
Houston Instruments
IBM
IDS
Inforunner
Infoscribe
MPI
NEC
Use ↓ to see more selections below.

Select the brand name of your
graphics printer from the list
on the left by highlighting it
and pressing ENTER. If you
have more than one graphics
printer, you can return to
this list and select another.

To cancel a selected graphics
printer, highlight the brand
name and press DEL.

↓ and ↑ move menu pointer
ENTER selects highlighted choice
ESC   returns to previous screen

F1 displays a Help screen
F9 displays the main menu
F10 displays current selections

A

■ *16* Highlight the brand name that you will be using and press ⏎. A list of models is displayed.

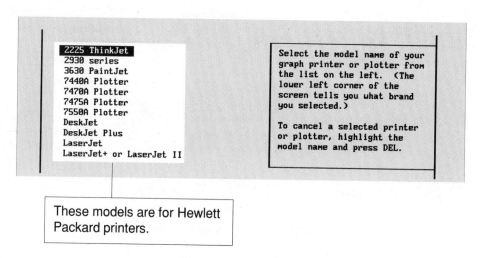

2225 ThinkJet
2930 series
3630 PaintJet
7440A Plotter
7470A Plotter
7475A Plotter
7550A Plotter
DeskJet
DeskJet Plus
LaserJet
LaserJet+ or LaserJet II

Select the model name of your
graph printer or plotter from
the list on the left. (The
lower left corner of the
screen tells you what brand
you selected.)

To cancel a selected printer
or plotter, highlight the
model name and press DEL.

These models are for Hewlett
Packard printers.

■ *17* Highlight your printer model and press ⏎.

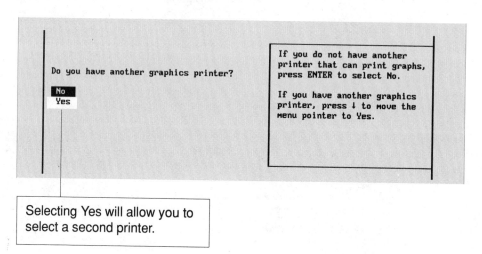

Do you have another graphics printer?

No
Yes

If you do not have another
printer that can print graphs,
press ENTER to select No.

If you have another graphics
printer, press ↓ to move the
menu pointer to Yes.

Selecting Yes will allow you to
select a second printer.

■ *18* With the highlight on No, press ⏎.

```
Do you want to name your driver set?        If you do not plan to create
                                            more than one driver set,
                                            press ENTER to select No.
    No
    Yes                                     If you are going to create
                                            more than one driver set,
                                            press ↓ to move the menu
                                            pointer to Yes. The Install
                                            program will automatically
                                            name your driver set 123.
```

■ *19* You will not be creating another driver set
(this is beyond the level of this book) so you
don't need to name this set. With the highlight on No, press ⏎.

```
                    S A V I N G   C H A N G E S

    When you press ENTER, the Install program will save your selections in
    a driver set called 123.SET.

    If you are using a two-diskette system, the Install program will prompt you
    to change disks.  Follow the instructions Install displays on the screen.
```

A

■*20* You've finished making your installation
selections, so press ⏎ . 1-2-3 saves your
drivers and names the file 123.SET. If you are
using a dual floppy-disk computer, follow the
instructions for installing the driver on the
remaining 1-2-3 program disks.

```
                    You have finished the installation process.

   o  If you want to see the contents of the driver set you just created,
      press F10.

      The list you see may differ from what you expect in a few ways.
      First, the Install program adds some drivers automatically.  Second,
      there are two drivers for your screen display -- one for text and one
      for graphs.

   o  If you want to return to the main menu, press F9.


   o  If you want to leave the Install program, press ENTER.
```

Press F10 to
see the
contents of
the driver set.

■*21* ⏎ to exit the Install program.

```
┌─────────────────────────────────────────────────────────────────┐
│                            E X I T                                │
├──────────────────────────────────┬────────────────────────────────┤
│                                  │ Select No to return to the     │
│                                  │ main menu and continue working │
│                                  │ with the Install program.      │
│  Do you want to leave Install?   │                                │
│                                  │                                │
│  No                              │                                │
│  Yes                             │                                │
└──────────────────────────────────┴────────────────────────────────┘
```

■*22* Highlight Yes and press ⏎. You are returned
to the Access System screen.

```
┌───────────────────────────────────────────────────────────────────┐
│  1-2-3  PrintGraph  Translate  Install  Exit                       │
│  Install 1-2-3                                                      │
│ ┌───────────────────────────────────────────────────────────────┐ │
│ │                     1-2-3 Access System                        │ │
│ │                   Copyright  1986, 1989                        │ │
│ │               Lotus Development Corporation                    │ │
│ │                    All Rights Reserved                         │ │
│ │                      Release 2.2                               │ │
│ │                                                                │ │
│ │  The Access system lets you choose 1-2-3, PrintGraph, the      │ │
│ │  Translate utility, and the Install program, from the menu at  │ │
│ │  the top of this screen.  If you're using a two-diskette       │ │
│ │  system, the Access system may prompt you to change disks.     │ │
│ │  Follow the instructions below to start a program.             │ │
│ │                                                                │ │
│ │  o  Use → or ← to move the menu pointer (the highlighted       │ │
│ │     rectangle at the top of the screen) to the program you     │ │
│ │     want to use.                                               │ │
│ │                                                                │ │
│ │  o  Press ENTER to start the program.                          │ │
│ │                                                                │ │
│ │  You can also start a program by typing the first character    │ │
│ │  of its name.                                                  │ │
│ │                                                                │ │
│ │  Press HELP (F1) for more information.                         │ │
│ └───────────────────────────────────────────────────────────────┘ │
└───────────────────────────────────────────────────────────────────┘
```

A

■*23* Highlight Exit and press ⏎. You are at a
DOS prompt.

```
A:>_
```

You have now installed your 1-2-3 program. You can run 1-2-3 and print both text
and graphics. If you need to change any equipment drivers in the future, follow steps
1–4 above and select the Change Selected Equipment option from the Main menu.
Then follow the instructions presented on your screen to make the appropriate
modifications.

APPENDIX B

Backing Up Your 1-2-3 Program Disks

Lotus 1-2-3 Release 2.2 is no longer copy-protected, which means that you can make backup copies of the program disks. This appendix is of particular importance to dual floppy-disk users. You should not use your original 1-2-3 disks on a regular basis because they may become damaged. To make backups, you'll need a DOS (or OS/2) disk, all the original 1-2-3 disks (seven if you have 5¼-inch disks, or three if you have 3½-inch disks), and a for-matted blank disk for every original 1-2-3 disk that you'll be copying, plus one more to use as a document disk. If you have a hard-disk computer, DOS will already be installed on the hard disk.

▪ *Formatting Your Floppy Disks*

Before you can copy information onto a disk it must be formatted for your system. Formatting disks on a dual floppy-disk computer is slightly different than on a hard-disk computer.

Dual Floppy-Disk Computers

▪ *1*   Place the DOS disk in drive A and start your computer. Ignore the date and time requests by pressing ⮐.

```
Current date is Wed 11-14-90
Enter new date (mm-dd-yy):
Current time is 12:16:45.08
Enter new time:

A>_
```

▪ *2*   Type **format b:** and press ⮐.

```
A>format b:
Insert new diskette for drive B:
and strike ENTER when ready_
```

B

■*3*   Place a new floppy disk in drive B and
press [↵].

```
Format complete

    1213952 bytes total disk space
    1213952 bytes available on disk

Format another (Y/N)?_
```

> This is displayed for a high-density drive (1.2 megabytes (Mb)).
> A low-density drive would show 360 kilobytes (K).

■*4*   Press [Y] to format another disk, then
press [↵].

■*5*   Repeat steps 3 and 4 until all of the blank
disks are formatted.

■*6*   When the last disk has been formatted, press
[N] [↵] to return to the DOS prompt.

```
Format another (Y/N)?n
A>_
```

Hard-Disk Computers

Before you can format a new disk, you must locate the FORMAT.COM file. You'll find FORMAT.COM with your DOS program files. Many times DOS is located on the root directory, but it is often installed in its own directory, in which case you will have to change to that directory before attempting to format a disk.

■ 1   Start your computer. Ignore the date and time
requests, if any, by pressing ⏎ .

```
Current date is Wed 11-14-90
Enter new date (mm-dd-yy):
Current time is 12:16:45.08
Enter new time:


C>_
```

> Read the
> Introduction
> before you begin
> this procedure—
> it contains useful
> information.

B

■2   Type **dir/w** and press ⏎ to check the contents of the root directory. Look for the FORMAT.COM file. Also locate the DISKCOPY.COM file. You'll use this file later to make backup copies of disks. If you do not find these files, go to step 3. Otherwise, move on to step 4.

```
C>dir/w

 Volume in drive C is WOODWARD
 Directory of  C:\DOS

 .                  ..               4201     CPI   5202     CPI   ANSI     SYS
 APPEND    EXE      ASSIGN   COM     ATTRIB   EXE   AUTOEXEC BAT   CAPTURE  COM
 CHKDSK    COM      COMMAND  COM     COMP     COM   CONFIG   SYS   COPY
 COUNTRY   SYS      DEBUG    COM     DISKCOMP COM   DISKCOPY COM   DISPLAY  SYS
 DRIVER    SYS      EDLIN    COM     EGA      CPI   EXE2BIN  EXE   FASTOPEN EXE
 FC        EXE      FDISK    COM     FIND     EXE   FORMAT   COM   GRAFTABL COM
 GRAPHICS  COM      GWBASIC  EXE     JOIN     EXE   KEYB     COM   KEYBOARD SYS
 LABEL     COM      LCD      CPI     LINK     EXE   MODE     COM   MORE     COM
 NLSFUNC   EXE      PRINT    COM     PRINTER  SYS   RAMDRIVE SYS   RECOVER  COM
 REPLACE   EXE      RESTORE  COM     SELECT   COM   SHARE    EXE   SORT     EXE
 SUBST     EXE      SYS      COM     TREE     COM   XCOPY    EXE
        54 File(s)    4347904 bytes free

C>_
```

■*3*   Change to the directory containing DOS by typing
cd followed by the directory name, then
pressing ⏎. My DOS files are located in my
DOS directory, so I will type **cd\dos**. If you do
not know which directory contains your DOS
files, check with your computer dealer or the
person who set up your system. When you've
changed to the correct directory, type dir/w to
see a file listing similar to that in step 2. You
should see the FORMAT.COM file.

```
C>cd\dos

C>_
```

Do not type a space between the \ and the directory name.

■*4*   Once you're in the proper directory, type
format a: and press ⏎. If you have a high-
density (1.2 Mb) disk drive and are formatting a low-density (360K) disk, type **format
a:/4** and press ⏎.

```
C>cd\dos

C>format a:
Insert new diskette for drive A:
and strike ENTER when ready_
```

B

■5 Place a new disk in drive A and press ⏎.

```
Format complete

    1213952 bytes total disk space
    1213952 bytes available on disk

Format another (Y/N)?_
```

This is displayed for a high-density drive (1.2 Mb).
A low-density drive would show 360K.

■6 Ⓨ ⏎ and repeat step 5 to format as many
disks as you need. When finished,
press Ⓝ ⏎.

```
Format another (Y/N)?n
C>_
```

■*Making Backup Copies of 1-2-3*

Before you back up 1-2-3, be sure to write-protect your original program disks
to prevent inadvertent erasure of information on the disk. New boxes of floppy
disks contain write-protect tabs. These tabs are small rectangular stickers that
are placed over the write-protect notch (see the "Disk Drives" section in the

Introduction). Place one of these tabs over the write-protect notch on each of your original 5¼-inch 1-2-3 disks. On a 3½-inch disk you simply push the small tab on the side of the disk and check to see that the hole is uncovered. If so, the disk is protected.

Dual Floppy-Disk Computers

Be sure you have formatted enough new disks to make a copy of each 1-2-3 disk plus one more to use as a document disk. If you just completed formatting disks in the previous exercise, go to step 2. Otherwise, begin with step 1.

■ *1*   Place the DOS disk in drive A and start your computer. Ignore the date and time requests by pressing ⏎ .

```
Current date is Wed 11-14-90
Enter new date (mm-dd-yy):
Current time is 12:16:45.08
Enter new time:

A>_
```

■ *2*   Remove the DOS disk and place the first 1-2-3 System Disk in drive A. *Never place your 1-2-3 disks in drive B*. You might damage them.

B

■*3*   Place a blank, formatted disk in drive B.

■*4*   Type **copy a:*.* b:** and press ⏎.

```
A>copy a:*.* b:
A:123.CMP
A:123.CNF
A:123.DLD
A:123.DYN
A:123.EXE
A:123.RI
A:LICENSE.000
A:LOTUS.COM
A:123.SET
        9 File(s) copied

A>_
```

■*5*   Remove both disks. Be sure to label the copy
so you don't lose track of which disk is
which. Place the next 1-2-3 disk in drive A
and another blank disk in drive B. Press F3
then ⏎.

```
A>copy a:*.* b:
A:123.HLP
        1 File(s) copied

A>_
```

■ *6*   Repeat step 5 until all your 1-2-3 disks have
been copied.

Store your original disks in a safe place and use the backup copies for your
everyday work.

Note   *Copying and Formatting Disks Simultaneously* You can simultaneously
format a new floppy disk and make a backup copy of a disk by using the DOS
DISKCOPY command. Place the DOS disk in drive A. Type **diskcopy a: b:** and
press ⏎. When prompted, remove the DOS disk and place the disk to be copied into
drive A. Place a blank, unformatted disk in drive B and press ⏎. Follow the screen
prompts for copying additional disks or terminating the procedure.

Hard-Disk Computers

Many hard-disk users use their original 1-2-3 program disks as backups, since
1-2-3 is copied onto the hard disk. So, you may prefer not to make backups of
your original 1-2-3 disks if you have a hard-disk computer. However, you can
use the procedure in this section to back up your regular data documents that are
stored on the hard disk. I recommend this highly, because hard disks occasionally
fail, and everything on your hard disk could be lost forever.

This exercise assumes your hard-disk computer has one floppy-disk drive. If
you have two floppy-disk drives, refer to the exercise in the previous section,
"Dual Floppy-Disk Computers."

■ *1*   Start your computer. Ignore the date and time
requests by pressing ⏎ .

B

■*2* Go to the directory containing DOS. The
DISKCOPY.COM file is located there. If
you're not sure where DOS is located, refer
to the hard-disk instructions in "Formatting
Your Floppy Disks" in this appendix.

■*3* Type **diskcopy a: a:** and press ⏎ .

```
C>diskcopy a: a:

Insert SOURCE diskette in drive A:

Press any key when ready . . .

_
```

■*4* Place the 1-2-3 System Disk in drive A; press
any key.

```
Copying 40 tracks
9 Sectors/Track, 2 Side(s)

Insert TARGET diskette in drive A:

Press any key when ready . . .

_
```

A high-density source disk (1.2 Mb) may contain more information than DOS
can copy in one attempt. In this case, you will be prompted to place the source
diskette back in drive A in order to copy the remaining information. Don't be
surprised if you have to go through this procedure three or four times. (By the
way, your 1-2-3 5¼-inch disks are not high density.)

■5 Remove the 1-2-3 System Disk and place a
blank disk in drive A; press any key.

```
Copy another diskette (Y/N)?_
```

■6 [Y]

```
Insert SOURCE diskette in drive A:

Press any key when ready . . .

_
```

■7 Follow steps 4–6 to copy the remaining 1-2-3
disks. Be sure to label each copy with the correct name of the original disk.

■8 When the last disk has been copied, press [N]
to return to the DOS prompt.

B

▪ *Index*

This book was produced on Ventura Professional Extension V.2.2. Page proofs were printed on a QMS PS-810 PostScript laser printer using LaserTool's PrintCache printer accelerator. Final camera-ready pages were printed on a Varityper 4200B-P PostScript typesetter.

Selections from The SYBEX Library

ACCOUNTING

Mastering DacEasy Accounting
Darleen Hartley Yourzek
476pp. Ref. 442-9

Applied accounting principles are at your fingertips in this exciting new guide to using DacEasy Accounting versions 2.0 and 3.0. Installing, converting data, processing work, and printing reports are covered with a variety of practical business examples. Through Version 3.0

Mastering DacEasy Accounting (Second Edition)
Darleen Hartley Yourzek
463pp. Ref. 679-0

This new edition focuses on version 4.0 (with notes on using 3.0), and includes an introduction to DacEasy Payroll. Packed with real-world accounting examples, it covers everything from installing DacEasy to converting data, setting up applications, processing work and printing custom reports.

SPREADSHEETS AND INTEGRATED SOFTWARE

1-2-3 for Scientists and Engineers
William J. Orvis
341pp. Ref. 407-0

Fast, elegant solutions to common problems in science and engineering, using Lotus 1-2-3. Tables and plotting, curve fitting, statistics, derivatives, integrals and differentials, solving systems of equations, and more.

The ABC's of 1-2-3 (Second Edition)
Chris Gilbert
Laurie Williams
245pp. Ref. 355-4

Online Today recommends it as "an easy and comfortable way to get started with the program." An essential tutorial for novices, it will remain on your desk as a valuable source of ongoing reference and support. For Release 2.

The ABC's of 1-2-3 Release 2.2
Chris Gilbert
Laurie Williams
340pp. Ref. 623-5

New Lotus 1-2-3 users delight in this book's step-by-step approach to building trouble-free spreadsheets, displaying graphs, and efficiently building databases. The authors cover the ins and outs of the latest version including easier calculations, file linking, and better graphic presentation.

The ABC's of 1-2-3 Release 3
Judd Robbins
290pp. Ref. 519-0

The ideal book for beginners who are new to Lotus or new to Release 3. This step-by-step approach to the 1-2-3 spreadsheet software gets the reader up and running with spreadsheet, database, graphics, and macro functions.

The ABC's of Excel on the IBM PC
Douglas Hergert
326pp. Ref. 567-0

This book is a brisk and friendly introduction to the most important features of

Microsoft Excel for PC's. This beginner's book discusses worksheets, charts, database operations, and macros, all with hands-on examples. Written for all versions through Version 2.

The ABC's of Quattro
Alan Simpson
Douglas J. Wolf
286pp. Ref. 560-3

Especially for users new to spreadsheets, this is an introduction to the basic concepts and a guide to instant productivity through editing and using spreadsheet formulas and functions. Includes how to print out graphs and data for presentation. For Quattro 1.1.

The Complete Lotus 1-2-3 Release 2.2 Handbook
Greg Harvey
750pp. Ref. 625-1

This comprehensive handbook discusses every 1-2-3 operating with clear instructions and practical tips. This volume especially emphasizes the new improved graphics, high-speed recalculation techniques, and spreadsheet linking available with Release 2.2.

The Complete Lotus 1-2-3 Release 3 Handbook
Greg Harvey
700pp. Ref. 600-6

Everything you ever wanted to know about 1-2-3 is in this definitive handbook. As a Release 3 guide, it features the design and use of 3D worksheets, and improved graphics, along with using Lotus under DOS or OS/2. Problems, exercises, and helpful insights are included.

Lotus 1-2-3 Desktop Companion
SYBEX Ready Reference Series
Greg Harvey
976pp. Ref. 501-8

A full-time consultant, right on your desk. Hundreds of self-contained entries cover every 1-2-3 feature, organized by topic, indexed and cross-referenced, and supplemented by tips, macros and working examples. For Release 2.

Lotus 1-2-3 Instant Reference Release 2.2
SYBEX Prompter Series
Greg Harvey
Kay Yarborough Nelson
254pp. Ref. 635-9, 4 ¾" × 8"

The reader gets quick and easy access to any operation in 1-2-3 Version 2.2 in this handy pocket-sized encyclopedia. Organized by menu function, each command and function has a summary description, the exact key sequence, and a discussion of the options.

Lotus 1-2-3 Tips and Tricks (2nd edition)
Gene Weisskopf
425pp. Ref. 668-5

This outstanding collection of tips, shortcuts and cautions for longtime Lotus users is in an expanded new edition covering Release 2.2. Topics include macros, range names, spreadsheet design, hardware and operating system tips, data analysis, printing, data interchange, applications development, and more.

Mastering 1-2-3 (Second Edition)
Carolyn Jorgensen
702pp. Ref. 528-X

Get the most from 1-2-3 Release 2.01 with this step-by-step guide emphasizing advanced features and practical uses. Topics include data sharing, macros, spreadsheet security, expanded memory, and graphics enhancements.

Mastering 1-2-3 Release 3
Carolyn Jorgensen
682pp. Ref. 517-4

For new Release 3 and experienced Release 2 users, "Mastering" starts with a basic spreadsheet, then introduces spreadsheet and database commands, functions, and macros, and then tells how to analyze 3D spreadsheets and make high-impact reports and graphs. Lotus add-ons are discussed and Fast Tracks are included.

Mastering Enable
Keith D. Bishop
517pp. Ref. 440-2

A comprehensive, practical, hands-on guide to Enable 2.0—integrated word processing, spreadsheet, database management, graphics, and communications—from basic concepts to custom menus, macros and the Enable Procedural Language.

Mastering Enable/OA
Christopher Van Buren
Robert Bixby
540pp. Ref 637-5

This is a structured, hands-on guide to integrated business computing, for users who want to achieve productivity in the shortest possible time. Separate in-depth sections cover word processing, spreadsheets, databases, telecommunications, task integration and macros.

Mastering Excel on the IBM PC
Carl Townsend
628pp. Ref. 403-8

A complete Excel handbook with step-by-step tutorials, sample applications and an extensive reference section. Topics include worksheet fundamentals, formulas and windows, graphics, database techniques, special features, macros and more.

Mastering Framework III
Douglas Hergert
Jonathan Kamin
613pp. Ref. 513-1

Thorough, hands-on treatment of the latest Framework release. An outstanding introduction to integrated software applications, with examples for outlining, spreadsheets, word processing, databases, and more; plus an introduction to FRED programming.

Mastering Quattro
Alan Simpson
576pp. Ref. 514-X

This tutorial covers not only all of Quattro's classic spreadsheet features, but also its added capabilities including extended graphing, modifiable menus, and the macro debugging environment. Simpson brings out how to use all of Quattro's new-generation-spreadsheet capabilities.

Mastering SuperCalc5
Greg Harvey
Mary Beth Andrasak
500pp. Ref. 624-3

This book offers a complete and unintimidating guided tour through each feature. With step-by-step lessons, readers learn about the full capabilities of spreadsheet, graphics, and data management functions. Multiple spreadsheets, linked spreadsheets, 3D graphics, and macros are also discussed.

Mastering Symphony (Fourth Edition)
Douglas Cobb
857pp. Ref. 494-1

Thoroughly revised to cover all aspects of the major upgrade of Symphony Version 2, this Fourth Edition of Doug Cobb's classic is still "the Symphony bible" to this complex but even more powerful package. All the new features are discussed and placed in context with prior versions so that both new and previous users will benefit from Cobb's insights.

Understanding PFS: First Choice
Gerry Litton
489pp. Ref. 568-9

From basic commands to complex features, this complete guide to the popular integrated package is loaded with step-by-step instructions. Lessons cover creating attractive documents, setting up easy-to-use databases, working with spreadsheets and graphics, and smoothly integrating tasks from different First Choice modules. For Version 3.0.

TO JOIN THE SYBEX MAILING LIST OR ORDER BOOKS
PLEASE COMPLETE THIS FORM

NAME _____ COMPANY _____

STREET _____ CITY _____

STATE _____ ZIP _____

☐ PLEASE MAIL ME MORE INFORMATION ABOUT **SYBEX** TITLES

ORDER FORM (There is no obligation to order)

PLEASE SEND ME THE FOLLOWING:

TITLE	QTY	PRICE
_____	____	____
_____	____	____
_____	____	____
_____	____	____

TOTAL BOOK ORDER _____ $_____

SHIPPING AND HANDLING PLEASE ADD $2.00 PER BOOK VIA UPS _____

FOR OVERSEAS SURFACE ADD $5.25 PER BOOK PLUS $4.40 REGISTRATION FEE _____

FOR OVERSEAS AIRMAIL ADD $18.25 PER BOOK PLUS $4.40 REGISTRATION FEE _____

CALIFORNIA RESIDENTS PLEASE ADD APPLICABLE SALES TAX _____

TOTAL AMOUNT PAYABLE _____

☐ CHECK ENCLOSED ☐ VISA
☐ MASTERCARD ☐ AMERICAN EXPRESS

ACCOUNT NUMBER _____

EXPIR. DATE _____ DAYTIME PHONE _____

CUSTOMER SIGNATURE _____

CHECK AREA OF COMPUTER INTEREST:

☐ BUSINESS SOFTWARE

☐ TECHNICAL PROGRAMMING

☐ OTHER: _____

THE FACTOR THAT WAS MOST IMPORTANT IN YOUR SELECTION:

☐ THE SYBEX NAME

☐ QUALITY

☐ PRICE

☐ EXTRA FEATURES

☐ COMPREHENSIVENESS

☐ CLEAR WRITING

☐ OTHER _____

OTHER COMPUTER TITLES YOU WOULD LIKE TO SEE IN PRINT:

_____

_____

OCCUPATION

☐ PROGRAMMER   ☐ TEACHER

☐ SENIOR EXECUTIVE   ☐ HOMEMAKER

☐ COMPUTER CONSULTANT   ☐ RETIRED

☐ SUPERVISOR   ☐ STUDENT

☐ MIDDLE MANAGEMENT   ☐ OTHER:

☐ ENGINEER/TECHNICAL   _____

☐ CLERICAL/SERVICE

☐ BUSINESS OWNER/SELF EMPLOYED

CHECK YOUR LEVEL OF COMPUTER USE

☐ NEW TO COMPUTERS

☐ INFREQUENT COMPUTER USER

☐ FREQUENT USER OF ONE SOFTWARE
  PACKAGE:
  NAME _____

☐ FREQUENT USER OF MANY SOFTWARE
  PACKAGES

☐ PROFESSIONAL PROGRAMMER

OTHER COMMENTS:

_____

_____

_____

_____

_____

_____

_____

PLEASE FOLD, SEAL, AND MAIL TO SYBEX

SYBEX, INC.
2021 CHALLENGER DR. #100
ALAMEDA, CALIFORNIA USA
                    94501

SEAL

SYBEX Computer Books
are different.

Here is why . . .

At SYBEX, each book is designed with you in mind. Every manuscript is carefully selected and supervised by our editors, who are themselves computer experts. We publish the best authors, whose technical expertise is matched by an ability to write clearly and to communicate effectively. Programs are thoroughly tested for accuracy by our technical staff. Our computerized production department goes to great lengths to make sure that each book is well-designed.

In the pursuit of timeliness, SYBEX has achieved many publishing firsts. SYBEX was among the first to integrate personal computers used by authors and staff into the publishing process. SYBEX was the first to publish books on the CP/M operating system, microprocessor interfacing techniques, word processing, and many more topics.

Expertise in computers and dedication to the highest quality product have made SYBEX a world leader in computer book publishing. Translated into fourteen languages, SYBEX books have helped millions of people around the world to get the most from their computers. We hope we have helped you, too.

For a complete catalog of our publications:

SYBEX, Inc. 2021 Challenger Drive, #100, Alameda, CA 94501
Tel: (415) 523-8233/(800) 227-2346   Telex: 336311
Fax: (415) 523-2373

LOTUS 1-2-3 CURSOR MOVEMENT

KEY	READY AND POINT MODES	EDIT MODE
Home	Moves to cell A1.	Moves to the first character on the entry line.
↑	Moves up one cell.	Finishes, enters edit. Moves up one cell
↓	Moves down one cell.	Finishes, enters edit. Moves down one cel
←	Moves left one cell.	Moves left one character.
→	Moves right one cell.	Moves right one character.
End	Moves to the end of the entry. Must be used with another pointer/cursor key.	Moves to the end of entry line.
End-↑	Moves up the column to the intersection of a blank and nonblank cell.	
End-↓	Moves down the column to the intersection of a blank and nonblank cell.	
End-←	Moves across the row to the intersection of a blank and nonblank cell.	
End-Home	Moves to the lower-right corner of the active area.	
PgUp	Moves up one screen.	
PgDn	Moves down one screen.	
Ctrl-→ or Tab	Moves one screen to the right (also called Big Right).	Moves five characters to the right.
Ctrl-← or Shift-Tab	Moves one screen to the left (also called Big Left).	Moves five characters to the left.
Scroll-Lock	Freezes in relative position while scrolling the screen display; displays SCROLL status indicator when activated.	
Num Lock	Activates numbers on the numeric pad and disables cursor and editing functions; status indicator reads NUM when activated.	

Note: In LABEL and VALUE modes, the cursor movement keys also complete data entry in the current cell before moving the pointer to the next cell.